While America Slept

While America Slept

A CONTEMPORARY ANALYSIS OF WORLD EVENTS FROM THE FALL OF FRANCE TO PEARL HARBOR

D. F. Fleming

ABINGDON - COKESBURY PRESS

New York • *Nashville*

WHILE AMERICA SLEPT
COPYRIGHT, MCMXLIV
By WHITMORE & STONE

Wartime Books

Wartime shortage of pulp, manpower, and transportation has produced a severe shortage of paper. In compliance with orders of the War Production Board, wartime books are printed on lighter-weight paper. This reduces thickness and weight. New books have more words to the page and smaller margins. This reduces the number of pages without reducing reading content.

Thinner books save paper, critical copper, and other metals. They help also to avoid wartime increases in book prices. Wartime books appear to be smaller, but their content has not been cut. They are complete. The only change is in appearance.

24654

SET UP, PRINTED, AND BOUND BY THE PARTHENON PRESS AT NASHVILLE, TENNESSEE, UNITED STATES OF AMERICA

Preface

☆

THE NINETEEN MONTHS COVERED IN THIS BOOK WERE THE most chaotic in our history for many decades past. It was a time when the illusory, unreal world which our isolationists had built up in their minds collapsed, while they clung to the hope that one final act of stubborn will power would "keep us out of war." It was a time of intense debate, when anyone who hoped to keep ahead of onrushing disaster had to speak quickly and plainly.

This book is therefore a record of one man's part in the greatest debate in our history, save only that tragic controversy over the League of Nations in 1919 which laid the basis for the second World War. In the discussions reproduced in these pages I tried to portray the forces which were driving us to war against our will and to describe our stake in this conflict, the introduction to total war in the air age.

A little later these events will be history, but today the war is not yet won. We are resolved that this time it shall be won, both militarily and politically, but will we carry through? There was a tidal wave of isolationist reaction after the last war. Reaction always follows war, especially if the struggle is long and bitter. Will the coming postwar relapse be severe enough to lose us the peace again?

For the next few years that question will loom larger with each passing day—and its urgency will increase. This is our last chance to get an organized, civilized world before the devastations of the international anarchy come home to us. If we miss this opportunity, the next world war will kill *our* cities, as this one is to destroy the cities of Europe and Japan.

This book is offered in the hope that it will help us to keep firmly on the course we now pursue until dependable international order based upon law is established.

I am grateful to radio station WSM, which broadcast these discussions, for enabling me to say what I believed to be true throughout the clash and clamor of this turbulent period. At all times the opinions expressed were entirely my own, and none of them necessarily represented those of the owners and operators of WSM.

D. F. FLEMING

Nashville, Tennessee
December 7, 1943

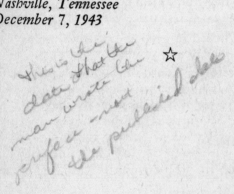

6

Contents

☆

7

AS HITLER ATTACKED RUSSIA

March 30–July 12, 1941

THE DEBATE CONTINUES

July 30–September 17, 1941

TOTAL WAR COMES TO US

September 24–December 10, 1941

☆

Milestones on the Road to
World War 2

1919

March 3—Round robin published committing one-third of
the Senate to oppose the League of Nations.

1919-20—Refusal of the Senate to consider Anglo-American
treaty guaranteeing France against attack by Germany.

November 18—First rejection of the League Covenant in the
Senate.

1920

March 19—Second rejection of the League by the Senate.

October 9—Zeligowski seized Vilna.

1921

October 18—Our separate peace treaty with Germany rati-
fied.

October—Article 16 of the Covenant weakened by interpre-
tation.

1922

February—Naval control of the Orient achieved by Japan
at the Washington Conference.

1923

January—Memel seized by Lithuania.

August 31—Corfu bombarded and seized by Mussolini.

1924

September—Article 10 of the Covenant watered down.

11

DESCENT INTO THE SECOND WORLD WAR

1931

September 18—Japanese attack on Manchuria.

1933

January 30—Hitler became Chancellor of Germany.

1935

January-September—Mussolini prepared openly to conquer Ethiopia.

August 31—First United States neutrality act embargoed arms to all belligerents.

1936

February—Our second neutrality law forbade belligerents to borrow money here.

March 7—Hitler occupied the demilitarized Rhineland.

July—Germany and Italy began conquest of Spanish Republic.

August to April, 1939—"Nonintervention" in Spain.

November 25—Japanese-German anti-Comintern pact signed.

1937

January 6—Congress forbade shipment of arms to Spain.

May 1—Third neutrality law prescribed "cash and carry" for nonmilitary articles.

July 7—Open Japanese conquest of China renewed.

1938

March 11—Austria seized by Hitler.

September 30—Czechoslovakia dismembered at Munich.

1939

March 11—Czechoslovakia suppressed by the Nazis.

March 22—Memel seized by Germany.

March 31—Franco-British pledge to defend Poland.

April 7—Albania occupied by Italy.

April 13—Chamberlain guaranteed Rumania and Greece.

April 28—Germany denounced 1935 naval agreement with Britain, 1934 ten-year nonaggression treaty with Poland, and made demands on Poland.

1939 *continued*

July 26—United States abrogated 1911 commercial treaty with Japan.

July 30—Congress leaders refused to amend the neutrality laws on Borah's assurance that there would not be a war.

August 23—German-U.S.S.R. nonaggression pact signed.

THE WAR BECOMES TOTAL AND GLOBAL

September 1—Germany invaded Poland.

September 3—Britain and France declared war on Germany.

October 7—300-mile neutrality zone around America decreed.

November 3—Arms embargo repealed and "cash and carry" substituted.

1940

March 12—Soviet-Finnish peace treaty signed.

March 28—Franco-British agreement for no separate armistice or peace.

April 9—German invasion of Denmark and Norway.

May 9—German invasion of Belgium, Luxembourg, and Holland.

May 10—Winston Churchill became Prime Minister of Great Britain.

May 15—Rotterdam leveled by air attack after Dutch surrender.

June 3—Dunkirk evacuation completed.

June 10—Italy declared war on France and Great Britain.

June 17—Pétain became Premier of France and asked for armistice.

June 22—Franco-German armistice signed giving Germans France's entire Atlantic coast.

June 27—Bessarabia ceded by Rumania to U.S.S.R.

July 3—British attack on French fleet at Oran.

July 18—Burma road closed for three months.

July 25—Export of petroleum and scrap metal to Japan licensed.

June 31—Our National Guard mobilized for maneuvers.

August 25—Esthonia, Latvia, and Lithuania incorporated into U.S.S.R.

September 12—The fifty destroyer–naval base exchange announced.

September 14—Conscription enacted.

September 23—British-French naval battle at Dakar.

September 25—A $25,000,000 loan made to China, and an embargo laid on scrap iron and steel.

September 27—German-Italian-Japanese ten-year military-economic alliance signed.

October 18—Burma road opened.

November 15—Coventry blasted by German air attack.

November 30—$100,000,000 loan made to China.

December 12—Hungarian-Yugoslav treaty of friendship signed.

1941

January 6—Lend-lease policy proposed by Roosevelt.

January 31—Japan got bases in French Indo-China.

March 11—Lend-lease act became law.

March 24—Seven billions appropriated for lend-lease.

April 6—Germany attacked Yugoslavia and Greece.

April 9—United States protection of Greenland assumed.

April 13—Japanese-Soviet five-year neutrality pact signed.

May 1—80,000 British troops evacuated from Greece.

May 6—Joseph Stalin became Premier of the U.S.S.R.

May 21—Sinking of the *Robin Moor* in the South Atlantic.

June 14—All assets of Germany, Italy, and their victims frozen.

June 16—All German consulates in the United States ordered closed.

June 21—Italian consular offices in the United States closed.

June 22—Germany invaded Soviet Union.

June 24—All Japanese assets in the United States frozen.

July 7—United States occupied Iceland.

July 12—British-Soviet mutual-assistance agreement signed.

July 30—United States recognized Czechoslovak government-in-exile.

1941 *continued*

August 1—All petroleum products embargoed to Japan.

August 4—United States formally pledged all-out aid to Russia.

August 14—Atlantic Charter published.

September 5—The destroyer *Greer* attacked near Iceland.

September 11—Shoot-on-sight order given to Navy.

September 22—Steamer *Pink Star* sunk.

October 15—Destroyer *Kearney* damaged.

October 16—Japanese Cabinet resigned.

October 17—All United States ships in Pacific ordered into friendly ports.

October 18—House of Representatives voted to repeal neutrality law and arm our ships to carry arms to Britain.

October 19—Tojo crisis Cabinet appointed in Japan. State of siege declared in Moscow.

November 1—Destroyer *Reuben James* sunk.

November 8—Senate voted for armed cargo ships in combat zones.

November 17—Tojo demanded a free hand and no curbs.

November 27—Our terms given to Japan.

December 4—The *Chicago Tribune* published in full the secret master war plans of the United States Army and Navy.

December 6—The President sent a personal appeal to Emperor Hirohito.

December 7—Pearl Harbor.

The Fall of France

This series of radio talks began at what was probably the most critical moment in all modern history. On May 22, 1940, the German armies reached the Channel, behind the Allied armies in Flanders, cutting off half a million men from all aid by land. It was the beginning of the disaster and miracle of Dunkirk. Certainly not since the decisive Marne battles of the first World War had the fate of all Western civilization hung so precariously in the balance.

This tragic May day had been preceded by two strangely contrasting periods. After Germany had obliterated Poland in September, 1939, almost in a single day, there ensued the great winter lull which Senator Borah termed "the phony war" and others the "sitzkrieg." Sitting behind the Maginot Line and the Belgian forts, the Allies felt secure; and so did we. On October 3, 1939, former President Herbert Hoover saw "no possibility that they can be defeated." The Allies controlled the seas and could "sit there until their enemies are exhausted." At the worst there would be a stalemate, even if Russia and Italy fought on Germany's side. Germany might try a quick, overwhelming attack; but there was "little reason to believe it can succeed." Therefore, concluded Mr. Hoover, "we need to keep cool. For after all we must keep out of this war."

We kept cool, except for our indignation about Russia's attack on Finland. The Allies themselves almost forgot about their war with Germany and mentally went to war with Russia. On February 23, 1940, Vice-Premier Chautemps proclaimed that France would not fail Finland. Prime Minister Chamberlain joined in attacking Russia two days later; and on March

11, as Finland was forced to make peace, the New York Times *reported that he told "a surprised and strangely silent House that Britain had not only refused to act as an intermediary in Russo-Finnish peace talks but had agreed with France to fight alongside the Finns, if Finland asked for help." In France, Premier Daladier announced that fifty thousand French troops were ready to go to Finland.*

The waiting winter passed, while all Germany was roaring with war preparations. In March it became evident that the British intended to cut the iron-ore traffic by sea from northern Norway to Germany. On April 9 Norway was invaded by Germany and rapidly overrun. On May 9 Holland, Belgium, and Luxembourg were as suddenly attacked. The next day Chamberlain resigned to an angry House of Commons and Churchill became Prime Minister.

As the German armies surged across the Low Countries, while their aircraft bombed the people out of the towns and then machine-gunned them on the roads, President Roosevelt went to the Congress and asked for a billion dollars to equip an army of seven hundred fifty thousand men. Nobody had any objection, though the President's goal of fifty thousand planes a year was widely thought to be visionary—until in 1943 we nearly doubled it.

But air fleets hoped for could not stop the German avalanche. On May 15 the main part of Rotterdam was obliterated from the air after the Dutch had formally ceased resistance. On May 17 the French lines were pierced on a sixty-two-mile front. Premier Reynaud declared that "unbelievable faults in Allied defense" would be punished. By May 22 the Germans had raced to the sea and cut the Allied armies in two.

IS IT VITAL TO US THAT THE ALLIES SURVIVE?

May 22, 1940

LAST THURSDAY, PRESIDENT ROOSEVELT DELIVERED TO THE Congress and the nation one of the most important messages ever written by any American president. It was not a declaration of war but a belated acceptance of the fact that war of the most desperate character is being waged on every free people. For the first time in history our outer defenses are in the gravest danger of falling. The American people have suddenly realized the immensity of the danger, and they are rising to meet it. As rapidly as possible we are now going on a war economy—to give the Allies the decisive fighting machines if that is still possible; to prepare ourselves for defensive existence in a hostile world if the worst happens in Europe.

Our people have watched for years the onward rush of aggression in its most brutal forms. Now they do not need to be told that it is approaching the proportions of a world tidal wave. Opposition to a swift girding of ourselves for whatever is ahead is conspicuous by its absence.

Yet one well-known voice has been raised to tell us that nothing alarming is afoot. On Sunday, Colonel Charles A. Lindbergh made over a national hookup a radio address in which he demanded that we "stop this hysterical chatter of calamity and invasion that has been rife these last few days. . . . . It is not," chided the Colonel, "befitting to the people who built this nation."

"Regardless of which side wins this war," he continued, "there is no reason, aside from our own actions, to prevent a continuation of peace relationships between America and the countries of Europe. If we desire peace, we need only stop asking for war. No one wishes to attack us, and no one is in a position to do so."

That is, according to Lindbergh, we have nothing to fear from a Europe ruled by the Nazis. Their suppression of every political party and every other form of free association in Germany; their pogroms against the Jews; their persecution of the churches, Catholic and Protestant; their brutal concentration camps and utter destruction of the

19

right of any German to think for himself—these are things which do not matter.

It is the world triumph of this system which Colonel Lindbergh asks us to regard with cold detachment. From his mount of Olympian calm he would require us to forget that the Nazi regime is running amuck on a world scale—that already the Nazis have terrorized and conquered the Austrians; overrun the Czechs; enslaved the Poles; seized Denmark and Norway, threatening the Norwegians with the death of traitors if they resisted; blitzkrieged the Dutch; and carried devastation through Belgium and northern France for the second time in twenty-five years.

That these successive tragedies should not be considered important is indicated clearly in Colonel Lindbergh's radio address of September 14, 1939, after the third of these disasters had occurred. Said Lindbergh at the height of the Nazi destruction of Poland: "This is simply one more of those age-old quarrels within our family of nations." Toward it "we must be as impersonal as a surgeon with his knife."

Why we must be so coldly impersonal was explained a month later by Colonel Lindbergh in an address on October 13, in which he said: "It is the European race we must preserve; political progress will follow. Racial strength is vital; politics is a luxury. If the white race is ever seriously threatened, it may then be time for us to take our part in its protection, to fight side by side with the English, French, and Germans, but not with one against the other for our mutual destruction."

In other words, the effort of Germany to dominate the Western world is to Lindbergh merely "politics," and he strongly implies that the triumph of the Nazi terror in Europe would be "political progress." There is not a word in his latest address which would indicate that the Nazi conquests are not a good thing. On the contrary, he announces: "That the world is facing a new era is beyond

20

question.   Our mission is to make it a better era."

That we are facing a new era is but too probable, for if the Allies fall we will live in a world instantly unrecognizable. Instead of living behind the screen of the easygoing, tolerant French and British empires, civilized, freedom-loving, living by the rules and standards that have been ours from the beginning, we would face utterly ruthless power which denies every single principle, without exception, upon which our free civilization is based.

The situation which will confront us at once if the Allies go down this summer was described by Walter Lippmann on Sunday in terms which it seems to me should be heeded by all. Said Lippmann: "Faster than we can conceivably build the means of defense, the victorious aggressor states will occupy by force or by subversive conspiracies the strategic outposts of our defensive system."

"For," continued Lippmann, "we cannot build a navy and air force and an adequate continental army as fast as the victorious coalition could take possession of Iceland, Greenland, Ireland, Portugal, Gibraltar, the Azores, the Cape Verde Islands, the Allied colonies in western Africa, the Netherlands Indies, Singapore, Hong Kong, the Philippines, and Guam; we cannot perfect our defenses rapidly enough to suppress the invasions of the fifth columns which are already prepared in several vitally important countries of this hemisphere. Once those outposts are in the hands of victorious, unfriendly, aggressive, and hungry powers, we shall not be allowed the time to arm ourselves adequately even if it were possible, which it is not, for one nation to arm itself adequately against the combined military forces of virtually the whole world.

"The American people," concluded Lippmann, "will not be in possession of the truth until they know clearly that a successful resistance by the Allies this summer is absolutely vital to the defense of the United States. Any attempt to conceal this truth is at best an innocent but a dangerous ignorance, and at worst it is treacherous alien propaganda."

This, it seems to me, is the sober truth. And if it is, nothing should be neglected which might prevent Allied disaster this summer. In the present crisis, is there anything which we can do to ward off decades of defensive existence, with enormous hostile military empires on both sides of us? One suggestion was radioed from Paris lately by the president of the American Chamber of Commerce. Is it not possible, he asked, for a couple of thousand fighting planes to be gathered together in this country and sent to France, largely by air? This suggestion was broadened by Senator Pepper, of Florida, who asked if the twenty-one American republics could not join in sending the two thousand planes. On Saturday, May 18, the twenty-one American republics did unite in a joint statement denouncing the German invasion of Belgium, Holland, and Luxembourg as "unjustified and cruel." Every one of the twenty-one republics is menaced as it has never been in its history. Why should they not join in something stronger than words if they have the power to do so?

I do not advance this suggestion as one who is technically qualified to recommend its feasibility, but in this supreme crisis no possibility should be overlooked. Thirteen years ago last Sunday, Charles A. Lindbergh did a splendidly daring thing. And when he gallantly flew across the ocean he reduced the Atlantic to a ribbon of water which could never be stretched into an ocean again. From that day forward the Atlantic could only contract, steadily and relentlessly, as it has every day since and as it will as far into the future as any man can see.

Constantly and inexorably our scientists are making the earth a unit for purposes of trade and war, and the one thing of which we may be most certain is that they will continue to shrink time and space and to increase the range and striking power of the engines of destruction—especially if world power is now to be surrendered to the most ruthless warmakers.

If today a great ocean flight could be made for the rescue of Western civilization, the Americas might escape the decades of tremendous defense expenditure, falling standards of living, and burdensome militarized life which are ahead of them if by winter only one large—but unprepared—democracy remains on the face of the earth.

We have said to the Allies that if they can hold out until winter the first of our fifty thousand planes will be there to see them through. But to survive the summer the Allies require many additional planes, and they must have them *now*.

As disaster engulfed the Allied armies beyond the English Channel, the British Parliament passed in less than three hours a bill giving the government the right to conscript every person, piece of property, and penny in the realm. The excess profits tax was raised to 100 per cent. Canadian war industries went on a twenty-four-hour day, including Sundays. Our own Congress voted more than three billions for defense by unanimous votes, excepting that of one lone member in the House. A two-ocean navy was planned, and great expansion of air power. The President appointed a seven-man Council of National Defense.

In London the British Fascist leader Sir Oswald Mosely was jailed, and in France fifteen generals were relieved of command and a Colonel Charles de Gaulle filled one of their places. As the German ring around the Allied armies closed in, King Leopold ordered the Belgian armies to surrender, on May 27. His Cabinet voted to continue the struggle and went to London. By May 29 the rescue fleet from England was beginning the historic evacuation from Dunkirk.

OUR DEFENSE PROBLEM IF GERMANY WINS

May 29, 1940

IF GERMANY DEFEATS FRANCE AND BRITAIN, WHAT WILL OUR defense situation be? No one could foresee all the tremendous consequences of such an event, but it would be strange indeed if we did not look ahead far enough to see some of the very grave problems which would at once confront us.

The first fact to be grasped is of such vital importance that to miss it is to miss the significance of everything which is going on in Europe. A German triumph will mean that some three hundred million Europeans will be organized into an enormous German military and trade empire, an area peopled by far more skilled workers and trained fighters than we have or can get. We have been told that Germany could not rule so many people, but by now it is totally clear that a people once disarmed of its heavy weapons can never revolt against determined conquerors. They can only work and obey. It is essential to remember, too, that a Germanized Europe can produce far more coal, iron, and other elements of military power than the United States can—for equipping armies and building navies. If Hitler wins, we shall at once confront a superior power across the Atlantic from Norway to Cape Town, South Africa—a power which is absolutely hostile to every principle by which we live.

It should be said at once that the conquest of any part of our continental territory is not to be feared, though that does not preclude air attacks upon our cities or the constant blackmailing threat of air attack such as England lived under for years past. Bombers can now be built which will fly the Atlantic from Europe and return nonstop. That their military effectiveness might be small will not be much comfort to many millions of people living in our Eastern cities. It is not necessary, however, for three-thousand-mile flights to be made from Europe to bring the shadow of air attack over our great cities. The vast subcontinent of Greenland, one of the most strategic flying spots on the globe, is but six hours' flying time from New England and as close to Europe as to us.

The fact that Greenland is also but three or four hours' flying time from eastern Canada brings us to the first of our enormous defense problems. Our Canadian neighbor is at war with Germany. Canada has an area of four million square miles defended by eleven million people, most of whom live along our northern border. We could not possibly allow a hostile force to become lodged in the Canadian North without doing our utmost to meet the menace far from our frontiers. Whether we wish it or not, we must assist in the defense of Canada against invasion from any quarter.

Yet it is in the South Atlantic that a German victory would give us our gravest defense problem. The Monroe Doctrine is our oldest and most cherished foreign policy. It requires us to defend against invasion all of Latin America, a rich, virgin continent containing seven million square miles, inhabited by a hundred million people who are thinly scattered over its vast area, and divided into twenty-one states, most of them necessarily weak. A very large proportion of our southern neighbors are not Europeans, and it is no disrespect to them to say that there are very few of these peoples which are strong enough to resist a European invasion in force.

It must be remembered, too, that much of South America is closer to Europe than to us and that the ocean is only sixteen hundred miles wide between the bulge of Brazil and the shoulder of Africa. The great harbor at Freetown, West Africa, now in British hands, is one of the finest harbors in the world. It lies 1,632 miles from Pernambuco,

Brazil, while our naval base at Norfolk, Virginia, is more than twice as far away. In German hands Freetown would put all South America in immediate peril, especially Brazil with her large German colonies. The German road to Freetown would also be fully protected by a screen of islands all the way down. The Azores, Canary, Madeira, and Cape Verde islands make a safe inside passage from Germany to Freetown. It is sometimes said that German victory would force us to seize the Azores, since they are only two thousand miles from our shores. But they are barely one thousand miles from Europe, and it is highly unlikely that a Hitler Europe would permit us to retain the Azores even if we occupied them.

The suggestion has already appeared repeatedly in the newspapers that in case of a Nazi victory we would have to abandon all of South America below the Amazon River, and there would be much to compel such a humiliating retreat on our part. The Atlantic coast of South America is seven thousand miles long. Could the American Navy defend such a distant expanse against both sea and air power, in addition to five thousand miles of coast line in North America? Would it be possible for our navy to operate at all below the narrow waters with the Freetown harbor in German hands? Would not the defense of the Monroe Doctrine be a back-breaking task—one beyond our strength?

That we would have to get air bases all over the northern part of South America for the defense of the Panama Canal goes without saying, for we are not at all certain that a few well-placed bombs would not destroy the Canal locks and with them the keystone of our whole defense.

The defense of the Canal brings us at once to a second tremendous fact: that a German victory in Europe means automatically a clean sweep for Japan in the Far East. At present our navy is at Hawaii, making it perilous for Japan to try to seize the Dutch East Indies with their immense stores of oil, rubber, and tin. But we have only one navy, and if Britain falls we shall need it at once in the Atlantic, while Japan takes over the Dutch Indies, the Philippines, and a thousand South Sea Islands now in the hands of Britain and France. The Marquesas Islands, particularly, lying two thousand miles south of Honolulu, would if taken by Japan become a distant but potential threat to American naval action in the whole of the South Pacific. From the tip of Alaska to the tip of South America there are ten thousand miles of coast line. Could any American navy defend these limitless reaches with the myriad islands of the Pacific, both north and south, in Japanese hands? Alaska alone stretches for twenty-one hundred miles through the North Pacific, a vast, rich hostage to fortune nearly half as large as the United States and with thirty thousand white people living in its huge arc.

A German victory in Europe would put the whole wealth of the Orient, including China's coal and iron, into Japan's hands, giving her plenty of time to bend the four hundred million Chinese to her will—and to develop a military and naval colossus on our western frontier.

We should have to expect also that a Germanized Europe and a Japanized Asia would co-operate in threats against the Western Hemisphere and in shutting us out of the markets of the world. As Dr. J. A. de Haas, Harvard specialist on international economics, said on May 25, we would at once be shut in by a system of world barter which would make our vast gold hoard valueless and force us to beg supplies of rubber, tin, and quinine from Japan.

Today we are in imminent danger of finding ourselves in a state of enforced isolation which would change profoundly, and for the worse, the life of every person in this country, and especially of our children and their children. In the words of the historian Allan Nevins, of Columbia University, written May 26: "Every farmer, every laborer, every businessman would feel the pinch. In desperation we

27

would have to turn ourselves to a heavily regimented economy, and at the same time we would have to contend with strong Fascist groups in the United States and irresistible Fascist parties in much of Latin America."

But if we should be able by strenuous effort to preserve a part of our liberties, we would still have to bend our backs for generations under the load and lash of militarism in order to live a cabined, confined life in our island continent. That is the prospect which is straight in front of us unless we speed to the Allies, within the next month or two, enough airplanes and other weapons to enable them to hold on until December. We are now living in our last moment of grace, when swift, determined action *now* will keep the world in which we have lived comfortably for a hundred and fifty years from being irrevocably destroyed.

Every effort which we can make now will in all probability have to be multiplied a hundredfold if we let the summer pass without acting. We probably have enough warplanes in our service to prevent an Allied disaster until our fifty-thousand-plane program can turn the scales. But as General Pershing recently warned, time is everything. No other democracy has been able to make up its mind in time. We are the last great people which can make the same disastrous mistake.

On May 29 the Germans drove a wedge across the pocket containing the Allied armies and an incalculable number of refugees; but the larger part of the trapped forces were able to proceed toward the sea at Dunkirk, which was shelled and bombed, but over which the British managed to maintain a local air superiority. Then, aided by an unusual calm, the British people took to the sea in everything that would float, to the tiniest of boats, and brought the major fraction of their shattered armies home, plus many French and Belgians. As

a salvage operation it was a thrilling epic. By June 4 some 335,000 men were saved, but their arms had to be left behind. Britain was virtually defenseless if strong hostile forces could cross the Channel.

OUR FIRST LINE OF DEFENSE
June 5, 1940

A WEEK AGO, ON MAY 29, MR. WENDELL WILLKIE, PRESIdent of the Commonwealth and Southern Corporation and a man generally accepted as one of the most hardheaded businessmen in the country, made an address in which he stated a truth which we can fail to understand and act upon—but only at very great cost to ourselves. Said Mr. Willkie: "It is clear that England and France constitute our first line of defense against Hitler. If anybody is going to stop Hitler from further aggression, they are the ones who will do it. Just putting the matter in a selfish light, if Britain and France can lick Hitler now, we may be saved billions of dollars, billions of tons of armament, billions of hours of wasted effort and unfruitful work. Just on the most selfish basis, it is enormously to our advantage to have them win."

In these few words Mr. Willkie has expressed exactly the tremendous stake which we have in the war in Europe —a war which Germany now seems likely to win. The Allies have won a great moral victory in snatching their Flanders armies from the German mincing machine, but their situation still remains extremely perilous. The German Army has suffered great losses, but it still has tremendous striking power—power which is already turned toward Paris and may soon crash through into the open again. The French have a great army, but it must fight all summer long under a constant hail of German bombs,

29

while German observers spot each daylight move that it makes. France has so few planes now, also, that only a fragment of the British Air Force is left to prevent German bombers from ranging at will over all France. Paris, Lyon, and Marseilles have already been heavily bombed, with many civilians killed; and these key cities may be bombed scores of times in the coming weeks, together with every other important point in France. Soon, also, Italy's great fleet of bombing planes is expected to attack France, and Fascist Spain may use her war-hardened army and air force against the French.

The plight of the British, too, is almost as grave. The Germans are now only twenty miles from England, closer than they could ever get during the last war. For the first time in eight hundred years there is real danger of an invasion of England in force. The Germans can now rain bombs upon England month after month, and they can launch a single great aerial offensive from many points at once—from Norway, Holland, Belgium, Germany, and northern France—backed by transport planes carrying parachutists and perhaps by armored planes which become tanks on landing. German big guns can also lay down a curtain of fire behind Dover in England, and a huge fleet of bombers can cover an attempt to land a big army from surface ships. Behind England, Ireland is almost defenseless and has a republican fifth column ready to welcome German landings. And added to all these avenues of German attack upon Britain is the overriding danger that incessant bombing of British munition and aircraft factories, docks, and communications may wear down Britain's ability to resist before the day for a mass invasion comes.

Throughout the summer we must expect blow after blow from the German juggernaut, and each drive will further weaken our first line of defense. Every month until winter comes will be critical for the whole future of our civilization.

For the first time in our history we have to face the
probability that the British Navy may be unable to defend
this hemisphere. Yesterday Prime Minister Churchill declared that Britain and France would defend their home-
lands to the last and that if the worst comes the British
fleet would retreat to the New World and continue
the war. That is the spirit which may pull the Allies
through; but it would be unwise for us to count on the
aid of the British fleet if the Allies fall, for there are two
developments which may make it impossible to save the
British Navy for our future defense. Even Mr. Churchill
does not know whether he may not be compelled to surrender the fleet to prevent the mass killing of the British
people from the air, Churchill is facing a man who
apparently has unlimited powers of destruction in his hands
and who is ready to destroy the British people, along with
many others, if they will not submit to him. If by autumn
some millions of British civilians have been bombed to
death and Hitler threatens to kill other millions in cold
blood, who can say that the British Navy will not be surrendered to stop the slaughter? Again, if a German blitzkrieg is launched upon Britain by air, sea, and land, might
not the navy be largely used up in its efforts to frustrate
the invasion? In attempting to prevent the subjugation of
England, the fleet might have to come into the narrow
waters of the Channel, beneath hundreds of German bombers and land guns.

But if the British fleet should retire to Canada, its retreat
would still be a world-shaking disaster to our security.
The British Navy is our mightiest bulwark against the in-
finitely destructive forces now in control of Europe, because its bases in the British Isles enable it to bottle up
the Nazi inferno in Europe. It cannot be too strongly
emphasized that the same fleet based on Canada would
lose the greater part of its value to us. It would enable us
to tide over the first critical period, until we could build

31

a great navy for the Atlantic Ocean, and would thus be a great comfort to us for a few years; but in reality it could do little more than defend Canada for a decade, until obsolescence claimed it. Its immense value to us as the strongest line of our own defense could be restored only if we were willing to make a titanic effort to reconquer its bases in the British Isles.

Such an effort would be greater than anything we have ever attempted. Yet the alternative would be to take our chances between German and Japanese empires containing a billion people and war-making resources far in excess of our own. Dorothy Thompson did not exaggerate in the slightest when she said yesterday that we are threatened with "the complete collapse of the world of which we are an integral part and the redistribution and reorganization of that world, socially, economically, politically, financially, and spiritually, in such a manner as will menace our institutions, our way of life, and our possibility of independent survival."

That is the grim truth. But can we as a people grasp it in time? Our public opinion is moving very fast indeed, but it takes time for even the grimmest truth really to stir a hundred and thirty million people to action—and if we are to be of material aid to the Allies during this crucial fighting season, we have but little time for debate.

Yet it is possible for a free people to make up its mind quickly. Yesterday evening two thousand people filled the War Memorial Building in Nashville to demand three things: (1) stronger aid to the Allies; (2) full production by our war industries of new weapons for our own defense; and (3) action by the government to prevent fifth-column activities here. At this meeting a reasoned address was made by Mr. Will R. Manier, Jr., a past-president of Rotary International, and the response to it was in the same spirit. There was instant and prolonged applause for each suggestion that aid to the Allies is in our own defense. Resolutions covering the purposes of the meeting were adopted by a unanimous rising vote, and hundreds of petitions were distributed to enable the remainder of the community to make its voice heard.

That was democracy in action. The call for the meeting originated spontaneously in the minds of three or four people. They wrote out a brief statement asking all like-minded citizens to assemble, and within three days two hundred leading citizens had signed the call, many of them asking the privilege of doing so as the news spread. The presidents of nearly every civic organization in the city, the American Legion, the Chamber of Commerce, and labor leaders all co-operated.

A few days ago a similar meeting was held in Louisville. What Louisville and Nashville have done can also be done in hundreds of towns, large and small, from Mexico to Canada. Since 1937 the President and Secretary Hull have done all that two men could do to arouse us to a realization that the slaughtering and looting of the gangster governments on both sides of us must be brought to a stop. But each time that our leaders warned us what was ahead, we here in the Mississippi Valley said: "Don't rock the boat, stop talking, and keep us out of war." Now the time has come for us in the Mississippi Valley to tell the Government in no uncertain terms that we do not want to live for generations hemmed in by huge predatory empires, sinking our substance in war equipment and drilling our sons for the constant menace of war—all in defense of a steadily-shrinking standard of living.

We have just voted five billion dollars for defense. What would our annual defense bill be if the Allies were crushed? To quote Wendell Willkie again, how many "billions of tons of armaments" would we need? How many "billions of hours of wasted effort and unfruitful work" would we be compelled to spend? On the coldest and most selfish calculation that it is possible for us to make, what *would* the cost to us be if the British Navy should be driven from Europe by German air power?

Under a ruling by Attorney General Jackson our armed forces began to surrender old equipment to manufacturers, who in turn sold it to the Allies. About six hundred thousand rifles, twenty-five hundred field guns and ammunition, a thousand planes, and other weapons were involved.

On June 9 the Norwegian government ceased all resistance and fled to Britain, while a million German troops swept across northern France, compelling the evacuation of Paris by the government on June 10, the day Mussolini declared war on the Allies. On June 11 the famous line of the Marne broke under German tank assaults; and our President obeyed the neutrality laws by adding the Mediterranean to the areas from which American planes, ships, and citizens were barred.

CAN DEMOCRACY SURVIVE?
June 12, 1940

Twenty years ago anyone who questioned the survival of democracy would have been thought demented. Now that democracy is in headlong flight and no one knows whether the flight can be stopped, I want to try to evaluate our chances of preserving democracy here if the worst happens in Europe. I give you my conclusion at the beginning: If the Allies lose we shall have to struggle desperately and indefinitely to preserve even a part of our own liberties.

What are the known facts upon which such a conclusion can be based? The first and inescapable fact is that the totalitarian state is the most efficient engine of power which has ever been invented. It takes an entire people by the scruff of the neck and extracts from them the last degree of effort of which they are capable. It leaves nothing to chance, permits nothing to be muddled, and drives from one goal to another with a relentless energy which is almost irresistible. If this be not true of the Communist state, it is undeniably true of Fascism. The first thing to be grasped about Fascism is that it is war. The Fascist state is born in violence, lives by violence, and must die a violent death. From the time that a Fascist party seizes power and crushes every freely associated group in the land, it preaches war, studies war, drills its children mentally and physically, and spends each day in the accumulation of arms. It kills every precept and feeling of right and wrong, exalts force and guile, and makes all of life a struggle on the level of the jungle. Fascism and war are at all times one and the same thing.

Democracy is a civilized way of life. For it peace is the goal. Democracy cultivates every humane, tolerant, and kindly impulse. But no people can live a civilized life if it has a Fascist neighbor. It must descend to the level of the jungle and stay there, or it will certainly perish.

There is a second characteristic of the Fascist state which makes it a deadly neighbor. It is utterly dynamic, always on the move, never quiet, because the controlling gang knows that it has suppressed a far better way of life, knows that it must keep the nation in a state of emergency in order to rule it, knows that it must keep bringing home loot to justify the strain and repression which it imposes on everyone. Unfortunately, it must be admitted that this dynamism generates power—power which will overwhelm any of its neighbors which cling to the easygoing, live-and-let-live ways of democracy.

Democracy suffers from an almost fatal handicap: in no single case so far has it been able to look ahead to forestall great dangers plainly visible on the horizon. Either the leaders are deaf, dumb, and blind, or the people remain inert and apathetic. There are today legions of Englishmen and Frenchmen who have warned daily for the past ten years that only concerted action with other nations could save Britain and France from the terrible fate which has overtaken them. But their leaders were selfish and stupid; they put every class and personal consideration before the national welfare. The Dutch and Belgian peoples also were in mortal peril, but their leaders clung to the old empty formulas of neutrality. They would be scrupulously correct and trust to the assurances of the Nazis. And all the while the Nazi fifth columns were burrowing under the foundations of the state.

Here at home we as a people knew what we should do in 1919. We knew that our supreme task was to lead an organization of free peoples against another world outbreak of stupid, criminal barbarism. But we were frustrated by false, shortsighted leaders. In recent years it cannot be said that our leaders did not warn us—month after month, year after year. But we ourselves clung to ancient shibboleths which the sciences of communication and destruction had robbed of any validity.

Most incredible of all has been the inability of the democracies to stand together. There has never been a day during the past twenty years when the free peoples could not have united in such fashion as to make large-scale war anywhere unprofitable to the aggressors. But the free peoples preferred to be picked off one at a time. They could not get alarmed. The danger was too far away. It was not their business. As a result, the wealth of the democracies is being taken over by the dictatorships at such a rate that soon the preponderance of power, of all kinds, will be in the hands of the "plunderbund."

When the skies are black with Fascist bombers and the roads choked with terrified civilians being constantly machine-gunned and bombed from the air, then the democracies do rouse themselves to splendid efforts. At long last both the British and the French have governments which will save them if governments can still avert disaster. Both in London and Paris men of vision, courage, and determination are finally at the helm. In both countries, too, all power has now been placed in the hands of these men.

But this, say some of our own confused ones, is no consolation, for if you have to go totalitarian to beat the totalitarians, what is the use? Many of our professional pacifists are now arguing that we must at all costs avoid recognizing that a state of war exists between us and the Fascist powers, since that would mean the end of our liberties. This reasoning, it seems to me, is the height of democratic futility. Of course a democracy has to give dictatorial powers to its chosen leaders for the duration of a totalitarian war, but there is no analogy whatever between this and the permanent enslavement of a people by a self-imposed group which bludgeons a nation into submission with the avowed object of ruling and driving it for the next thousand years. We gave all powers to our president during the last war without anyone's losing a night's sleep about it. And if the British and French peoples can succeed in breaking the conqueror's grip on their throats, they will take back their ancient liberties from hands ready and willing to surrender them.

If the Allies are defeated, democracy can only make a last-ditch stand on this continent. At once four hundred million Europeans would be welded into an economic block under German command—a block with buying power so huge as to take our South American markets by storm. Simultaneously, the Fascist fifth columns in every Latin American state, some of them millions strong, would reach for control, backed by the mightiest power and the most overwhelming prestige in all history. The naval shipbuilding yards under German rule would exceed our own by

37

five or six times—with plenty of coal, iron, and skilled man-power to operate them. It must always be remembered, too, that German-Italian victory means that the vast resources of the entire Orient will be behind the Japanese Navy.

No one who believes in democracy and loves its freedom as much as I do could bring himself to say that democracy in our own country would be finally doomed. But if the Allies are defeated, two things are as clearly forecast as the future can ever be: (1) We would have to regiment ourselves permanently for defense, with all the galling oppressions that permanent militarization involves. (2) The gigantic costs of defense would constantly lower our standard of living at the same time that the military trade methods of Fascist Europe strangled our foreign trade. For this reason permanent regimentation of our civilian life would be unavoidable, in order to divide less and less among us and to preserve internal peace during the process.

There may still be some who would prefer to meet this situation when it comes crowding in upon us from the Atlantic, the Pacific, and Latin America, and upon every radio wave, with no possibility left of help in the last extremity—and with our own Fascist-minded elements to be continually contended with. But the American people have risen in their might during the last two weeks. They are speaking to their congressmen as they have never spoken before, and they will continue to speak by every mail—as individuals, as organizations, and as whole communities—until the arms which have a good chance of halting the Germans now are sent to the Allies in full quantity. We are determined not to be the last beleaguered island of freedom, the last democracy which could not bring itself to keep great danger at a distance.

It is not too late, either, to save democracy on a world scale—the only scale on which there is any safety for it. The free peoples still have the preponderance of potential power. And when their entire future is at stake, free men can achieve in deeds what mass-driven helots cannot. So long as any part of France or any part of the British Isles can be held, the cause of world democracy is not lost. So long as the British fleet and air force can be kept in action *in Europe,* the victory of the gangster powers cannot be registered. The next six months will be the most critical in the history of Western civilization; during that time the united efforts of all free men can prevent the destruction of our common heritage. The Battle of France is the beginning, not the end, of the final struggle to prevent the extinction of democracy and free institutions. The current battle may be lost; the war must not be.

On June 14, a week after Hitler's second big drive opened, his troops entered Paris, which had been declared an open city along with all other towns of twenty thousand population. By Sunday, June 16, the Maginot Line, behind the "protection" of which France had fatally split into Fascist and anti-Fascist factions, was completely flanked, the Germans marching behind it to the Franco-Swiss border. On the same day the death of the Third Republic was signalled by the resignation of Premier Paul Reynaud and the coming to power of eighty-four-year-old Marshal Pétain.

By a narrow vote of 12 to 10 the Pétain Cabinet decided to quit the war and make an honorable "soldier's peace" with Hitler instead of continuing the conflict from Africa with the French fleet and air force in co-operation with the British Navy. On June 22 Pétain's representatives signed an armistice with Germany in the same railroad car in the forest of Compiègne in which Germany's surrender of 1918 had been registered. By its terms France was split into two parts—occupied and unoccupied—to be slowly crucified, body and soul. But on the day that Pétain agreed to her crucifixion General

39

Charles de Gaulle radioed from London an appeal to his countrymen to keep up resistance. He was forming a French National Committee which was "resolved to maintain the independence of France and the honor of alliances to which she is committed and contribute to the war efforts of the Allies until final victory."

On June 20 the President appointed two distinguished Republicans to his Cabinet: Henry L. Stimson became Secretary of War; Frank Knox, Secretary of the Navy. And Senator Burke, of Nebraska, introduced a bill for selective, compulsory military training of the nation's manhood.

AFTER THE FALL OF FRANCE
June 26, 1940

IT IS PROBABLY IMPOSSIBLE FOR ANYONE TO GRASP TODAY the full significance of what has happened in France during the last two weeks. The French government was confronted with a tragic alternative: it had to cease resistance in France and retire to Africa to continue the struggle; or else it had to bow to Germany and Italy, give up the struggle entirely, and take whatever Hitler chose to give. To continue the war meant that France would be administered directly by Germany and if the war were finally lost everything would be lost; to surrender meant that some few privileges might be saved if France would become a loyal servant of Germany and help her to conquer Britain.

The Reynaud government would not surrender; and it could not find enough support in Parliament, among the Army leaders, or from the President of the Republic to continue the struggle. Hence Reynaud resigned and the Rightist elements put through the surrender. Laval, whose dickering with Mussolini during the Ethiopian crisis prevented the League of Nations from disciplining Mussolini then, was sent to Rome once more; and he is now vice-premier of France. The aged Marshal Pétain, the man thought best able to get on with Fascist dictator Franco as France's ambassador to Spain, is the premier, apparently destined to do for the French Republic what the eighty-six-year-old Hindenburg did for the German Republic.

It is not the right of any non-Frenchman to attempt to utter at this time a conclusive judgment upon what these French leaders have done. They had a cruel choice to make, and in defense of their gravest act—the breaking of France's word to Britain that she would make no separate peace—they could reply that Britain did not adopt conscription in time to get a large army to France.

This is true, and it is a failure which must hang heavily on the shoulders of recent appeasement governments in Britain. Yet the failures of recent French governments are just as basic to France's defeat. For these failures, too, the parties of the Left must bear a share of the responsibility. They demanded social reforms when every energy which France had was required for national defense. Basically, France fell because she was divided, because all her parties played politics for many years when the country was in mortal peril. Hitler sprang all of his early seizures of power and some recent ones during French cabinet crises. He never needed to wait for one very long, for the French Right and Left were always at each other's throats. He advanced from one triumph to another chiefly because the French and British conservatives swallowed all his early protestations and deceits and clung to peace as the only way of preserving their own dominant positions in France and Britain.

Now the French Rightists have elected to go over to Hitler. They have turned over to him outright more than half of France, and in the remaining fragment they will maintain a puppet government which must do his will. What French territories are to be directly annexed to Germany and Italy they do not yet know. Nor will it matter very much while the Fascist empires rule Europe, for all France will become tributary to Berlin and Rome. In order to sustain the national morale a little, many brave words are now being spoken in France about the immortality of her people and the uncrushability of her soul. In the long run France may live again, but until Hitler's power is crushed she must toil and sweat for his purposes and for no other. I know that there are many who still say, "But surely the French will revolt." In former times that could have been expected, but modern weapons do not permit revolt. All of France's heavy weapons are being turned over to Germany, and she can never have any again. They are too bulky to be concealed. All that the French can hope to do is to hide a few small bombs, rifles, and machine guns—weapons which would be utterly useless until German power is ready to collapse for other reasons. A hundred German bombing planes and tanks can now keep all France permanently in subjection, backed as they will be by unlimited quantities of all other weapons. It is conceivable that if the Nazis have to fight Britain and Russia over a long period, the French and the Czechs and the Poles might be able to give the Nazi regime a final push by revolting. But when the war ends, the prospect of revolution by any conquered people will have vanished, for all the peoples conquered by Germany will be so thoroughly disarmed and their patriotic leaders so constantly exterminated that the very possibility of revolt will cease to exist. Nor will it occur through any period which we can foresee. The Nazis will not be so foolish as to let anyone rearm as they were permitted to, first secretly and then openly.

Willingly or unwillingly, the Pétain government now becomes the tool of Hitler. Its claim that it has made peace with honor is pathetic. As much of the French Navy as can be got into French harbors is by the promise of Hitler's armistice not to be used against England, but everyone knows that this is merely a German ruse to get control of the ships. Henceforth, all French resources will be used by Germany against England. From now on, also, France must be blockaded and bombed by England as a part of Germany. Hitler has at last succeeded in splitting the two great European democracies. Only one now remains.

Politically, Hitler has but one problem left: to separate the two great democracies which still exist—Great Britain and the United States—and to immobilize the United States until Britain is destroyed. Then the whole Atlantic world would be wide open to his penetration—ideological, economic, and military.

Already, too, there are important national figures who are beginning to say that we must get along with Hitler and that they are the ones to manage it. That would mean, of course, that we must stop criticizing the great conqueror, whatever he does. It would mean the muzzling of free speech and press, for nothing has ever infuriated Hitler like the condemnation of editors in the free countries. To begin to accept Hitler now would be the beginning of appeasement and of our gradual submission to his system.

Is that the road which the free American people choose to take, when the British Empire is still in control of the seas and fighting with all its might for ultimate victory? The fall of France has, of course, altered to some extent what we can do to prevent the creation of a Hitler world empire. There are nevertheless, powerful aids which we can still give to Britain to prevent our greatest line of defense from falling:

(1) We can resist the defeatist suggestion that Britain is already lost, so there is nothing we can do. A democracy which abandons a sister democracy thus readily is not too likely to survive when its own turn comes.

(2) There is always the crucial matter of planes. It is planes now in existence, not those which we plan to build, which will decide the battle for Britain before Thanksgiving Day.

43

(3) We can amend our laws to permit the sale to the British of World War destroyers and other small craft which would be of great value in keeping the sea lanes open. Britain must now draw all her supplies from far-distant points overseas.

(4) We can give our prompt and effective support to Secretaries Stimson and Knox, the newly appointed heads of the War and Navy departments. Two objections are being made to these men: they are able, distinguished Republicans who ought not to serve under a Democratic president; and they are "interventionists." If calling them interventionists means that both men have for years foreseen what is now occurring, that both have foreseen a terribly dangerous isolation crowding in upon the United States —if these be the charges against them, they are but added reasons for their prompt confirmation by the Senate.

This is not the time for the Senate to give notice to Hitler that we are already in full retreat before him. The fate of our world hangs upon what we do or fail to do before November. If by then Hitler has not conquered Britain, he probably never will. But if by November he has defeated Britain, we are in for many decades of defensive struggle as the last stronghold of democracy in a Fascist world.

We Adopt Conscription

JULY 3–AUGUST 28, 1940

On June 27 the President declared a limited national emergency to validate the seizure or control of all foreign shipping in our waters. Two days later legislation was completed for the registration and fingerprinting of all aliens.

In Europe, Russia delivered an ultimatum to Rumania and occupied the province of Bessarabia, a disputed area whose loss in 1918 the Soviets had never recognized. A little later, on August 3, 1940, the three small Baltic states, Estonia, Latvia, and Lithuania were to be incorporated into the U.S.S.R. as Soviet Republics. The eastern half of Poland had been seized by Russia during Hitler's invasion of Poland, and parts of Finland in the winter of 1939-40. These operations were to supply Russia with a buffer zone extending from the Baltic to the Black Sea, which was very swiftly fortified.

HITLER'S THREAT TO US
July 3, 1940

DURING RECENT WEEKS WE HAVE UNDERGONE THE GREATEST revolution in our thinking which has ever occurred. From a people with an island mentality, satisfied that no real harm could ever come to us, we have become a nation profoundly alarmed for our whole future and anxious not to be left alone in a hostile world.

45

On Sunday, June 16, the *New York Times* published a full page of dispatches covering all parts of the country, every one of which reported an overwhelming demand for aid to the Allies, short of sending troops, and for an immense armament program for ourselves. From Boston and Atlanta, from Chicago and St. Paul, from Omaha and Dallas, from San Francisco and Portland the news was identically the same. Neither regions nor parties made any difference. With one voice the nation demanded action in its own defense.

In these and many other reports there is evidence of a national unity which promises to save us from the divisions which have been so disastrous to some democracies abroad. As a people we are convinced that the Hitler system is a grave threat to our whole way of life.

Yet there are some who still say: "It cannot happen here. Can the man be so mad as to think he can master us?" What, in the cold light of what we know, are the probabilities of a Hitler attempt upon the New World if Britain is conquered? So far as words can constitute a threat, Hitler did his worst to us in his interview with Karl von Wiegand on June 13. In that interview Hitler disclaimed any intention to conquer the United States or to interfere in South America. By the record of past experience, no graver threat against us could be uttered than for Hitler to say he has no plans for us. Let us look at the record.

On October 14 and 19, 1933, Hitler took Germany out of the Disarmament Conference and the League of Nations—acts which plainly said that he meant to smash the peace settlements of 1919 and make another German bid for world power. But the plain intent was denied. Said Hitler on the same day: "While claiming boldly those rights which the treaties themselves have given us, I will say boldly that there are otherwise for Germany no grounds for territorial conflict."

46

At that time Germany needed arms for no purpose other than territorial conflict. And when German rearmament had a good start, Hitler raised the question of abolishing Austria. In his address of May 21, 1935, he asked for "self-determination" for Austria, but he expressly declared: "Germany neither wishes nor intends to interfere in the internal affairs of Austria, to annex Austria, or to conclude a union with Austria—Germany will also respect all other provisions of the Treaty of Versailles, including the territorial provisions." Words could not be plainer, yet in March, 1937, after a great fifth column had done its work inside of Austria, Hitler suddenly fell upon Austria with his new army and destroyed her independence. At the same time the Germans solemnly told everybody that they wanted only peace with the Czechs.

In March, 1936, Hitler suddenly tore up the freely negotiated Treaty of Locarno by marching his troops into the Rhineland. On that occasion, also, he shouted loudly: "We have no territorial demands to make in Europe." After Austria there was Czechoslovakia. Again a huge fifth column was organized inside the victim, and the launching of Hitler's army was prevented only by the pitiful surrender of the democracies at Munich. While Chamberlain and Daladier were hurrying to do Hitler's will, Hitler roared into the world's microphones: "If this problem is solved there will be no further territorial problems in Europe for Germany. We do not want any Czechs." Six months later Hitler's armies suddenly reduced all the Czechs to subjection.

The rest of the story need not be told in detail. Hitler's technique was perfectly clear from the beginning. It was to take one step at a time and proclaim that after that 'he would be satisfied. Each conquest was preceded by the most intense fifth-column attack upon the victim from within and carried out under a great smoke screen of

47

propaganda designed to confuse and reduce to inaction everyone outside.

In every case, too, these tactics succeeded. One of Hitler's first acts was to make a ten-year treaty of nonaggression with Poland. Yet he tore up that treaty and made war on Poland six years later. A little later Denmark was compelled against her will to sign a nonaggression pact with Germany. Holland was often assured that Germany had no intentions upon her, and Belgium was induced to break her alliance with France and to rely on Germany's promises to respect her neutrality.

It can, therefore, be only a danger signal when Hitler tells any country that he has no designs upon it. No greater warning could be given. It would seem incredible that Hitler should expect the tissue of lies in his interview of June 13 to deceive anyone. Yet he has amply proved in the past the validity of his principle that the more audacious the lie, the more likely it is to be believed. Consider, for example, his statement that "the so-called fifth column conveys nothing to me, because it doesn't exist except in the imagination of fantastic minds or as a phantom created by unscrupulous propaganda for obvious purposes." Could anything be more audacious than that—at a time when organized Nazi fifth columns are being unearthed in nearly every country in South America?

Yet his superlative attempt at deceit is to be found in the statement: "It has never been my aim or intention to destroy the British Empire." It is scarcely thinkable that Hitler expected anyone in the British Empire to believe that one, but he did expect some Americans to be deceived. His purposes in giving out this interview were undoubtedly two. First, he expected once again to fool those who might spoil his whole game by intervening before their own turn came. Hitler is acutely aware that it was American power which blocked Germany in 1918. And, in spite of all confident announcements, no German can be certain that our power would not be decisive again if exerted in time. Hence the obvious strategy to put us back to sleep again until the decisive battle with Britain has been fought. If our isolationist minority will only rise to that bait, Hitler's final attempt to paralyze the next victim while he finishes off its neighbor will have succeeded.

Then he would be able to face us in control of all Europe and Africa, with six times as many navy yards as we have and with Japan in secure control of naval-building resources only less vast in our rear. "But," we can hear Hitler's unconscious American allies saying, "surely he would be satisfied with Europe and Africa. Not even Hitler can be so mad as to think he can rule the whole world."

About this hope there are three things to be said. First, it is obvious enough that Hitler has cleverly and purposely deceived all his previous victims with assurances that his aims were strictly limited—and that this grab was his last. Second, the ambitions of the Nazis have inevitably grown with each succeeding conquest, until now, without any question, their vision covers the whole of this small planet. There is involved here the saddest reflection that any American can make. In 1918 we had in Woodrow Wilson a leader with a great, sane vision. He led us to visualize a shrinking world organized for peace and stability on the basis of a free union of many free peoples. But we allowed a clique of bitter politicians, who thought of their own power above all else, to take from us and destroy that sound, practical vision of an organized world of free peoples. Now all our powers must be summoned to prevent the unification of the world by force. We fight a defensive battle at great disadvantage, when we could have been leading the world into a new era of truly civilized life.

There is a third reason for expecting that Hitler would expand his operations to the New World if he conquers Britain. A part of the explanation of his never-ending conquests is to be found in necessity. He has started out to make Germany wholly independent, but he finds that after each conquest the goal eludes him. He still lacks iron and oil and foodstuffs—and they are to be had a little farther away. That is why Stalin is grabbing buffer lands and arming them with all haste. He knows that Hitler cannot be really independent, even in Europe, until he gets Russia's great wheat and oil lands—in both cases the finest in all Europe.

There is for the Nazis no place at which they can stop. If they rule all Europe, they will still need the coffee, cotton, and rubber of Brazil, the wheat and meat of Argentina, the oil of Venezuela and Mexico. Nor can their regime of brutal suppression and terror be safe while a single great people stands upright and free, a living challenge to that tyranny. While any weak peoples remain to be despoiled or free ones to be suppressed, the Nazis will be driven onward by what seems to them compelling necessity. They have set out on a road from which there is no turning back. It is not possible for any people, even the German "master race," to make itself truly self-sufficient and independent unless it rules virtually the whole of the earth.

Nor is it feasible for free, tolerant, humane, pacific peoples to live side by side with rapacious, brutalized empires which have put behind them every Christian and ethical principle upon which our civilization is built. We are in the midst of a world war which cannot end until one system or the other has triumphed. The next few months will be crucial. If by November, Hitler's battle for Britain has not been won, it is not likely to be. What we who are still free do or fail to do in this brief interval will loom large indeed in the pages of future history.

☆

On July 3 the British Navy acted to settle the uncertainty about the future of the French fleet. French ships in Britain were seized; those at Alexandria agreed to internment; and those at Oran, which refused, were attacked. A battleship and several other ships were sunk. Some crippled ships escaped to Toulon. On July 9 the French Parliament voted itself out of existence in favor of a totalitarian dictatorship under Marshal Pétain, who assumed full legislative powers. The vote was 395 to 3 in the Chamber of Deputies and 225 to 1 in the Senate, about two thirds of the total membership in each chamber. Pierre Laval was designated to draw up a new constitution.

COULD WE DEFEND
SOUTH AMERICA?
July 10, 1940

A HUNDRED AND SEVENTEEN YEARS AGO THE UNITED STATES forbade the transfer of any further territory in this hemisphere to any Old World power. Since 1823 the Monroe Doctrine has been our most important foreign policy, the only one upon which all Americans have agreed. But in all this time the Doctrine has been easy to enforce because the British Navy prevented any actual attempt to upset it. Now for the first time we are having to decide what we would do if the British Navy should no longer control the Atlantic, and we find that the problem would be of very great proportions indeed. Stated briefly, there would be nearly four hundred million Europeans regimented by Germany into one vast military and economic unit, with naval and air bases in Africa only 1,657 miles from Brazil.

Both the government and the Republican National Convention have declared that we will defend the whole of this hemisphere. But there are many who believe that neither our navy nor our air force could operate in the Atlantic below the bulge of Brazil. Certainly it would re-

51

quire a very great effort on our part to defend the whole of South America. The task of defending the Panama Canal by air would alone be an immense undertaking if German power were established anywhere on the southern continent. We would require a ring of air bases many hundred miles south of the Canal, bases which it would be essential to acquire by friendly means. Should we be driven to seize them from any of our southern neighbors, our difficulties would multiply very rapidly. The method of co-operation, lately applied in the Havana conference of twenty-one American states, is much the best way.

Great as the military problem would be, however, it would be overshadowed by the danger of an economic conquest of South America by a Nazi-controlled Europe. There is a school of semi-isolationists which has argued that we should let the Old World go hang and develop the New World as "our garden." We could develop rubber plantations in Brazil, it was said, and depend on the tin mines of Bolivia, thus making ourselves almost self-sufficient.

But such dreams of hemisphere security overlook entirely the fact that South America's trade is mainly with Europe. She has great surpluses of cotton, grain, and meat—things of which we already have too much. These goods must be sold in the Old World or not at all. The fact is that South America would be helpless before the barter methods of a German Europe. The Germans would give Argentina huge orders for meat and pay for them in manufactured products—on their own terms. The Argentinians could accept the proffered list of goods or do without. The Brazilians, also, would be compelled to take what was offered them in exchange for, let us say, an order for ten million bags of coffee. It would be better to get the German goods, however bad the bargain, than to have the coffee rot. Thus most, if not all, of the Latin American peoples would fall under the complete economic domination of a

Nazi Europe, and neither our battleships or our warplanes could prevent it.

It is to forestall the loss of Latin America by these means, already proved effective in the Balkans, that our government is sponsoring a huge organization which would buy up all the surplus products of Latin America and resell them to the Old World, or otherwise dispose of them. This bold proposal has been attacked by some as a chimerical idea. It is admitted, too, that such a corporation might operate at a loss of several hundred million dollars a year. Yet it is practically certain that nothing short of these heroic means would prevent the economic conquest of Latin America without the firing of a shot. A Nazi-controlled Europe would be the mightiest economic unit ever invented, and it would operate with a ruthless war mentality in every year of peace between its wars. No half measures would be of any use in attempting to hold our own economic position in our own hemisphere. That such an inter-American corporation would involve governmental control of our foreign trade is also no argument against it. If we permit the world to go totalitarian, we cannot avoid adopting *some* totalitarian methods in self-defense.

It is all to the good that our government is joining with the government of Brazil to build a great steel plant in Brazil to forestall Germany's doing it. Many other similar measures may be required. But we cannot begin to solve the problem, if the worst happens in Europe, by money power, by making loans. We shall have to think always in terms of commodities, of actual goods.

The task of preventing the military and economic conquest of the virgin resources of South America by a Nazi Europe would tax our ingenuity and power to the limit. But there is a third kind of Nazi invasion which would be still more difficult to meet. It cannot be too often reiterated that Fascism is war and that every Fascist regime fights by every means short of war during periods of so-called peace.

The propaganda war never ceases for a moment. The organization of fifth columns does not wait for war to begin. On the contrary, they are always ready to operate before the guns begin to go off.

That the Nazis and Italians are organizing fifth columns throughout Latin America is known to every reader of the newspapers. Some three weeks ago an investigation in the small republic of Uruguay disclosed a super-Nazi organization which directed Nazi Bunds throughout the whole continent. Nazi propaganda, as distinguished from political organization, is operated from Buenos Aires. A secret Nazi lodge controls the organizers. In an effort to block further investigations and to provide a cloak for further activity, the German legation in Montevideo has announced the disbanding of the local Bunds and the deeding of their property to the German legation—a ruse which deceives no one.

Everywhere below us there are fertile fields for the Fascist organizers. There are nearly two million Germans in Brazil, most of them Nazified either voluntarily or by pressure. As in Europe, the Nazi organizers coerce the reluctant into their organizations by threatening harm to relatives in Germany. This form of terror is now being applied also to the Norwegians, Dutch, Belgians, and French who are in South America. All these peoples are also being blackmailed by demands for money to protect their relatives or interests in Europe. Every South American country has its Nazi organizations, many of them openly flaunting storm-trooper uniforms. Mexico is uneasy over a fresh influx of German tourists. Colombia has lately dismissed all Germans from her air service, but most air lines in South America are owned and operated by Germans. Argentina is moving to curb the Nazis, but the fact that at the same time she has forbidden public criticism of Hitler and his ways helps to muffle and blind public opinion. Both Uruguay and Argentina are passing large armament appropriations, and we have a small fleet of warships at

Montevideo to support the government of Uruguay against Nazi revolt if necessary. The calling out of our National Guard is projected to replace the regulars if there should be further trouble.

These are probably wise precautions, but it would be most unwise to permit ourselves to be distracted from the main theater of events by the Nazis. Their ostentatious activity throughout Latin America at this time is undoubtedly designed to draw our attention away from England while Hitler attempts to take over the British fleet. It is in the British Isles that the fate of Latin America is being settled. If Hitler loses in England, the Nazis will never be a grave menace in this hemisphere.

If Hitler wins in England, we shall have more than we can do to the south of us. There are also three million Italians in South America, about half of them tied into Fascist organizations controlled from Rome. And should Hitler conquer England, the whole cultural force of Fascist Spain will aid the Fascist drive on Latin America. Inside each country, too, there are native fifth columns—most dangerous of all—composed of disgruntled politicians hungry for power, army officers who see a brighter future for themselves under warlike dictatorship, young people who have been led astray by Nazi or Fascist professors or by free trips to Germany, and reckless adventurers who are all set to become little Führers.

How are we to prevail against forces such as these if Hitler subdues England and bears down upon our Latin neighbors with unparalleled success prestige behind him? Mr. Walter Lippmann recently came to the conclusion that if Hitler defeats Britain "it will be beyond any power we possess, or can quickly mobilize, to defend Latin America. Strategically, economically, and ideologically, South America will be beyond our reach. . . . . The plain truth of the matter is," continues Mr. Lippmann, "that the fate of the Monroe Doctrine and the security of the Western Hemisphere will be decided in the battles that will be fought around the British Isles and at Gibraltar. If the French resistance is broken, if the British Isles are subjugated, and if Spain and northwestern Africa are dominated by Hitler and Mussolini, the strategic defenses of the Western Hemisphere will have been shattered. After that we shall be able to fight only a rear-guard action in the outposts of our security while we attempt at infinite cost and sacrifice to arm ourselves sufficiently to maintain our very independence."

I cannot find in these words of Lippmann the slightest exaggeration. They ought to shake from us the last trace of complacency and rivet our attention and effort on the British Isles every day this summer and autumn. There the British are putting up a tremendous battle against a Hitler world empire. There our fate is being determined. If the British win, we shall be spared the shouldering of terrific and perhaps unbearable responsibility in Latin America. Never before have we had such an opportunity to ward off unlimited danger and keep it at a distance. But never before has the need for quick decision and action been so imperative. A year ago it would have seemed incredible to any American that the British Empire and the United States would allow themselves to be defeated and the control of the Atlantic Ocean to be taken away from them. Today that catastrophe should still be something which we will permit to happen only if we have no power whatever to prevent it. What we do in the next few months will determine not whether we can keep out of war but whether perpetual war can be kept out of the Americas.

In a radio address on July 14 Prime Minister Churchill declared: "We shall seek no terms; we shall tolerate no parleys. We may show mercy; we shall ask none." On July 19 Hitler replied that if Britain did not sue for peace, she would be annihilated. At home a law authorizing a two-ocean navy by 1946 was enacted July 12. In Japan firebrand Yosuke Matsuoka became Foreign Minister and General Tojo Minister of War.

THE ECONOMIC CONSEQUENCES
OF A GERMAN VICTORY
July 24, 1940

TONIGHT I AM GOING TO TRY TO DESCRIBE WHAT A NAZI victory over Britain would mean to us economically—in terms of the plain man's bread and butter and of his economic security; in terms of the business man's profits and of his future in a Fascist world. In discussing this subject I am deeply conscious that no one can hope to foresee all the consequences of a Nazi triumph, but I feel as strongly that we must understand the main outlines of its meaning.

For many years our economists have understood that a European tariff union would create for us a competitor of unparalleled economic power. That is one of the reasons why our failure to back the League of Nations was so shortsighted. The League offered us a heaven-sent chance to work for a stable union of free peoples everywhere, but especially in Europe. There we had everything to gain from promoting a prosperous continent containing many free peoples living under the capitalistic system and trading freely with the world. But we threw away the immense opportunity which the League of Nations offered us. Too many of our people thought of it only as a liability for us to carry instead of a last chance to help create a decent, hu-

57

mane world whose orderliness would profit us more than any other people because our world interests were the greatest.

Now, instead of a United States of Europe governed by liberal ways of living and trading, the victory of Germany would mean a Europe forcibly unified and dealing with the rest of the world on a permanent war basis. Doubtless the Germans would maintain some camouflage appearances of local autonomy. Mussolini would still make speeches in Rome; other native puppets would be said to reign in other places; but the finance, industries, and tariffs of Europe would be ruthlessly controlled by Berlin. Everywhere businessmen and bankers who were willing to conform would get business, and the others would be boycotted and ruined.

To know what a Germanized Europe would be like we have only to look at the practices by which the Nazis have already conquered half of Europe. The first Nazi economic principle is that all property is at the service of the state. If it suits the state to spur some armament industries by permitting sizeable profits, they are allowed; but the cash reserves of all other industries, even of savings banks and insurance companies, are remorselessly taken. No man can buy or sell unless it suits the state to give him permission. The state directs his whole activity. In 1933 Fritz Thyssen, the lord of Krupps, contributed much money to put Hitler in power. Now Thyssen is a trapped refugee in Switzerland, lately urging his former workers to revolt—long after they have lost all power to revolt.

In any Fascist land, labor also takes what is given it—after every labor union has been destroyed and labor is driven to its utmost. From both capital and labor the Fascists drain away the huge sums to be spent on armaments, on the enormous political police which keeps everyone in subjection, and on the great propaganda machine which operates ceaselessly in foreign countries.

58

Another key aspect of Fascist economy is that it is based on things, not money. For ten years the Nazis have had no gold—not enough to back two per cent of their paper money—but it has not mattered. The Nazis have simply used their buying power to destroy completely the system of free international trade to which we still cling. The method is to buy from each country only as much as Germany sells to it—and to dictate the terms. Germany pays in her own paper marks, at what seem to be high prices to foreign producers of, say, cotton or wheat. Then Germany determines the prices which she will pay in manufactured goods and gains both ways. Against this method of trading the business interests of other states are helpless, because they are dealing with a great government, not with other businessmen, and because they have the choice of taking what Germany gives them or of seeing their raw materials rot or go unsold.

Against these methods the Balkan nations have been powerless. What would be the position of the twenty Latin American states if confronted with a Nazi Europe wielding the buying power of four hundred million people? In my judgment the American who knows most about the working of the Nazi economic system is Mr. Otto Tolischus, a veteran *New York Times* correspondent in Germany until his recent expulsion. Tolischus says that all Nazi transactions with other peoples are measured in terms of hours of labor and so rigged that it is really the military power of buyer and seller which fixes the rates of exchange. It is his deliberate conclusion that Germany "as the mightiest country in the world could herself determine how much foreign goods her fiat marks would buy and how much German goods the currencies of other countries would buy in return. Germany could determine employment and living standards in all countries that must trade with her."

It must be obvious to anyone that the twenty Latin

American republics, with great surpluses of raw materials which must be sold in Europe, would be individually helpless before a Nazi Europe. Probably nothing less than a tight tariff union of the United States, Canada, and the whole of Latin America would offer any hope of avoiding economic subjection to Berlin—and such a union might easily bring a decision in Berlin to seize South America with the superior military and naval power which Germany would soon control. The Nazis are wholly confident that they will never need to use military means to conquer South America, and they have every reason to believe that their overwhelming economic power, aided by Nazi agents, propaganda, and native fifth columns, would make the use of guns unnecessary.

Our own situation here in the United States might be a little better, but how much? No American businessman could buy or sell anywhere in the world without dealing or competing with a government monopoly backed by the military power of a vast empire. Perhaps the United States Steel Corporation might hold its own for a time, but could any ordinary manufacturer attempt it? What, too, would our wheat and cotton farmers do? Would they submit to the total loss of their exports, or would they set up a loud demand for German manufactured goods in exchange—goods which would be made by skilled labor paid the wages of sweated labor in Germany and the wages of slave labor in the rest of Europe? The prospect for American labor in competition like that is dismal indeed. But the position of American capitalists would be no better. As Walter Lippmann has recently warned, our capitalists would be competing with a gigantic economic unit in which capitalism was dead in everything but name, in which there would be no great overhead of bonds and other debts to carry.

In these circumstances what would our capitalists do? When Nazi agents approached them and said, "You can have a large foreign business with us on our terms or be boycotted and get none at all," what would the decision be? It must never be forgotten for a moment, either, that a Germanized Europe means automatically a Japanized East Asia, in which another five hundred million people and vast resources would be organized on the same basis for crushing the trade of all democratic rivals.

For many years our politicians have been telling us that political isolation was the thing, but no one wanted or even imagined economic isolation. But if Germany defeats Britain, how can we avoid economic isolation?

There would be two alternatives open to us. One would be to go totalitarian ourselves so far as foreign trade is concerned. Even great United States government corporations could not compete with a Germanized Europe on a basis of equality, but they could do something to make our end of the deal a little bigger. Such a course would automatically involve heavy regimentation at home—to stifle the surpluses we could not readily sell; to keep order among us while a shrinking standard of living gave us less and less to divide and as enormous armament costs took permanently what we would like to put into automobiles, clothing, and other consumption goods.

There are, it is true, some who still think that our gold would save us. Today we do have the world's gold; but if Hitler wins, its value will be very slight—perhaps less than the same weight of coal. The Nazis have proved conclusively that they can operate Germany at full speed on a managed currency and that they can impose that currency upon all weaker nations. If Hitler wins, he will take whatever gold he can get and send it to us for goods, and at the same time he will impose his managed currency system upon every people which does business with Europe.

This is not a pretty prospect for anyone who loves democracy or for a people which has grown up with every expectation of possessing its full share of the products of the whole earth by free and fair trade. But consider the

61

alternative to a closed, regimented economy in our own defense. If Britain falls and we do not at once wall ourselves in, we would be invaded by fresh hordes of Nazi agents, operating upon our cotton, wheat, and other export interests, tying up with Fascist-minded businessmen and boycotting those who hate their system, disintegrating our national life as they have that of all their previous victims. If we continued to drift before the storm, what could prevent us from becoming a German economic colony ourselves?

Whether we tried to weld this hemisphere into an economic unit, as now proposed, or whether we retreated to defend a shrinking life in North America, a Hitler victory over England would mean inescapably a long period of total war for us—war first perhaps on the propaganda and economic fronts for years, but war every month, week, and day of each year, with constant and feverish preparation for a final conflict of arms.

The Nazis are convinced that we would be one of the softest prizes to pick off as well as the richest. The United States, they say, is not a nation; it is just a vast agglomeration of mongrel breeds which will be an easy prey to the German "master race." We shall easily set race against race, class against class and labor against capitalists; for labor is gullible and selfish, say the Nazis, and capitalists will do anything for profits.

Today ninety per cent of all the people in the world still want only to live and trade in peace. Yet the ninety per cent are well on the way to being dominated and controlled by three gangster governments which together speak for less than ten per cent of the people in the world. Today only the British people and their outnumbered air force stand between Hitler and world dominion such as has not existed since the Roman Empire. How shall we be able to justify in the future the omission of any efforts which might enable the British to hold on in defense of our world until winter comes?

On July 25 the President prohibited the export of petroleum and scrap metal without a license. Up to this time Japan had been purchasing 65 per cent of her oil and 85 per cent of her scrap metal here. On July 31 an embargo was laid on the export of aviation-type gasoline to all countries outside the Western Hemisphere.

THE CRISIS IN THE FAR EAST
July 31, 1940

FOR SEVERAL WEEKS I HAVE TRIED TO EXPLAIN IN THIS RADIO period why I believe it is imperative that Great Britain should not be defeated by Germany if any action on our part can prevent it. It seems to me to be overwhelmingly clear that a Hitler victory brings to us not only military danger, especially by way of Latin America, but far greater perils to our economic life and to our free American ways of living.

For the past three months we have had our eyes riveted on Europe, where the crucial struggle is being fought. But it is always to be remembered that on the other side of us Japan is trying to do exactly the same thing that Germany is attempting in Europe. If Hitler conquers Europe and Africa, Japan will almost inevitably take over the whole of the Far East. Indeed, she is moving in that direction at the present time with a speed that does not permit us to overlook what is going on behind us.

A new government has just been formed in Tokyo—a

government of men whose avowed purpose is to take as many of the Oriental possessions now in European hands as they can, and as soon as possible. For more than three years Japan has been endeavoring to subdue the vast Chinese nation by bombing and killing and by such other means as the fostering of the opium traffic. She has seized all of China's seaports, all of her large cities and railways. Yet Japan has not been able to conquer China. The Chinese government still controls a large area in western China and causes constant trouble for Japan throughout the whole of China. Japan alone cannot conquer the Chinese. Her one hope is to force and cajole other powers to shut off all supplies to Free China and to continue to supply Japan with the war materials she requires. This policy, too, appears at this moment to be at the point of success. Early in the summer Japan forced the French government to close the rail line from Indo-China into Free China. Japanese inspectors now sit along that railroad to see that no supplies of military value go into China.

This Japanese success left only two other lines of supply open to China, both long and difficult. One was the trail across the great desert to Russia; the other was the Burma Road, a thousand-mile highway across the mountains, which the Chinese built in recent years at incredible effort, nearly all of it by hand labor. Now in the last two weeks the Japanese have induced the British to close the Burma Road to all military traffic for the next three months on condition that Japan try to make peace with China.

This appeasement move has been defended by Prime Minister Churchill as a temporary agreement designed to ease tension with Japan while Britain is "engaged in a life-or-death struggle." I am inclined, too, to believe that the present British government does not intend to sell China out to Japan permanently. The Chamberlain group would have done so more readily, but the Churchill government knows that the appeasement of predatory empires simply does not work. They have nevertheless tried, by the Burma Road concession, to keep Japan from attacking Hong Kong and Singapore this summer while Britain fights for her own life at home. If Hitler does not invade England successfully within two months, it is probable that British policy toward Japan may stiffen in the autumn.

In the meantime, the United States is the only remaining check upon Japanese ambition, and what we do to prevent Japan from seizing the vast resources of the Orient will have to be done soon. In saying this I do not suggest for an instant that we should move to protect British interests in the Far East while Britain is occupied at home. On the contrary, it has seemed to me for years that we should stand firmly against Japanese aggression in the Far East, regardless of British policy. If there is any following to be done in the Orient, British policy should follow ours, not our policy theirs. British economic interests in the Far East are at the present time much larger than ours, but this is not the primary consideration. The British might lose all their holdings in the Far East and still remain a great power on the opposite side of the world. We must live permanently as a neighbor to the Far East, and conditions there are of permanent importance to us. If we have to deal with a strong, free Chinese republic, that will be one thing; if we must deal with a huge, closed empire controlled by militaristic Japan, that will be quite a different matter.

So far, however, our government has not felt strong enough to do more than restrain Britain from too-hasty retreat in the Far East. A year ago, on July 18, 1939, when the British were about to surrender to Japan in the Tientsin area, we denounced our trade treaty with Japan. In January that treaty expired, but we continued to sell to Japan the war materials she required for the conquest of China. American oil, cotton, machinery, trucks, and money have still kept Japan in the war business. It was only on Friday last that President Roosevelt issued an order requiring licenses for the export of aviation gasoline and lubricating oil, tetraethyl lead, and number one heavy scrap iron. The President having declared these materials essential to national defense, it is to be presumed that they will not in the future be poured into Japan's war machine. These materials alone are not vital to Japan, but the addition of crude oil and all kinds of scrap iron to our embargo list would have an important bearing upon Japan's war effort. In 1939 we supplied 65 per cent of Japan's petroleum imports and 85 per cent of her scrap iron. In that year more than two million tons of American scrap iron went to Japan.

Whether our government should now shut off the flow of oil and iron to Japan is one of the most important questions before it. One restraining factor has been the probability, amounting almost to a certainty, that Japan would reply by attempting to seize the Dutch East Indies with their large supplies of oil and iron ore, rubber and tin. But if, as is generally believed, the present Japanese government means to move on the Dutch Indies anyway, our action will not determine its decision. Doubtless the Japanese have large stores of oil and scrap iron accumulated, enough to see them through a campaign against the Indies and also against British Hong Kong and Singapore. Had we embargoed oil and iron sales to Japan at the start of her war upon China, this would not be true.

Now the crisis is approaching in the Far East as well as in Europe. Japan's power, however, is by no means unlimited. She has a million men bogged down in China, and the Chinese have enough munitions stored up to last them for a year of heavy fighting. Doubtless the Japanese Navy and Army can still make a big effort in the South Seas; but Japanese economy is already strained, and there should be limits to the territory which Japan can spread herself over successfully if the democracies will defend their holdings.

Secretary Hull protested vigorously on July 16 against the closing of the Burma Road, but the British replied that the United States showed no inclination to take steps in the Far East which would make it unnecessary for them to appease Japan. Hence our government must decide during the next three months whether to exert enough economic pressure on Japan to justify us in strongly urging Britain to open the Burma Road in October. It is essential, too, that public opinion should understand what is at stake.

We cannot afford to forget the real issue—whether the Chinese people are to be free or enslaved to Japan. It is no longer possible to say that the Chinese will not fight or that they will not help themselves. They have done wonders in opposing the industrialized might of Japan—Japan backed by the oil and iron and machinery of the United States. For a hundred years the Chinese have regarded us as their friends; but if they are compelled by our war materials to submit to Japan, we will lose the very great asset of Chinese friendship at the same time that we gain an Asia monopolized by an unfriendly and aggressive Japan.

If at this time we take no effective steps to restrain Japan's conquests and to aid China, the Chinese will be left with only one line of communication to the outside world—the road to Russia—and with only one friend left —Soviet Russia. In that case either of two things may be expected: Russia and Japan may divide China between them, or Russia may continue to aid China against Japan and thus become China's only dependable friend. In either case Soviet influence would extend over a great part of China.

For the past ten years no one of the great democracies has taken timely action to defend its position in the world. The result is that France is conquered, Britain is fighting for existence, and the United States is arming feverishly to live, if necessary, a circumscribed existence in a hostile world. Yet it is very probable that the British Empire and the United States still have the power to prevent the world from being taken over by the gangster powers—if they can achieve teamwork in both the Atlantic and Pacific. But the time of the Anglo-Saxon powers is now very short. The next year will probably determine whether they are to lose control of the world and whether progress toward human freedom is to be set back for a long period, perhaps for several hundred years.

On July 31 the House of Representatives passed a five-billion-dollar supplemental defense bill, and three hundred thousand members of the National Guard and regular Army—85 per cent of the total—went into field maneuvers.

WHERE DOES COLONEL LINDBERGH LEAD US?
August 7, 1940

ON SUNDAY LAST TWO RADIO ADDRESSES WERE MADE TO THE American public which outlined as clearly as two speeches could the great dangers which confront this nation.

The first address was by Colonel Charles A. Lindbergh, and the second by General John J. Pershing. Lindbergh began by characterizing the great alarm for our future which has lately swept over this country as "hysteria" and "surface foam." He charged that there were American "interests" trying to put us into the war in Europe, without naming any of the alleged interests. He then tried to put us to sleep again by saying that "our eyes are turned once more in the direction of security and peace; for if our own military forces are strong no foreign nation can invade us, and if we do not interfere in their affairs none will desire to."

That kind of lullaby was sung to the Danes and the Norwegians, the Dutch and the Belgians by Nazi appeasers months and years ago. But Hitler needed some things which these people had and he took them over without a pretext or a qualm. If Hitler should conquer England, also, he would urgently need the riches of South America and he would take them—by propaganda, by economic war, and by military force if necessary—without the slightest regard for our feelings; and no amount of "minding our own business" would deter him in the slightest. Few people who have followed the events of the last seven years doubt that there is an irreconcilable conflict in progress between the gangster regimes and everything for which this nation stands. Every informed person also knows that Hitler is the head of a world revolution and that for years his plans have covered the whole of the earth. If anyone doubts the scope of Hitler's plans, I beg him to read either of these books by Hermann Rauschning: *The Revolution of Nihilism* or *The Voice of Destruction.*

The actual situation which surrounds us was conservatively stated by General Pershing in his Sunday address as follows: "A new kind of war is loose in the world, fought with all weapons, including treason, fought most insidiously during what some of our countrymen call peacetime. It is a war against the civilization that we know. It is a revolution against the values which we have cherished and which we wish our children to cherish in the future. It is a revolution which denies the dignity of man and which banishes the hope of brotherhood and comradeship on earth."

It is these ruthlessly destructive forces which Colonel

Lindbergh advises us will never desire to interfere in our affairs if we will only make peace with them now. He urges that "we must take the lead in offering a plan for peace." To the charge that no treaty with Nazi Germany is worth anything, he replies that "co-operation is never impossible when there is sufficient gain on both sides." How does Lindbergh propose to get advantages for us in a treaty with a Nazified Europe containing four hundred million people and far greater fighting power than we possess or can get? Hitler made a treaty of nonaggression with Poland in order to crush her later at his convenience. He forced similar treaties on his other weaker neighbors in order to overrun them when their time arrived. No one can point to a single treaty that Hitler has kept a moment longer than has suited his strategy of conquest.

What ground then does Lindbergh stand upon in asking us to accept a Nazi-dominated Europe? His reason is clearly set forth in his Sunday speech. He says, "I have a different outlook toward Europe than most people in America"—as in truth he has—and he tells us that he got it by traveling through Europe. He relates how he found the Germans thriving mightily under the adversity of their defeat. He "saw the phenomenal military strength of Germany growing like a giant at the side of an aged and complacent England. . . . . The underlying issue," says Lindbergh, "was clear. It was not the support of democracy. It was not a crusade for Christianity. It was not the preservation of the small and hopeless. The issue was one of the oldest and best-known among men. It concerned the division of territory and wealth between nations."

In these words does Lindbergh make his own the Fascist doctrine than any nation has a right to take what it wants from its neighbors. It is not without significance, either, that the speaker who preceded Lindbergh at the Chicago meeting said openly that in this world "might makes right." That is the Prussian doctrine which we defeated in 1918, and which is the only rule governing the conduct of Germany and her imitators today.

It is the law of the jungle, without any frills on it, which Lindbergh asks us to accept. To make his position on this point utterly plain, he says: "When I saw the wealth of the British Empire, I felt that the rich had become too rich. When I saw the poverty of Central Europe, I felt that the poor had become too poor. That something would happen was blazoned on the skies of Europe by mounting thousands of fighting aircraft."

What does Lindbergh mean by Central Europe? There is not a line in his speeches to indicate that he thought the Austrians and the Czechs too poor, that he pitied the poor Poles and Danes, the Norwegians, Dutch, Belgians, and French, and thought that they should take to robbing their neighbors; nor is there a word of regret or apology for the devastation and looting of all these peoples by the Nazis. No, the whole of Lindbergh's speech indicates that by "the poverty of Central Europe" he meant German poverty. This is what justified the devastation of a continent, the killing of countless myriads of people in their homes and on the roads, the driving of tens of millions of people into helpless flight. It was German poverty which justified to Lindbergh the killing of a dozen small nations, the systematic looting of everything they possess, and the deliberate attempts to exterminate whole peoples, as in the case of the Poles.

Let us examine this poverty of Germany which is alleged to justify the greatest pillaging expedition since the time of Attila. Lindbergh complains through several paragraphs that no one would believe how powerful Germany is. One of the myths that he lists as having been fed to us is "that Germany lacked enough food, fuel, and raw material to wage war." If she did not lack material things, why did she need to fight? But if Germany could afford in the space of seven short years to pile up enough armed power

to conquer all Europe, what becomes of the poverty excuse? What would have been Germany's condition today
if the Nazis had put the fifty to seventy-five billion dollars
which they have poured into armaments into things to eat
and wear and use? The whole of Germany could have been
rebuilt and the German people given the highest standard
of living in their history instead of the hard subsistence
standard which has been their lot.

Today we are not far from complete international
anarchy, and the Nazi-Lindbergh doctrine that the poor
have a right to take forcibly what they want from the
rich leads straight to total anarchy, both between and
within the nations. If it is right for a poor young giant
Germany to lay all Europe in waste in order that she may
seize the wealth of a rich old England, it is right for any
group to organize a strong-arm Fascist party in this country and take for themselves whatever they want from
whoever happens to have it. That is literally and exactly
what the German Nazis did when they came to power in
Germany. It was not only the Jews who were robbed, despoiled, and thrown out of their jobs. The whole Fascist
racket is at bottom organized gangsterism, and he who
espouses it internationally must be prepared to have its
virus eat into the vitals of his nation. For centuries we have
been slowly and painfully repressing international gangsterism. If it now escapes all bounds, the consequences will
be felt in the homes of the humblest citizens everywhere.
If it is right for nations to run amuck merely because they
are powerful, it is right for any thug who is physically
strong or who can get a submachine gun to take what he
likes from anyone who has anything, murder notwithstanding.

To compensate us for living in a world like that, what
does Colonel Lindbergh offer? There is in all his speeches
to date the injunction that whatever happens we must not
fight Europe, and his reason is always the same: that only

a war with the colored races—in which he sometimes hints the Russians belong—is justifiable. In his latest speech he seems to point toward Japan. It is only by co-operation with Europe, German-dominated or not, he says, "that we can maintain the supremacy of our Western civilization and the right of our commerce to proceed unmolested throughout the world."

The Nazi propaganda mills never invented a more deceptive doctrine than that. If Germany dominates Europe, Japan will control East Asia; and the last thing that these two predatory regimes will do is to fight each other when the richest prize in all the world, the Americas, lies between them. Giant German and Japanese empires cannot fight each other while thousands of miles of land mass lie between them, but they can co-operate to squeeze between them across the fluid ocean highways the last remaining island of freedom and the richest spot on the globe. By Lindbergh's doctrine, too, they would be fully justified in combining to take our wealth from us. Their greatly superior strength would give them full title to it.

No greater service could be done to Nazi Germany than to put out at this time vague plans for peace with her. From the beginning of his great career of conquest and looting, Hitler has been certain that the democracies would fall before him, one by one, because of divided counsels. So far he has been right, largely because he has spared no expenditure of money or effort in sowing dissension in advance of his armies. He has frequently boasted, also, that the American democracy will be the easiest to dissolve from within. Is he to be right?

The time is very close when the American people will have to show whether they have the sense to remain united and free or whether they will divide and lose their heritage. General Pershing put our plight in a few words when he said: "More than half the world is ruled by men who despise the American idea and have sworn to destroy it. They know that while one great people remains independent and free, because it is strong and brave, they can never crush finally the people they have conquered. The example of liberty here will always continue to inspire the resistance to tyranny over there."

That is the inescapable reason why we cannot avoid playing a part in the world conflict which is now raging. What is that part to be? General Pershing pleaded that we send to the British at once at least fifty of our World War destroyers. He made it plain that the British desperately need small warships to repel the coming invasion and that the lack of them may soon mean the difference to us between continued safety and a back-to-the-wall struggle for generations. Said Pershing: "The most critical time is the next few weeks or months. If there is anything we can do to save the British fleet during that time, we shall be failing in our duty to America if we do not do it."

Here is a definite, concrete decision for this nation to make. If we cannot make up our minds to take timely action now to keep the law of the jungle from breaking all bounds in Europe and Asia, flooding out into all the oceans which surround us, it will do us no good to complain of the endless burdens of defense which will follow.

There is a growing opinion that fifty or sixty of our destroyers, sent from what Pershing terms "our immense reserve of destroyers," will have an even chance of pulling Britain through. If that is true, no great people ever had an opportunity to escape decades of siege as cheaply. But time is short. We are compelled to decide soon whether we shall give the British the weapons they must have to survive or whether we shall take the path of appeasement, and we must make our voices heard by those in authority. Before we follow those who preach appeasement, we should remember Pershing's warning that the appeasers in seven European democracies "led their countries into disaster."

German air raids on England increased alarmingly, five hundred planes being used in a day.

OUR DECISIVE MOMENT
August 14, 1940

FOR SEVERAL WEEKS I HAVE TRIED TO EXPLAIN WHY I BElieve that we cannot permit Nazi Germany to seize control of the Atlantic Ocean. My reason remains the same: German victory would mean unending expense, strain, and danger to us and a perpetual attack upon our institutions. I have not argued that we should save Britain for Britain's sake—though a powerful argument on that score can be made—but for the sake of our own safety. May I add in all earnestness that no American should be deterred from helping to defeat Hitler by dislike of Britain. If there be those who hate Britain for her former subjection of Ireland, I beg them to remember that Ireland now enjoys freedom, for every practical purpose—a freedom which she will certainly lose to an antireligious, revolutionary tyranny if Hitler conquers England, for free government anywhere is a maddening offense in the nostrils of the Nazis, especially freedom that is close to German-subjugated peoples. And if there be those who hate England for other historical reasons, I ask them to remember that since the American Revolution, Britain has been steadily granting self-government to her peoples. Canada, Australia, New Zealand, Newfoundland, and South Africa—all have reecived full self-government. India and Southern Rhodesia are near to it, and all other British colonies of any size have some degree of self-rule. It is this relaxing control of the British which would be replaced by the hard, ruthless exploitation of the Nazis and the Japanese.

But our own great stake in Britain's survival is the thing

which must guide our action in this critical summer. What does a German victory over England mean to us? I list the following consequences as so plainly evident that no informed person can doubt their fulfillment if Hitler wins: (1) overwhelming naval control of the Atlantic by a Nazi Europe, which would have six times as many naval-building shipyards as we have, with ample men and materials to operate them; (2) German economic control of South America, based upon the regimented buying power of five hundred million people reinforced by full naval sway over the South Atlantic and a mass propaganda assault backed by the unlimited prestige of success; (3) Japanese rule of the whole of East Asia, with its six hundred sixty million people and its indispensable stores of rubber, tin, tungsten, antimony, quinine, and other products—rule backed by a Japanese naval control of the entire Pacific Ocean which we would be powerless to challenge; (4) a burden upon us of many billions a year for defense—not for a brief period, but for the long pull—permanent conscription, the growth of a militaristic class, and a steadily falling standard of living to accord with shrinking trade and mounting taxes; (5) a defensive position for all free institutions here which would keep us in constant internal struggle.

It is in the light of these tremendous burdens and dangers to us, which a Hitler victory would inevitably bring, that I wish to discuss the proposal advanced by General Pershing and dozens of other American leaders that our government send fifty or sixty of our World War destroyers to aid the British.

First consider the need. The British started out with one hundred seventy-five destroyers, of which thirty have been sunk and as many more sent to dry dock for extensive repairs. This leaves about one hundred destroyers to protect many hundreds of merchant ships arriving in England weekly, to keep the blockade in operation in all oceans, to work with the British battle fleets from Scotland to Suez, and to help defeat a German invasion of England. To break up a German invasion nothing could be more useful than the small, swift, zigzagging, yet powerful, warships of the destroyer type. In a decisive battle many of them could be lost and yet victory gained. Sixty of our destroyers in action around England in the two crucial months just ahead could easily mean the difference between living in a free world and living a cribbed, confined life in a world of Fascist terror.

But have we the ships to send? We have two hundred thirty-seven destroyers—a much larger number than any other naval power now possesses. If we send sixty to England, we will still have one hundred seventy-seven, a superiority over any single power.

What then prevents the sending of the destroyers? Let us consider the objections as cold-bloodedly as we can:

(1) It is said that such an act would get us into war with Germany, that is, into direct physical combat. That is possible; but the repeal of the Arms Embargo did not bring us into direct action with Germany, and the sending of several hundred of our army and navy planes early in the summer did not. The destroyers could be turned back to manufacturers in the same way and resold to Britain.

Would that be a violation of neutrality? It would unquestionably be a violation of the laws of neutrality which Hitler has ground to dust in his invasion and conquest of free nations from Norway to Belgium. We have also to remember that we are already at war with Nazi Germany, by every means short of armed combat, and that the struggle between their system and ours is irreconcilable and to the death. The Fascists have made war into a permanent, glorified thing. They have openly organized their peoples to wage war at all times, by propaganda and by economic weapons when it is not expedient to use military means. There can never be peace between such a system in control of Europe, Africa, Asia, and South America on one hand and a free, peaceful, liberal United States on the other. All that we have to decide is whether we will throw enough weight into the scales *now* to keep ourselves and our children from fighting on the defensive permanently.

(2) A second objection to sending the destroyers has been raised by some of our Navy officials. They say: "Suppose Britain should be defeated anyway? Then we would need every ship we can get." A month ago some officials in Washington concluded that Britain was done for. But Britain is still fighting magnificently, and surely her defeat should not be assumed while there is any reasonable chance of preventing it.

The reasoning of the Navy men is perfectly natural, and I do not for a moment censure them for it. They say: "We have twelve thousand miles of coast line in North America, and now the Havana conference has given us as much more to defend in South America. If we are to do that, we cannot spare even a rowboat."

It is this opinion which some commentators have told us must be final, must not be questioned. Yet some Navy men are strongly of the opinion that the sixty destroyers should be sent at once. Rear Admiral Yates Stirling, retired, said on August 9: "In my opinion, those destroyers should be furnished to Britain. They will be fighting for America most effectively by being added to the British Navy. That navy is all that stands between Hitler and his ultimate goal: the resources of the Americas and the enslavement of their peoples." On the same day, also, Admiral H. S. Yarnell, until very recently commander of our Asiatic fleet, took identically the same view; and the next day Admiral William H. Standley, former chief of naval operations, urged that Congress declare a state of national emergency which would permit the President to send the destroyers at once and to help Britain "without stint or limit."

No one can deny that if Britain were defeated we would need the sixty destroyers in addition to the one hundred seventy-five we would have left; but then we would need thousands of destroyers, tens of thousands of warplanes, and the two-ocean navy which we have voted but which can hardly be completed before 1946. *Then* the sixty destroyers would be a drop in the bucket of our needs. *Now,* manned by British crews around the British Isles, the same sixty destroyers would have at least an even chance of turning the scales and dissipating the great nightmare which hangs over our future.

Of course there would be risks, yet when did a people ever have a chance to risk so little for such huge gain? Not to take the risks of sending the destroyers and whatever else is necessary, says the columnist Frank Kent, "seems like national insanity on a grand scale."

Why then, isn't it done at once?

(3) In answer, Mr. Kent puts his finger on a third reason —that this is a political year with us. The fear of offending a segment of voters in some key states paralyzes both parties, in his opinion; and he is moved to say: "In so terrible a crisis it is an awful thing to think that the curse of politics is preventing the people from getting the truth from their leaders and blocking the country from the only course that holds out hope for freedom."

What is the wise policy for this country as the crest of the world crisis bears down upon us? When all the factors have been surveyed, can there be any other policy than one of sending to the British all the destroyers, airplanes, and other supplies that they require to pull them through until winter? Now, every dollar's worth of American arms used in the Battle of Britain may save the spending of a million or ten million dollars. Now, every ship sent may save the construction of a hundred costly vessels. Now, every plane sent may save us the building of a thousand or ten thousand planes.

Today is the decisive moment. Will it be written soon that the world lost its freedom because the Americans could not decide to risk a fourth of their destroyers? Will it be recorded that the United States became a militarized, impoverished nation because her leaders could not make up their minds to send the thousand airplanes which would have kept the gangster regimes from taking over the world? Will it be remembered for centuries that the greatest of the democracies was paralyzed at the most decisive moment in all world history by a political campaign?

These are questions which must soon be answered, and each American citizen must bear his share of the responsibility for the answers. Each of us has a little influence, and now is the time to use it. If you are convinced that we dare not permit Hitler and Japan to take control of the world in the next three months, make your views known as clearly and as forcefully as you can to the President and to the members of Congress, regardless of party. I am not suggesting that you write a dozen letters, or that you rest content with one letter, one telegram, or one speech. I am pleading that each person do what he can in this greatest of world crises.

By November we shall know whether England—and, with her, world democracy—still lives under the autumn fogs which will begin to blanket her. By November we shall know whether our great industrial power will have time to enable the British to overpower the gangster nations. Between now and Thanksgiving Day we must make certain that our entire future as a nation has not been mortgaged because we failed to take some comparatively small risks in August and September.

By this time the Germans were using a thousand planes over
England, whose navy was stretched dangerously thin by the
defection of France. On August 15 Churchill proposed to ex-
change naval bases on British possessions for fifty of our over-
age destroyers. In the Far East, Britain withdrew the last of
her forces from China, and our marines took over the British
sector in Shanghai.

IS CONSCRIPTION NECESSARY NOW?
August 21, 1940

FOR THE PAST MONTH THE NEWS CHANNELS HAVE BEEN
full of debate over the proposal to adopt conscription. Is
it possible to sift these arguments and arrive at a reasoned
conclusion? I have read everything on the subject that I
could find, and my own conclusion is that the arguments
against conscription will not stand up. But let me examine
the contentions of the opposition.

To begin with, both sides are agreed that conscription
is the only method to use in fighting a war. There is no
argument about that. There is only opposition to conscription in what is called "peacetime." This reasoning
assumes that until there is a formal declaration of war
peace persists. In former times that might have been true,
but no one who is even partly familiar with what has happened in the past nine years can honestly call our present
state one of peace. The world is in the grip of vast revolutionary wars which have ruthlessly destroyed the independence of a dozen nations and which may have complete control of the other side of both the Atlantic and
Pacific oceans three months from now. If that happens, I
know of no credible witness who foresees a life of peace
for this country, for the first thing to grasp about Fascism,
especially the German brand, is that its very lifeblood is

Is Conscription Necessary Now?   *August 21, 1940*

force, the permanent use of force. There can be no such thing as peace in a Fascist country; there can be only periods of arming, propaganda war, and economic war between military and naval wars. The existence of every remaining democracy in the world depends upon a clear understanding that Fascism can never become peaceful without ceasing to be Fascism.

But whether or not our country is in danger has already been settled by the Congress in appropriating more than ten billion dollars for emergency defenses. We are about to order many thousands of complicated war machines—warships, bombers, tanks, artillery. It is not thinkable that we shall fail to provide the men to operate them and the infantry to support them.

At this point it is asked, "Why bother to train the men when everybody knows the weapons won't be ready for months and years?" The reply is that this is precisely what Hitler did. He trained his men while the weapons were being made, and he would not have Europe under his feet today if he had not.

Driven from this position, the isolationists question whether conscript armies could save us anyway. Senator Taft actually argued in the Senate lately that universal service did not save France, Holland, and Belgium when they were confronted with "a highly professional force acting with perfect harmony and timing." Ignoring the fact that Germany's armed might is based on conscription, Taft proposed that we get this "highly professional force" by lowering the army enlistment period from three years to one year and three months—a step which would tend strongly to deprive us of any professional force at all. The truth is, of course, that any great army must have both professional soldiers and conscript reserves.

But the word conscription is offensive to many. It is undemocratic, they say. Of course no American likes to be ordered about, in the army or out; yet if each American

82

has a share in the government of the country, he also has a share in its defense—a share which each man cannot reject or determine for himself. In endorsing conscription in his acceptance speech, Wendell Willkie was careful to declare for "selective service" as "the only democratic way in which to assure the trained and competent manpower we need in our national defense."

There is the crux of the matter. Which is the best way to raise a great army for scientific warfare, in which the close co-ordination of thousands of complicated machines is required? We can take a great census of our total manpower, registering with at least some degree of accuracy what each man can do best, and then select for every kind of service. Or we can put on a big emotional recruiting campaign, turn the heat on the unemployed, pin white feathers on all athletic-looking youths, and drive into the army the boys who are most sensitive to these appeals and pressures. Is that really the way to get a democratic army or a skilled one?

I do not suppose that selective service is fair to every man without exception, or that it is proof against draft dodging, or that it always puts the right man in the right place; but the selective method cannot be as inefficient as the method of forced volunteering.

Nevertheless, the opposition to selective service is pinning its hopes on a delaying campaign—the same kind of campaign which defeated the League of Nations in the United States in 1919. It is to be remembered, too, that the leaders of the fight against conscription are, with one or two exceptions, the direct heirs of the group of senators who kept us out of the League of Nations, telling us that there would not be another great war for a century and that our future needed no protection. Today our new isolationist leaders say with one voice: "Let us wait until January 1, and in the meantime put on a great recruiting campaign and raise the base pay in the Army to equal that in the Navy." Great play has been made of the higher pay in the Navy. The Navy has all the men it has asked for, they say. That is true, but there are one hundred thousand more enlisted men in the lower-paid Army than there are in the Navy. The pay of the two services is going to be equalized, but does anyone seriously suppose that raising the pay in the Army by thirty cents a day will get us a great army and, ultimately, millions of trained reserves?

What do our young people say on the subject? A Gallup poll issued on August 11 registered 62 per cent of those between twenty-one and thirty for selective service and 66 per cent of the entire population. The vote for conscription carried every single state in the union without exception. Both President Roosevelt and Mr. Willkie have endorsed it unequivocally, though Senator Taft allowed himself to say that Willkie's "selective service" did not necessarily mean a draft. Most of our national leaders are supporting the swift passage of the Burke-Wadsworth conscription bill, a measure sponsored by two strong opponents of the Roosevelt administration.

Yet the passage of the bill before the national election is by no means certain. A strong fight is being made against it by many sincere pacifists and by citizens to whom danger still seems remote. Needless to say the mail of isolationist congressmen is being swelled heavily by the followers of Father Coughlin, by the Communists, by the Bundists, and by other fifth-column elements.

The opposition to conscription is being led in the Senate by the same group of men which opposed the repeal of the arms embargo. They are the men also who, led by Senator Borah, told us a year ago that there would be no war in Europe. They now pose as the calm, cool men who still know what is ahead. In a radio address of August 9, Senator Nye dismissed all fear of a Hitler Europe and talked about "this pother of conscription," "whipped-up hysteria," and "being led down the pathway to war." In a similar address Senator Wheeler said that conscription "would slit the throat of American democracy" and greatly please Hitler. He neglected to say that Hitler ignored all of Britain's warnings for years because she did not adopt conscription and that her national life is at stake as a result. Senator Holt declares, "Show me a dictatorship and I'll show you conscription"; but he does not mention that democracies have always used conscription whenever necessary. He dismisses warnings of German aggression across the ocean as "just plain poppycock." This group freely alleges that, in the words of Senator Nye, "the only emergency in this country is the one conjured up by those who want to send our boys to Europe and Asia."

Perhaps I may be permitted a personal word on this point, not because my experience in the last war was in the slightest degree notable, but because it was typical of that of multitudes of others. I enlisted in early 1918 and served six months overseas. I thought it was a long way to go to fight but could not doubt that there were forces loose in the world which had to be stopped. As a private soldier I had some officers whom I respected. I also obeyed ignorant, conscripted corporals, supertough sergeants, and shallow, cocky lieutenants—with no particular pleasure but without jumping to the conclusion that conscription was a bad way to raise a wartime army. It was the only way then and it is the only way now. But now the danger to our country is far greater than it was in 1918. Then we had mighty allies to screen us safely while we hastily made an army. Now that screen is wearing dangerously thin. It may well be that the lack of small warships will permit it to be broken in the next three months. In 1918 we were not menaced by the creation of enormous hostile empires on both sides of us. Today we are. In 1918 we had only old-style German militarism and imperialism to meet. Today we confront a Germanism which is a hundred times more dangerous and which operates ceaselessly on all fronts, military

85

and nonmilitary, night and day, in so-called peacetime and in time of open warfare.

Today there are no battlefields left in Europe upon which our armies could fight. That should be clearly understood. But today the battle between gangsterism and freedom is world wide, and it will be fought to a decisive conclusion. Today, too, the forces of freedom and democracy have been in disastrous retreat for nine full years, and they are still retreating.

Of course conscription is distasteful to us, but our fatal apathy in world affairs until lately has made it inescapable. Of course it will be costly, but if Hitler is defeated we can soon dispense with it. If victory is coming to him, we are already very late in adopting conscription. This is a political year, and the vote of a few states in which isolationist or anti-British feeling is strong may determine the election. But in these days our democracy cannot afford a single failure to function. It is on trial for its life.

On August 22 Japan called home forty diplomats from service abroad who had liberal or democratic tendencies, and a new United States–Canadian Joint Defense Board was constituted.

SOME FALLACIES WHICH ENDANGER US
August 28, 1940

TONIGHT I WISH TO CONSIDER SOME OF THE FALLACIES which have helped to destroy a dozen free governments abroad and which work to undermine our own. It is human to discount danger and to believe what we want to believe.

The first refuge from reality to which we fled when the dictatorships were created was a belief that they would soon fall from internal reasons. For years we steadily alleged that the Soviet regime in Russia could not last for economic reasons: it simply would not work. Then when Mussolini and Hitler came to power, we said: "But what will happen when the leader dies?" I have been asked that question dozens of times, nearly always with an air of suggesting that there could be only one answer. It is possible, too, that a disastrous struggle for power might break out when the leader dies, but it is most unlikely, since the huge one-party machine which the leader heads has every reason to set up a new chief quickly and continue to rule. None of the tens of thousands of little autocrats under the big one wants to lose his fat job of lording it over his area. When, also, every suspicion of opposition to the gang in power has been ruthlessly stamped out, there is no group anywhere which can raise its head. The army is the only body which could revolt, and it will not because the regime pours the whole substance of the land into its coffers and holds out perpetually the promise of conquest, glory, and loot. Once a totalitarian regime has been forced on a people, it can never be broken except by some great national disaster; and the chances are ten to one that the disaster must come from defeat in war.

A second fallacy which has gripped us for twenty years is that the conquest of weaker nations by others is "none of our business." The vast majority of our intellectual, business, and labor leaders knew at the close of the last war that the world had become so small that we must take a hand in its government. There was no altruism about it; the scientists and inventors had already destroyed time and space to such a degree and at the same time increased our need of the products of every corner of the world so greatly that it was a matter of extreme urgency for us to be able to live thereafter in an orderly world. But a group of our senators decreed to the contrary, and we soon followed them in proclaiming that we were not our brother's keeper and that all we had to do was to "mind our own business." How often have we heard that blind and selfish phrase rolled unctuously or tartly from the tongues of isolationist leaders! Yet with every passing month the earth was shrinking steadily for all the purposes of trade and war.

What was "our business" in those years after 1918? Would it not have been far more "realistic," as the hard-boiled men like to say, for the United States Government to keep its ear constantly tuned for the fall of the smallest sparrow among the nations? In 1918 the United States was incontestably the greatest power on the globe. In military and economic strength and in moral leadership we stood upon a pinnacle of power and responsibility such as no other nation has ever attained—until our Senate leaders told us to forget about the responsibility!

Then for ten years we sought money above all else, with our uneasiness suppressed, until the towers of money suddenly crashed about our ears and the looting of weaker nations began. We were deeply uneasy when the first depredation occurred in Manchuria in 1931, and our alarm has steadily increased with the mounting roll of nations assassinated. Today we still have great potential strength, but we have reached the pass that if the British Empire falls we shall at once be overshadowed, both in Europe and Asia, by gigantic empires with potential strength far greater than ours. Then we would be one of the world's smaller powers, whom it would be nobody's business to help if we were attacked.

We are very close to finding ourselves in this plight because of a third fallacy which has soothed our dreams—that our oceans are a secure defense for us. This is the greatest of our illusions—the one which seemed most to make practical our pell-mell retreat from the world after the last war. I would be the last person to deplore the existence of those oceans or to wish to abolish them. They can never be abolished and they are a great defense asset. But they have seemed to be a safe defense during the last century and a quarter only because no superior navy in either ocean was hostile to us. As far back as 1814, when the British Navy was hostile, the slowness of sailing ships did not prevent the taking of Washington and the burning of our capitol. The essential thing to remember about oceans is that primarily they are not barriers but the easiest and greatest highways in the world.

Today the airplane has shrunk our oceans to ribbons of water, and each month that passes sees them narrower. They are still useful for defense, especially if we have far-flung outlying bases in all directions; but very soon no power can prevent the bombing of our cities if gangsterism rules the opposite shores. Last Friday, August 23, an announcement was made by Major General Henry H. Arnold, head of our Army Air Corps, which means definitely that the immunity of the whole of the United States from attack is about to be ended. General Arnold revealed that in October our Army will have a bomber boasting a wing spread of 212 feet, carrying the largest cannon ever sent aloft, having a gasoline capacity of 11,000 gallons, and capable of flying to Europe from New York and returning nonstop, not only to New York, but all the way across this continent to Los Angeles.

This announcement does not mean that our country can be invaded and occupied by air. No one believes that to be possible yet, but it does mean that our cities in the interior soon can be bombed by planes based on Europe. It means that within a few years Chicago and St. Louis and Kansas City can be attacked as well as New York and San Francisco, even in the unlikely contingency that all of the nearer bases would be in our hands. If the great screen of protective power which the British air and naval forces constitute is removed, any blackmailing dictator who may rule Europe can back his demands, let us say for a free hand in South America, with the power to bomb all of our great cities, even if he cannot occupy them. If it be granted that there will be some delays and some effective defense prepared, the fact still remains that the physical security of every large city on the globe is doomed shortly to disappear. If that is not true five or ten years from now, it will be true a little later. More than once during the past week incendiary bombs have started night fires in London, and great buildings have been wrecked by explosive bombs day and night. Tomorrow, historically speaking, our own cities will be open to similar attacks—unless British cities can withstand that kind of pounding for many months and unless the British air force finally overpowers the regimes on the European continent which have made war a total destroyer of men's homes and institutions.

As a nation which has since 1919 put its trust in a refusal to help defend other people's liberty, we have one last, final chance to prevent the destruction of a strong and kindred people. If Great Britain is submerged, we shall stand alone, without a powerful friend in the world and with enormous naval and military power developing on both sides of us. That would be a dangerous and enforced isolation such as no isolationist ever dreamed would actually come upon us.

Should that situation develop, there is still another fallacy upon which some are disposed to rely—that there would be revolts in many of the conquered lands. The answer to this hope, as I see it, is that there has been no revolt in either Italy or Germany. This has not been because great numbers of people did not want to revolt but because they were helpless to do so. With all power in the hands of the ruling group, revolt is hopeless. Rebels could hope to have only a few hand weapons against countless war machines. The mere organization of a revolting group is nearly impossible. The Gestapo constantly roots out everyone who shows any signs of having ideas of his own. Every single person is under the direct control of some member of the ruling gang.

In the conquered provinces, too, the same state of affairs soon exists. The big weapons are all in the hands of the conquerors. If there is trouble in any town it is crushed so brutally that it does not arise again. One bombing plane can keep hundreds of square miles in subjection once a people has been beaten and disarmed. Why sacrifice one's life uselessly when there is not the slightest chance of achieving anything? Conquered peoples can indulge in a little passive resistance of a mild character, but they can revolt only when the master race itself has been mortally stricken in war or, conceivably, by famine and disease. The power of modern weapons is such that seventy million Germans could easily rule the whole of Europe and Africa over a very long period, just as a like number of Japanese could dominate the entire Orient.

Toward Lend-Lease

The Burke-Wadsworth selective service bill passed the Senate on August 28 by a vote of 58 to 31 and the House on September 7 by 263 to 149, becoming law on September 14.

Abroad, Rumania was compelled by her Axis overlords to cede the Dobruja to Bulgaria and half of Transylvania (about twenty thousand square miles) to Hungary. King Carol abdicated in favor of his son, and General Ion Antonescu took over the government.

An Italian invasion of Egypt was fifty-five miles past the frontier, and another drive pressed from Ethiopia into Kenya. The British Navy made an unsuccessful attack on Dakar in French West Africa in behalf of a British-French expeditionary force led by General de Gaulle, September 23, and French planes bombed Gibraltar in reply. Simultaneously, Japan took over North Indo-China from France without serious resistance. London underwent its fifth all-night air raid on September 12.

On the same day, President Roosevelt informed Congress that he had completed an exchange of fifty old destroyers for ninety-nine year leases on eight sea and air bases on British territory scattered from Newfoundland to South America.

DO THE NAZIS AIM AT WORLD DOMINATION?

September 25, 1940

THERE ARE MANY PEOPLE WHO FIND IT DIFFICULT, IF NOT impossible, to believe that the Nazis are aiming at world empire. Nobody could be so foolish as to attempt that, they say; yet Hitler has said that "the impossible is always successful," and he has proved his point many times already.

Where does the truth lie? Do we have any reliable evidence for judging whether the Nazis are bent on world domination? The most detailed evidence published so far is to be found in two recent books by Hermann Rauschning. The title of the first is *The Revolution of Nihilism*. It was published a year ago, and there were twelve printings within three months. Rauschning's second book is called *The Voice of Destruction*, by which he means Hitler's voice. I suggest that you ask for one or both of these books at your local library.

The Rauschning books are everywhere accepted as a revelation of Nazi aims, because no one doubts the honesty of Rauschning's report. He was the Nazi President of the Danzig Senate until 1934, and as the leading citizen of Danzig he often had personal talks with Hitler and was in the inner councils of the Nazis for years. He joined the Nazi movement as a cultured, highly-educated young conservative who believed that the movement was a genuine effort to regenerate Germany on constructive lines. That was during the years when the Nazis were making their seductive campaign promises. Rauschning left Germany in 1934, when he was finally convinced that the Nazis were out to destroy everything which is of value in our civilization. From his first association with the Nazis to the last page of his recent book, Rauschning is a German patriot, one whose greatest desire is to see Germany a constructive, accepted member of the family of nations.

What, then, does this authenic witness tell us about the aims and ambitions of the Nazis? In the first place, he makes it clear throughout both volumes that the Nazi movement is a revolution against all existing order, that its chief urges are to destroy and to dominate. He was slow and most reluctant in coming to the conclusion that the Nazi revolution was truly nihilistic, that is, bent upon destruction for its own sake. Now he is wholly convinced that the habit and desire to destroy are so deeply rooted that the Nazis must continue their destroying career until stopped by superior force.

It has long been apparent to all who watch the situation that Germany is in the grip of a giant "racket." There is no other word which applies as accurately. Rauschning gives the details of the nation-wide grabbing of jobs, houses, lands, and every other valuable thing which followed the advent of the Nazis to power. Government, business, and industry—all had to turn over jobs and wealth to the great army of adventurers which chiefly composed the Nazi party. Most pitiful of all, perhaps, was the subservience of the German upper classes. These people had fallen for the Nazi tirades against Communism. They thought them genuine and believed that they could admit these bullies to power and then tame them down into useful tools of the aristocrats, *Junker* landlords, and industrialists.

What actually happened is described by Rauschning as follows: "The old upper classes wanted to remain on top. Bared of any shame or dignity, they clung to their positions, followed all the party doings they were told to follow—anything not to lose their positions. . . . . The greatest blame for the men's rapid loss of courage must be placed on the women. Unwilling to give up their luxurious cars, to be turned out of their palatial residences, they dinned into the men's ears the thought of the future, and of their children's future. The new social classes, on the other hand, pushed upwards ruthlessly, by every means. Never before has there been such corruption, such lack of stamina, in Germany!" [1] An eminent bank president admitted openly that he was not going to take any personal risks. He would

---

[1] *The Voice of Destruction*, G. P. Putnam's Sons, 1940, p. 99.

do as he was told. It was in this fashion that the German upper classes realized, when it was too late, what they had done in helping Hitler to power. Since then some of them have fled from Germany. Fritz Thyssen, the former master of the great Krupp works, who helped to finance Hitler to power, has been a refugee in Switzerland for many months. For a while he issued appeals to his workers back in Essen and all over Germany to resist the Nazis—long after they had lost all power to do so. Since the Nazis overran Europe, Thyssen has been silent, probably waiting, as Switzerland herself does, for the night when the Gestapo will knock at the door.

Soon after Hitler came to power he was able to boast to Rauschning: "I make use of members of the old ruling class itself. I keep them in fear and dependence. I am confident that I shall have no more willing helpers. And if they become refractory, I can always return to the ancient classic method." [2]

At this point I am sure that some will say, "But isn't there a constructive side to Nazism?" And the reply must be that in one sense there is. The Nazis have abolished unemployment and given millions in Germany a sense of being needed instead of being useless and derelict, a sense of being a part of a huge going concern. This is a fact which the remaining democracies may well ponder. No one in Germany is now allowed to go hungry or to be without a job. Quite to the contrary, the whole population has been overworked, overstrained for years—and for what? First to provide those terrific armaments of which we now know the size and purpose. Then the Nazis built, in addition to many useful things, party stadiums so huge as to stagger the mind and government buildings in Berlin large enough to house government offices for the whole of Europe. From Berlin concrete roads broad enough to carry the

[2] *Ibid.,* p. 282.

military traffic of a new Roman Empire now radiate in all directions.

The Nazis have indeed built the engines of domination. It is no longer necessary to demonstrate that they intend to rule all Europe. That has been apparent from the beginning. Rauschning only proves what we know from every sign coming out of Germany: that the plans for picking off Germany's neighbors one at a time were made years before the Nazis came to power in 1933. The same plans also call for the complete control of the whole of Russia.

If Britain is conquered, the Nazis will have Europe and Africa securely in their grasp, and Russia can be dealt with when they see fit. Only this week the Axis has announced that Africa is theirs. If the resistance of Great Britain can be crushed, then the enormous buying power of the whole European continent, plus Africa, will be turned upon South America, together with the prestige of unlimited success and a propaganda drive backed by hundreds of millions in money. Said Hitler in the summer of 1933, when Brazil was mentioned: "We shall find everything we need there. . . . . We shall not land troops like William the Conqueror and gain Brazil by the strength of arms. Our weapons are not visible ones." [3]

No one of us can look forward with any complacence to a struggle for South America against a Hitlerized Europe, with the cards stacked against us. Such a Europe would desperately need the great resources of South America, and the means for taking them were perfected long ago.

But aside from this danger, the Nazi regime is driven incessantly by its belief in nothing except violent activity. Rauschning searched in vain for something which the Nazis really believe in—some philosophy, some ideal, some purpose to benefit humanity—and he found nothing, only the desire to dominate, to breed a race of master rulers which

[3] *Ibid.*, pp. 61, 63.

would control the earth itself. Said Hitler just after President Hindenburg's funeral: "The revolution cannot be ended. It can never be ended. We are motion itself, we are eternal revolution." [4]

That this is profoundly true is the deepest lesson in Rauschning's books. In his words, "The National Socialist regime is now the prisoner of its own system of domination. It can no more dispense with its pursuit of hegemony than with its government by violence at home. It is following the law of its existence, and cannot be diverted from its path either by threats or by good will." [5]

The Nazis cannot stop the conquest and domination of foreign peoples because they are always coming close to some rich land to loot and because the dangerous example of some remaining free people is always still to be erased. But there is a still more compelling reason. If they gave up domination of the conquered nations and said, "Now we will live as brothers together; you shall help us to govern and to decide what shall be done," then the same rights would have to be granted to the German people—and the job of the master ruling class would be gone. Then, as Rauschning says, "All the things that are of the essence of the present regime would have to go—violence, terrorism, thraldom, and the daily quota of engineered enthusiasm and unison under duress. Then justice and the liberty of the person, freedom of thought and speech and action, the freedom of the immortal spirit of man, would have to be readmitted into Germany." [6]

To do this would be a stultification of Nazism, root and branch, to which the Nazis could not possibly agree. The Nazis must therefore proceed with the unlimited expansion of their dominion of conquest and looting. They could

[4] *Ibid.*, p. 75.

[5] *The Revolution of Nihilism*, Longmans, Green & Co., 1939, pp. 284-85.

[6] *Ibid.*, p. 298.

not stop if they would. They are driven by everything which they are and have done to go on until they are stopped somewhere by superior force.

On September 25 the United States encouraged China's resistance to Japan by a loan of twenty-five million dollars, and the next day an embargo was laid on all types of scrap iron and steel which might reach Japan. On September 27 Berlin announced the completion of a tripartite military alliance linking Germany, Italy, and Japan together.

THE TRIPLE ALLIANCE GIVES US NOTICE
October 2, 1940

FOR THE FIRST TIME IN OUR NATIONAL HISTORY AN IMPORTANT alliance has been made which is aimed primarily against the United States. I refer, of course, to the German-Italian-Japanese military alliance which was published last Friday.

This treaty announces that the three powers will "assist one another with all political, economic, and military means when one of the three contracting powers is attacked by a power at present not involved in the European war or in the Chinese-Japanese conflict." What the signatories mean by "attacked" is not stated. From all past practice we know that they regard any form of attack as legitimate—propaganda, economic pressure, or military action—whether or not it is called war. The Japanese still deny that their giant campaign of conquest in China is war. In the words of the treaty just quoted, the Sino-Japanese War is termed a "conflict."

The first thing to be said about the new treaty is that it is an indication of weakness on the part of the three aggressors. Hitler now knows that he has few chances of beating the British into submission before winter. The German people must therefore be prepared for another hard winter of war, during which the bombs won't all fall on London. The Italians, also, who never wanted this war, must be steeled to undergo their first winter in it. The short war that Mussolini was so anxious to have begins to lengthen. And for the Japanese the prospect is still worse: they must tighten their belts for a fourth winter of war—the war which was only to be the first Chinese "incident." Conditions are not yet desperate in Japan, but the strain is beginning to be severe.

In this predicament the three conquerors have come to the conclusion that the slow-to-move United States is the decisive factor in the world struggle. If we have time to mobilize our great industrial power, it will defeat them; and it begins to look as if we would have the necessary time. Hence the noisy warnings from Berlin, Rome, and Tokyo that if we do not stay quiet until they have conquered the rest of the world, they will gang up on us. The Italian press has been particularly vocal in trying to appeal to isolationist and pacifist sentiment in the United States at this important moment in our national life. Signor Gayda, Mussolini's mouthpiece, said on Friday that the triple-alliance treaty is "a warning to those American circles who consider themselves protected by President Roosevelt's favor and are tracing, at least in speech and print, plans of interference and intervention in a war that does not concern and cannot touch America and that is being fought in regions vital to Italy and Germany, who on their part do not even think of entering regions vital to America.

"These circles know," continued Gayda, "that any folly on their part would now expose them, on two land and sea fronts, to a war on two whole continents, and to ruinous loss of all the positions that the work of their people has conquered."

Gayda's protestations and warnings will of course not deceive anyone who knows even a little about the activity of the Italians and Germans in South America. But the most revealing threat to us is today's message from the president of the Japanese press association to the American publisher Roy Howard. A terrible crisis is impending in the Pacific, says the Japanese publisher, and it can be prevented "if America abandons the fortifications at Pearl Harbor, Guam, and the Midway Islands, gives up its support of Chiang Kai-shek, and restores trade to normalcy."

There you have it. All we have to do is stop our curtailment of war supplies to Japan, cease helping China, give up all plans to fortify Guam, where we have no fortifications, and demolish our great naval base at Pearl Harbor, Hawaii. Pearl Harbor is our greatest defensive base in the whole Pacific region. It is also on our side of the ocean. But to solve the present crisis we are invited to raze our fortifications there.

Such a demand would be humorous if it did not reveal, clearly and accurately, the mentality we have to deal with both in the Atlantic and the Pacific. The Pearl Harbor demand should convince the last lingering doubter that a policy of appeasing any of the predatory powers is sheer suicide. It is plain enough that they have agreed to intimidate us from helping Britain and China further until they have won control of everything beyond the oceans which join us to Europe, Africa, Asia, and South America. The three powers have agreed to threaten us from both sides in the hope of distracting and confusing us into inactivity.

In this situation what should our reaction be? There are some who dismiss the alliance as of little significance to us. They point to Japan's growing economic weakness and to the fact that the alliance is a far greater threat to Russia than to us. It will now be very difficult for Russia to venture to support Turkey when the Axis powers move into Greece. Strong pressure will also be brought upon Russia to stop sending war supplies to China—and this pressure may possibly be successful. Russia is now back in the position of being threatened on two fronts—gripped by the fear which has ruled her policy for two decades. Will she accept Persia and Afghanistan—baits to keep her busy until England is defeated—from triple-alliance powers, or will Stalin be more astute?

No one of us can answer that question now. At least our own problem has been much more sharply outlined. As I see it, the German-Italian-Japanese alliance has made three things so plain that Americans are not likely to disagree seriously about them in the future: (1) that we are in the midst of a true world war which is due to continue for years and which will determine the future of every nation; (2) that it is more than ever necessary to aid Great Britain in the main theater of war; and (3) that we should not surrender control of either the Atlantic or the Pacific unless we are compelled to do so.

The last war was a world war in the sense that dozens of nations took part in it, but it all centered in Europe. This war has two centers, both vital to us, since on both sides of us strong powers are fighting to create enormous closed empires. We shall do well not to take our eyes off the main battle, that which centers on Britain. While Britain stands we do not have to undertake the backbreaking task of defending the whole of this hemisphere. While Britain controls the Atlantic, we do not have to face superior navies in both oceans. No threats or diversions should deflect us from widening the stream of material aid which we are sending to the British. Each day that London stands up under the German rain of bombs keeps the war on the other side of the ocean, and each day's resistance gives us time to prepare to defend this hemisphere if the worst should happen in Europe.

Keep our eyes on the main issue, yes. Yet it does not follow that we can do nothing in the Pacific. The United States, Australia, New Zealand, the Dutch Indies, and the British still have the power to block Japan. They have the economic resources which Japan must have to conquer East Asia. They have the naval and air power and the naval bases which can enforce a blockade of Japan that will release her grip on China and leave the future of the Pacific to all the peoples that live on that greatest of oceans. But strong co-operation between the English-speaking powers is just as essential in the Pacific as in the Atlantic. We ourselves do not have the power to stop Japan's career of conquest in Asia, and the peoples whom she is conquering are not strong enough to resist her alone. As matters now stand, there is nothing to prevent Japan from creeping down through Indo-China and Siam to Singapore. With Singapore once in her hands, the Dutch Indies, Australia, and New Zealand could be picked off one at a time, not to mention the Philippines, which now have Japan's bases on two sides of them.

Neither the peoples on the other side of the Pacific nor we ourselves alone can restrain Japan—and give the great Chinese people a chance to live a free, democratic life. But by acting together the non-Japanese peoples on the Pacific may prevent all East Asia from falling under Japanese domination. Such a policy means: (1) that China be strongly supported; (2) that the great bases now in the hands of the democratic powers—Pearl Harbor, Singapore, Port Darwin in Australia, and Manila—be jointly used; and (3) that concerted economic pressure be brought to bear upon Japan.

The British, fighting for their lives in Europe, have tried to appease Japan. They yielded to Japanese pressure and insult at Tientsin. They abandoned Shanghai and closed the Burma Road at Japan's behest. The result is that Japan pushes south toward Singapore and makes a military alliance with Britain's deadly enemies in Europe. Appeasement has had the result that it always has wherever tried. Now that it is clear that the remaining free peoples all over the world have a strong community of interest and that they have virtually no choice but to stand together, the first consequence of the new triple alliance should be the reopening of the Burma Road and the speeding of aid to China. Our government has just loaned another twenty-five million dollars to China. With the Burma Road opened we shall receive from China tungsten, which we badly need, in exchange for war materials.

The three aggressor powers have formally put us on notice that they intend to hang together until they have taken complete control of Europe, Africa, and Asia. We cannot longer be in the slightest doubt as to their aim to dominate the earth. They give us the plain choice of defending our world position while we have powerful friends and bases on the other side of both oceans or of waiting until we face the pack alone.

On Monday, October 7, Undersecretary Welles had a conference with the Soviet Ambassador. On Tuesday our subsidy on wheat shipments to China, from which the Japanese Army largely benefited, was canceled, and Canada stopped sending copper to Japan. Prime Minister Churchill announced that the Burma Road would be opened on October 17. All Americans in the Far East who were not urgently required to remain were strongly advised to come home, and steamship offices in China and Japan were flooded with Americans. This exodus disturbed the Japanese people and led a Foreign Office spokesman to give out a statement on October 9 saying: "There is no reason to be so nervous. We wish Americans to understand that there is nothing to be alarmed about."

SHALL WE APPEASE JAPAN?
October 9, 1940

DURING THE PAST WEEK THE UNITED STATES HAS BEEN CHAL-
lenged more deliberately and menacingly than ever before
in her national history. On Friday last the Japanese Foreign
Minister Matsuoka issued a statement in which, among
many other strong warnings to us, he said: "I fling this
challenge to America: If she in her contentment is going
to blindly and stubbornly stick to the *status quo* in the
Pacific, then we will fight America. For it would be better
to perish than to maintain the *status quo*."

This is the usual dictatorial trick of using words to mean
the opposite of the truth. One would suppose that the map
of the Far East which we recognize as legal is very, very
bad and that Japan has a divine mission to change everything. Matsuoka repeats the new Japanese formula for making words lie. He says that Japan is trying to create "a
new order of mutual prosperity" in East Asia. But no single
person outside of Japan will be deceived. Everybody knows
that for years the comparatively small Japanese nation of
seventy million people has been trying to enslave six hundred million people in East Asia with fire and sword, with
rapine and opium, with bombs and threats.

Now Matsuoka tells us that war or peace is "purely in
the hands of the United States at this moment." In 1932 I
observed the sessions of the Council and Assembly of the
League of Nations at Geneva, during which Matsuoka, as
Japan's chief delegate, used similar methods in attempting
to block a judgment by the League upon Japan's conduct
in Manchuria. I remember especially one long session of
the Council during which Matsuoka tried for two hours to
prevent the Earl of Lytton, who had headed the League
Commission of Investigation in Manchuria, from saying
that he still concurred in his report. But President de Valera

104

of Ireland, in his capacity as President of the League Council, patiently but firmly defeated Matsuoka. Weeks later, when it was clear that Japan was going to be condemned as no nation ever had been in all history, Matsuoka stalked from the Assembly room, taking Japan out of the League of Nations.

He could do that, but he could not convince the assembled representatives of fifty nations that Japan was right; and his present attempt to intimidate the American people will have no more success. We have learned during the past two years that there is no safety in the fear of war. Being afraid of war does not keep war away any more than failing to oppose gangsters causes them to let you alone.

Japan's open drive for the rule of all East Asia compels us to make a vital decision. Shall we wait until she has seized the resources for truly great naval power, or shall we bring her career of unlimited conquest to a stop now? For nine years we have watched with growing disgust and concern the brutal Japanese campaign to dominate Asia. Now the Japanese have gambled everything on a drive to intimidate us at the decisive moment. But they have also compelled us to recognize that the decisive moment is here. An opportunity such as a nation has only once in a century is forced upon us. What use shall we make of it?

The case of doing nothing is presented by General Hugh S. Johnson in the *Saturday Evening Post* for October 5. In a long article which makes the fullest use of his strong vocabulary, Johnson argues for inactivity. He asserts that our great danger is in Europe and seeks to show that our fleet has no business in the Pacific. He sets up six arguments for what he calls "this strange diversion of our great defensive force" and knocks them all down without once looking the double peril of a Hitlerized Europe and a Japanized Asia in the face. Johnson talks of "sticking our unwelcome and gratuitous neck out in Asia," alleges that we can do nothing until we have first spent ten billions

105

in the Pacific, and terms any thought of opposing Japan's career of conquest as "a policy of foreign aggression" on our part, "which we have no business to pursue." Johnson ridicules the idea that China could be democratic, writes off our Open Door policy and the Nine-Power Treaty as being "dead as a dodo," contends that we can't depend on the British because they closed the Burma Road, and assures us that we need not be uneasy about a combination of the conquering powers against us. These powers will collide with one another, he says, "long before they threaten us," and he challenges anyone to call him an appeaser.

Now let us look at the other side of the picture. Japan is now in a public military alliance with Germany and Italy, the openly avowed and sole purpose of which is to keep the United States and Russia quiet until they can be dealt with singly. We still have the phenomenon of ten per cent of the people in the world—the Germans, Italians, and Japanese—trying to dominate the other ninety per cent by terrorizing everybody while they pick off the nations one at a time. The next victim on their list is the British Empire. If Britain fell they could then choose at their leisure whether to smother South America or Russia.

General Johnson is right in saying that we must not be diverted from continuing powerful aid to Britain. There the main battle is being fought, and it is imperative that we never forget the main issue. But that does not mean that nothing can be done about Japan.

It is altogether probable that if we continue to aid Japan's conquests with our natural resources she will succeed in mastering the whole of East Asia. But Japan cannot become a colossus unless we keep on helping her to do so. She started on her career of world conquest from a very slender base. She has been at war for three years, and the economic pinch is beginning to be severe. She has a million troops and more mired down in China and yet has only half conquered the Chinese. Her finances are badly strained. She is vitally dependent upon her foreign trade with the United States, the British Empire, and South America. Our country and Britain unquestionably have the power to bring her drive to become the master race of East Asia slowly but surely to an end. Nor is it necessary to send our fleet to attack Japan, though it is vitally necessary that we should not permit Singapore to fall into Japan's hands.

There are now but two places in the world where Japan can get the oil which keeps her war machines running. One is the United States; the other, the Dutch East Indies. That is why Japan is now plunging for the Dutch Indies, which also contain our supplies of rubber, tin, and quinine. Singapore must be held in order to protect the oil of the Indies, and also as the Asiatic bastion of a long-range blockade of Japan.

If Singapore is defended by our warships, in co-operation with some British ships and the considerable Dutch Navy in near-by waters, Japan would attack that power area only at great peril and disadvantage. The forces already in the Singapore regions, especially air and land forces, are important. Australia and New Zealand are also ready to make large contributions. As matters stand we can help our friends in the Far East to hold their bases, aid them in drying up the supply of oil that keeps Japan's bombers roaring over China, and enable all of the peoples in the Far East to develop their own lands in peace. To foil Japan it is necessary to take some risks, but we do not escape risks by doing nothing. By remaining inert we invite the creation of an enormously powerful Japanese navy in the hands of a truculent enemy.

Successful resistance to Japan means primarily naval action, with the American-British-Dutch-Australian combination resting on the defensive in their own waters. We have a powerful navy, which was built for use in great national emergencies. It is not needed in the Atlantic and will not be while Britain has the firm grip which she still holds on that ocean. Our newly acquired bases in the Atlantic will also soon push our Atlantic defenses a thousand miles into that ocean. Why should the two great naval powers abandon either ocean to pillage and conquest? Especially, why should the United States, which must always live between those oceans, give up either ocean to a self-elected master race unless absolutely compelled to do so?

In recent months I have learned to respect the observations of Rear Admiral H. E. Yarnell, who was until recently commander of our Asiatic fleet. Yarnell said today, after a conference with our Navy heads: "Washington is not going headlong into war. It is trying to avoid war. But the new triple alliance is aimed directly at us. We may be better prepared for a showdown with Japan now, while she is bogged down in China, than we will be six years from now"—that is, when our proposed two-ocean navy is completed.

That, as I see it, is the nub of the situation. We do not want war with Japan, but it is time we dealt with her firmly. It is reassuring that our reply to Japan's provocative threats is the calling up of all our naval reserves and the ordering of our people home from China and Japan. It is doubly reassuring that Britain has defiantly ordered the reopening of the Burma Road into China. Surely the end of retreat before Japan has at last been reached. It is almost impossible to believe that the United States and Britain will be separated again by appeasement influences in their dealings with Japan. We have all learned that where there is appeasement there is no peace and that to have a government which cannot act, constantly and courageously, is just about the same as having no government. There is no occasion for any precipitate action on our part, but all our experience of the last nine years supports a policy of firm and constantly increasing resistance to Japan's predatory ambitions.

WHY DO WE HAVE CONSCRIPTION AGAIN?

October 16, 1940

TODAY IS AN IMPORTANT DAY IN AMERICAN HISTORY. IT IS the second occasion in twenty-five years on which American men have registered for compulsory military service. It is a day on which it is important for all of us to pause and ask why it is that we should be obliged to resort to this drastic step so soon again.

Twenty-three years ago we mobilized our men to defend our rights upon the seas, to make the world safe for democracy, and to end war. Yet today we have by statute given up our right to use the North Atlantic Ocean, democracy is fighting for its very life, and war of the most desperate character rages, not on one side of us, but on both sides. Who is responsible for this state of affairs? What acts, what policies, what leaders have brought us back to a far more dangerous pass than existed even in 1917?

An explanation of our present predicament was made on Monday by Colonel Charles A. Lindbergh—a statement which ought to be very carefully scrutinized by all who are concerned about the future, both for what it says and what it does not say.

Lindbergh contends that we are in danger today simply and solely because of the leadership of President Roosevelt and Secretary Hull in foreign affairs. In a short address he speaks disparagingly of our present leaders nine different times and argues that all we have to do to be safe is to throw these leaders out. Can it be as simple as that?

Lindbergh begins by saying that it is amazing that he should have "to enter a plea for American independence," and it turns out that his idea of independence is complete aloofness from what is happening in Europe and in Asia. He says no single word about the strangling pressure of the enormous gangster empires that are now being rapidly created on both sides of us.

He begins by telling us that we won our independence when there were only four millions of us—but omits to mention the vital aid which France supplied us. He says we ejected Spain from the New World when there were only seventy-five millions of us and asks why we should be afraid of anything now that we are a hundred and thirty millions.

For many months past it has been evident that Nazi Germany was bent upon conquering an enormous empire which would include all of Europe and Africa, not to speak of the wheat and oil lands of Russia. It has been equally clear for years that Japan was engaged in the conquest of the whole of East Asia. On both sides of us empires are in process of creation which would command absolutely the labor and wealth of more than five hundred million people. These empires, we well know, would be operated as closed economic units wielding tremendous buying power. It is because a hundred and thirty million Americans may find themselves located between gigantic empires that we are arming and mobilizing. Since Colonel Lindbergh last spoke, all doubt that these predatory empires would squeeze the Western Hemisphere in a giant nutcracker has been removed by the publication of the triple alliance among Germany, Italy, and Japan, and by the tirade of intimidating threats against us which has poured out of Tokyo. We have felt the first great diplomatic squeeze—and at a moment when the gangster powers are still helpless to operate on us. Yet the only reference in Lindbergh's speech to the progressive extinction of free peoples which has been going on for nine years is the phrase: "Under this leadership we have alienated the most powerful military nations of both Europe and Asia."

That is equivalent to saying that we should have been

quiet when Japan took Manchuria, shown no concern when Italy seized Ethiopia, raised no protest when Czechoslovakia was murdered, and kept silent while Hitler's brutal tyranny swept over the finest and most civilized nations in Europe. By the same argument we should keep our mouths shut if the tremendous propaganda and economic power of a Fascist Europe floods down upon South America. We should resist only when the military power of a Nazi Europe and a Japanized Asia reaches our own borders —when large elements in our own population would already be corrupted by an enormous fifth-column campaign.

Colonel Lindbergh may believe that this is wisdom, but it is a policy which no great democracy could accept. It is to the eternal credit of the American people that they and their leaders have protested against each major outburst of international brigandage and terror as it occurred. I have before me an account of the nation-wide protest against the Nazi barbarities upon the German Jews which occurred in January, 1939. Thomas E. Dewey, Alfred E. Smith, Herbert Hoover, Alfred M. Landon, and scores of other national leaders of every religion, race, and political creed joined in the universal condemnation. These protests were not only right; they were in the line of self-preservation; for if barbaric brutality spreads unrebuked and unopposed, it will corrupt and conquer every free nation without exception. We cannot give the earth over to gangsterism and expect to keep the gangster mind and gangster methods out of the life of our own country. The earth is far too small for that. Yet in Lindbergh's address there is not the faintest suggestion of disapproval for the barbarities in Europe and Asia which for years have disgraced civilization itself, and which continue to increase in magnitude and atrocity.

On the contrary, Lindbergh, like Matsuoka of Japan, puts the whole responsibility upon us. "We can either throw the world into chaos," he says, "or lead it to new heights

111

of civilization." I only wish that we had such a choice. But the chaos is here; it is not of our choice, and any policy of doing nothing about it removes the last possibility of our leading "to new heights of civilization." The blunt fact is that the world is in the hands of lawless elements which could not stop if they would.

Lindbergh makes it perfectly clear that he would let the aggressor powers go just as far as they can. He condemns England for fighting "for land" and says we are now taking the same road. To give the Chamberlain government credit for fighting "for Poland" of course goes much too far. England fought in September, 1939, for the identical reason that we are helping England today—to avoid having to fight alone when all friends and allies have been conquered.

It is possible that we may let England and China fall—and face alone a totalitarian world which acts by the sole principle of taking what it can. But if that happens, it will not be because our present leaders did not see ahead and try to prepare us. Lindbergh speaks of "the men who were unable to foresee these conditions." But for years past Secretary Hull has incessantly warned us, as on October 27, 1937, that "order in international relations is just as vital as in the relations within a nation." On October 7, 1937, President Roosevelt issued a warning in which he traced the international lawlessness that was already rampant and cautioned: "Let no one imagine that America will escape, that it may expect mercy, that this Western Hemisphere will not be attacked, and that it will continue tranquilly and peacefully to carry on the ethics and the arts of civilization."

We were warned early enough, but it takes a long time and the pressure of tremendous events to move the people of a great democracy to action. Of late we have bestirred ourselves mightily. The great preparations we now have under way Lindbergh speaks of as "this alarm and confusion" and indicates that much of what we are doing is unnecessary.

No one can be sure of that any more than he can tell what use we shall have to make—or be able to make—of the armaments we still have on paper. The one thing that we certainly know is that all over the world the initiative is still in the hands of the destroyers who are looting and enslaving nation after nation.

It is indeed tragic that we should have to come to conscription so soon again. But if we seek to place the responsibility, we shall have to go back to the close of the last war and find out what leaders prevented the United States from entering the League of Nations, from taking any part in administering the peace settlement, from bearing our fair share of the risks and burdens of keeping the world in order. When these leaders are discovered there will indeed be crushing responsibility to assess, and not only in the United States. In Britain and in France also there were postwar leaders who sabotaged the League and thought they could make balance-of-power politics work again. When responsibility for the world's present plight is to be distributed, there is enough to go around among the principal nations.

But one central fact is clear: in 1919 the three great democracies had the power and the responsibility to keep the world in a reasonable degree of order, and they refused to do it. Now one of the great democracies is gone, and many smaller ones. Now the democracies that are left must first prevent predatory conquest from engulfing the earth. That is the task which we cannot escape. Then the free peoples must see to it that the peace is not thrown away and the world surrendered to chaos again.

On October 22-23 conferences were held by Hitler and Ribbentrop with Pétain, Laval, Franco, and Ciano. On October 28 an Italian ultimatum to Greece was refused and Italian forces attacked from Albania. Rumania had been occupied by German troops a fortnight earlier.

ARE WE GOING TO WAR?
October 30, 1940

I WISH TO CONSIDER TODAY THE QUESTION WHICH HAS BEEN brought to the front of most minds by the national campaign: To what extent can we avoid taking part in the world war now in progress? Very different answers have been given to this question lately, and, for my part, I have found many of the answers given by both sides disquieting —some of them gravely so. I do not pretend to have access to any unique fountain of wisdom, but, as I see it, the speakers on both sides are leaving unsaid some things which ought to be remembered, even in the heat of the campaign.

In the first place, the orators are using the word "war" in the old traditional sense to mean fighting with guns. But fighting with guns and bombs is only one phase of the world war which is now in progress, and it may not be the most decisive element in the fighting. I can see no way for our people to meet the crisis which confronts them without a general realization that the totalitarians have made war their permanent way of life. They have wiped the very word and idea of peace out of their minds, except as a propaganda weapon. Said Hitler in 1933: "War is eternal, war is universal. There is no beginning and there is no peace. War is life." [1]

These words describe exactly what has been taught with deadly intensity to the youth of Italy and Germany for

[1] Rauschning, *The Voice of Destruction*, pp. 6-7.

114

many years past. There is no secret about it. Every person who has followed the Fascist regimes knows that Fascism is war. It is born of violence, lives by force, and wages war by every means at its command each day of every year. First the nation is conquered and then the whole of its energies turned into war upon other peoples. War is waged just as relentlessly for years before the guns go off as while they are firing, and we shall delude ourselves completely if we suppose that a treaty of peace can be made with any Fascist power. The stopping of the guns merely means that the war goes into other channels—channels which can easily be more deadly to us than the war with tanks and bombers.

Trade and commerce used to be a thing of competition, perhaps of sharp practices; but it was a peaceful exchange of goods and services from which both sides gained. Trade was carried on by individuals and by comparatively small groups of men for their own gain and to everybody's advantage. Governments interfered with it by levying protective tariffs and by other devices, but no government tried to make its own foreign trade an engine of war. Now the totalitarians have mobilized every atom of trading power which they possess and forged it into a means of waging perpetual, never-ending war. Their massed buying power sweeps over the borders of weaker nations like a conquering army, seizes their markets on a conqueror's terms, holds them—partly by economic power and partly by intimidation. The wealth of many peoples is sucked into the conqueror's war machine and used to extend his military sway.

Almost everything depends upon our ability really to comprehend that if the Nazis win their present military campaigns they will mass the buying power of half a billion Europeans and Africans into one huge economic thunderbolt and hurl it at Latin America before directing it finally against us. Which of the twenty Latin American states can resist barter offers for the whole of their great surplus crops

115

when they produce crops of which we have huge surpluses ourselves? Once a so-called Nazi peace is imposed upon Europe, all our two-ocean navies and myriads of planes will be powerless to prevent the economic conquest of our weaker neighbors.

The Fascist machines may not even need their other weapons of waging war while the guns are silent. But if the new triple alliance wins its present desperate thrust for world power, it will be due very largely to the power of its fifth columns. Most governments have always had a secret service and employed some spies. But now the Germans and Italians have elevated propaganda into a major activity of the state and of the whole nation. Every loyal subject is a militant soldier in the propaganda army, fighting day and night permanently. The propaganda general staff directs a huge organization. It has immense funds at its command. The investigation recently initiated by Secretary Knox concluded that the Nazis have recently spent two hundred million dollars on propaganda and fifth-column work. Many thousands of trained agents permeate the whole life of the peoples next to be taken over. Every conceivable means is used to weaken and confuse. Every human weakness is made use of until the ground has been prepared for the military invasion. Personal ambitions, class conflicts, party antagonisms—all are fostered to the fullest. The wisdom of appeasement in every form is continually suggested, while both persuasion and force compel those of kindred race to enroll in the fifth-column armies of invasion.

It is essential to remember, too, that all three forms of war—propaganda, economic pressure, and military action—supplement and reinforce each other in periods of supposed peace and open war alike. The war is fought implacably in every realm of life and against every free people. Nor can any free nation escape it. The totalitarians give us no choice. Every thoughtful person knows that we have been in this total, permanent world war for years past—and there is no way by which we can resign from it. It cuts too deep.

The new triple allies not only proclaim their intent to take over control of the world; they seek to destroy our way of life completely and irrevocably. They work ruthlessly to kill all respect for weakness, all belief in truth, all recognition of conscience, all regard for the pledged word, all love of liberty. They smother all freedom of expression—by petition, press, radio, or word of mouth. They kill belief in Christianity, brutalize youth, strangle the human spirit, and destroy every free man's self-respect as they sweep nation after nation. I need not call the long roll of strangled nations again. It is an appalling fact that Greece is the sixteenth nation to be assaulted since Italy invaded Ethiopia in 1935.

It is not, I think, possible to escape more than momentarily the knowledge that we are caught in a life-and-death struggle between two utterly irreconcilable ways of life—a war which must go on until one side or the other is decisively defeated. We are in the midst of a world revolution of destruction which has gathered such terrific momentum that it is still sweeping everything before it. The best that we can look forward to is years of grueling struggle.

It would be foolish not to recognize also that there are dangerously incalculable forces working on the other side. The British can take the bombing for a time at least, but can they live huddled in foul holes in the ground for many months and retain the will to go on? The conquered peoples of Europe do not *want* to submit to a tyranny so highly organized that it cannot be shaken off for generations. But can they go hungry and cold all winter without coming to the point where they will give up all hope of freedom for the promise of some kind of peace and normal living? We may well remember that it was this desire for peace which made the Munich surrender possible—and that the conquered peoples have lived under unbearable strain too long already. We know now that France was defeated during a winter of waiting as much as by a summer's fighting.

We must hope that the British and the Chinese will stick it out—and we must see to it that they do. Fortunately, we are virtually all agreed about that.

Does that mean that we shall declare war? I can see no ground for believing that we shall—unless we are wantonly attacked by military force. The coming of permanent war has almost made declarations of war obsolete anyway.

Shall we send great conscript armies to Europe or Asia again? There is little reason for thinking so at present. We are not fighting the last war but an entirely different one. None of our friends want troops or have now any place to use them. Nor can any need for sending great American armies abroad now be foreseen.

Will it be necessary to use our navy to prevent a world triumph of the totalitarians? I do not see how anyone who weighs the tremendous strategic value of Singapore in the East, or of Dakar in West Africa, not to speak of the Azores and other islands which lead from Europe down to South America, can be certain that the use of our navy will not be required to ward off a state of permanent siege for us by huge closed empires on both sides of the United States.

Will our whole economic power be needed to win the war? Of this there is no room for doubt. Whether we permit any American men to fight directly in the war which will decide the future of every free people, we know that our supplies and weapons forged in our factories will win the war if it is won at all. We are irrevocably in the war, and we dare not quit until the world has been made a reasonably decent place to live in again. We

dare not believe that the strongest free people in the world
will choose to live permanently in a world given over to
brigandage, a world in which this country would become
a lesser power among colossal ones.

Never at any time has our whole future as a people been
so dangerously at stake as it is now. If the totalitarian aggressors are defeated, we have no domestic problems, economic or social, which cannot be solved—and we shall
have the time and the resources to solve them. But if the
dictatorships should win, either soon or after a patched-up
truce, we would have neither the time nor the money to
build a sounder social structure. On the contrary, both
permanent militarization and the inroads of the economic
war would compel our standard of living to fall steadily.

That much seems to me as certain as anything can now
be. But I do not believe that anyone can foretell just how
much of our power will need to be thrown into the
struggle, or in what form or when. That will depend upon
(1) the development of events abroad which are beyond
our control and (2) the clarity of our determination not
to be left to bear alone the full propaganda, economic, and
military assaults of a Hitlerized Europe and a Japanized
Asia.

WHAT KIND OF NEW WORLD ORDER?
November 13, 1940

Two days ago we celebrated the twenty-second Armistice Day. For most of us it was a sad day—a day of remem-
brance for the war which we won on the battlefield and
of mourning for the opportunity to make peace which we
failed to use. Let us take a look backward to see where

we have come from and then glance forward in an effort to see where we are going.

In recent years our people have been largely misled about the causes of our entry into the war of 1917. We went to war in April, 1917, because the German government repealed all of its pledges to us not to engage in unrestricted submarine warfare. We had taken our stand upon long-established rights to travel the seas, in our own ships or in those of the belligerents, in wartime as well as in peace; and at last we had no choice but to enforce that right or surrender it. We chose to fight. But behind that decision was a conviction which had been mounting for years that German ruthlessness could not be allowed to bestride the earth. Most of all we rebelled against the senselessness and horror of a world war which struck at the foundations of all civilized existence, which violated everybody's rights, and which could not possibly compensate any victor for the senseless loss and damage which had occurred.

That is why Woodrow Wilson wisely summoned us to fight to make the world safe for democracy and to end war. If he had asked us to fight merely to punish the Germans for the killing of our people, he would not have gone down in history as a farsighted statesman. It was not mere rhetoric when in the last sentences of his war message he said: "It is a fearful thing to lead this great peaceful people into war, into the most terrible and disastrous of all wars, civilization itself seeming to be in the balance. But the right is more precious than peace, and we shall fight for the things which we have always carried nearest our hearts, for democracy, for the right of those who submit to authority to have a voice in their own governments, for the rights and liberties of small nations, for a universal dominion of right by such a concert of free peoples as shall bring peace and safety to all nations and make the world itself free."

Again, on May 26, 1917, in his message to the Russian
120

people, Wilson looked forward to the end of the war and said: "And then the free peoples of the world must draw together in some covenant, some genuine and practical co-operation that will in effect combine their force to secure peace and justice in the dealings of nations with one another. The brotherhood of mankind must no longer be a fair but empty phrase; it must be given a structure of force and reality. The nations must realize their common life and effect a workable partnership to secure that life against the aggression of autocratic and self-pleasing power."

Here was a purpose worthy of fighting and dying for. It was the only possible objective which could snatch a gain from the disaster of the war itself.

In a message to Congress on February 11, 1918, President Wilson said: "We believe that our own desire for a new international order under which reason and justice and the common interests of mankind shall prevail is the desire of enlightened men everywhere. Without that new order the world will be without peace and human life will lack tolerable conditions of existence and development. Having set our hand to the task of achieving it, we shall not turn back."

What a warning was there! But alas, we did take our hand from the plow and turn backward, with the result that today the world is without peace and human life lacks "tolerable conditions of existence and development," precisely as Woodrow Wilson predicted. Never at any time had the need for an advance step in human government been so terribly demonstrated, so overwhelmingly proved. At the climax of the war Wilson went down to Mount Vernon, on July 4, 1918, and packed into one great sentence what mankind had to get out of the holocaust then raging: "What we seek is the reign of law based upon the consent of the governed and sustained by the organized opinion of mankind."

That was the new order for which we fought in 1918, and with us many, many millions of Englishmen, Frenchmen, and others. I know well that the others, as well as we ourselves, strayed from their new order at the peril of another wanton attempt to dominate the earth which would strike down free nations like flimsy frame houses in a tornado and imperil the freedom of every living human being.

Wilson's great objective was repudiated, first by his own people and then gradually by the other peoples; but it can never die, because it was hammered out of the immense agony of 1918. Woodrow Wilson was only the voice which spoke for ten million dead and scores of millions maimed and blighted—millions who should have continued to live in peace and usefulness.

Yet the majority of us soon permitted ourselves to be told that we need not concern ourselves about the world's peace. All we had to do was to "mind our own business," and return to "business as usual." That was what we did. We launched into an era of getting rich quick, by gambling on everything from Florida sands to the dangerously inflated paper values which exploded in Wall Street during October, 1929, spreading ruin and the seeds of war around the earth.

But all the while there were millions of the most thoughtful Americans who were sick at heart that the plainest lesson in all human history had been rejected. The younger generation had also to be given some explanation for the betrayal of the future which had occurred in the United States Senate. In 1919 the treaty of peace had been rejected, undeniably because the League of Nations Covenant was in it; but afterward we were told that the treaty was rejected because it was very bad in itself.

There had also been in the Congress some men who opposed our entry into the war in 1917. The sons of these men became—and remain, some four of them at least—the most vocal in telling us that the international bankers, the munition makers, and the British propagandized us into the war in 1917. All of these allegations were false. We went to war, not because of anything that was said, but because of a long series of things which the Germans *did*. Afterwards we accepted the claims of the isolationists because they furnished some plausible explanation for our incredible failure to try, with might and main, to make peace in the world while we had the power in our hands.

On November 11, 1918, the United States stood upon a pinnacle of power such as no nation had ever attained. In military power, naval power, economic power, and—best of all—in moral leadership, we had an opportunity such as the centuries rarely offer to consolidate a great victory and to make the world a decent, safe place in which to live.

But having won the first round of a truly great and urgent struggle, we threw in the sponge and quit. If the world wanted to stay peaceful and democratic, let it. Our example was soon followed also by the other powerful democracies. Everything drifted and everything went wrong. Today there are hundreds of millions of people living despairing lives under the brutal heel of predatory conquerors. Today gangster powers have amassed armed forces greater than any which existed in 1918. Today they are reaching for control of the earth itself, and nothing will stop them except superior armed force.

On November 13, 1940, we are back very close to where we were on April 7, 1917. Nearly two years ago we passed a law forbidding our ships or citizens to go into belligerent waters. This summer we decided that for our own safety we could not allow British sea power to be defeated. About that we are agreed. Both of our parties and virtually all of our national leaders are for it. But today German submarines are gnawing at the vitals of British sea power, with very great advantages in their favor that they did not have in 1917. German submarines almost won the war in 1917 before our navy took the field against them. By April, 1941, we may very well have to choose between sending our navy against them again and seeing a Germanized Europe control the Atlantic Ocean. The strain on British shipping is already terrific. As it grows, can we maintain the rule that no American ship may carry a single pound of supplies to the beleaguered British?

We shall probably have to decide much sooner, also, whether we are going to permit Japan to take over Singapore and the control of the Pacific Ocean.

For many months past our ears have been full of the cries of the conquerors—one on each side of us—for a new world order. What is this new order when all the bombast is squeezed out of it? Every one of us knows what this new order is. On one side of us it means a half billion Europeans and Africans regimented in a vast slave state to serve a master race—the same Germans whose ambitions for world hegemony we frustrated in 1918. On the other side of us the Japanese New Order in Greater East Asia also deceives no one. It means that there, likewise, another half billion people are to be compelled to labor for the wealth of Japan, for her military and naval power and glory.

This is the "new order" which now faces us—one which threatens to make us the ham in the totalitarian sandwich. The world is now in the hands of the men of violence. It is their new order which we must accept or reject. We lost our chance to build and we may not have another. But as we gird ourselves for a last-ditch defense of freedom we might well post on every public square in the land and emblazon over every post office those immortal words of Woodrow Wilson: "What we seek is the reign of law based on the consent of the governed and sustained by the organized opinion of mankind."

☆

IS APPEASEMENT STILL POSSIBLE?
November 27, 1940

IT IS ALTOGETHER PROBABLE THAT THE NEXT FEW MONTHS will require far-reaching decisions on our part with reference to the second World War. The probabilities are that we shall have to support the British cause with stronger and stronger aid or prepare to accept a German-Japanese victory. There are one or two other possibilities, but the one certain thing is that the dynamic situation which we are in will move rapidly in some direction. Things will not stand still.

Is it then still possible to appease the aggressors and compromise with them? I want to discuss this question because there are powerful voices being raised in this country in behalf of a policy looking in that direction. I refer especially to the widely reported attitudes of Ambassor Joseph P. Kennedy and Mr. Henry Ford.

On November 16 Henry Ford was quoted as saying in an interview that nobody must win this war. If either side wins, he said, there will be another war, but "if neither side wins and America is the 'big brother' and makes them quit this senseless fighting, then there will be an end to war. I hope neither side wins," concluded Mr. Ford. "I don't think either side will win!" Similar sentiments were also quoted from Mr. Ford in the *New York Times* on November 21.

These statements show conclusively that Mr. Ford does not see any particular issue at stake in Europe. He does not see a regimented, servile German people on one side, which has been armed to the teeth and used as an instrument for looting all Europe, and on the other side a British people holding the last citadel of freedom in Western Europe. Mr. Ford does not see in Germany a gangster regime

125

which has fastened itself upon the German people and made war and conquest the permanent business of the whole nation. He does not see that the Nazi regime, having squandered fifty billions of dollars on armaments must proceed to hold up the world at the cannon's mouth. Mr. Ford makes no mention of the Nazi intention to become Europe's master race. He gives not the slightest indication that a German-dominated Europe and Africa would be a perpetual menace to us, immediately felt through South America.

On the contrary, Mr. Ford puts the free and enlightened civilizations of Norway, Denmark, Holland, Belgium, France, and Great Britain on exactly the same footing as the sadistic tyranny of the Nazis. He does not see the slow development of free institutions in these countries for a thousand years suddenly blacked out by utterly ruthless and brutal force. He does not recognize in Germany and Italy a tremendous revolution of destruction which can only go forward and could not stop if it would. According to Mr. Ford, we are just having another cat-and-dog fight in Europe, and he says, "I hope neither side wins."

There was a time in the first World War when Woodrow Wilson advocated a "peace without victory." He anticipated correctly that victory for either side would leave the other crushed and embittered, aching for another war. Perhaps a stalemate in 1917 might have had good results. The Germany of that day was not a wholly lawless state. Internally it was governed by laws which were known and could be depended on, whereas today there is nothing in Germany that corresponds to our conception of law. There is only force arbitrarily used. But Wilson was not able to manage a stalemate. The forces which had been turned loose were too mighty for any man to stop at an inconclusive point. Then, as now, any reckless ruler could start a world war which only the combined power of many nations could stop. Where such gigantic forces are involved, there is only one chance in a million that both sides will become fully exhausted at exactly the same moment.

Today, if a nicely balanced stalemate could be arranged for the moment, it would be a world calamity, for it is not possible to make peace with a Fascist state. Fascism is war; it scoffs at peace, disavows it, dedicates itself wholly to the use of force—military, economic, and psychological. The very idea of peace is destroyed. The Fascist state is devoted to perpetual repression within the state and to never-ending external aggression. Hence it is idle to talk about a peace which would leave the Fascist regime in control of Germany, Italy, and Japan—and of Europe and Asia.

It is possible for the democracies to make a truce with the Fascist states, but it is a disastrous possibility since it could only mean a breathing spell until the Fascist regimes became strong enough to resume the shooting war. In the meantime, the economic and propaganda wars would go right on with redoubled intensity. The Fascist state never demobilizes in any important respect; it always continues to pile up power for the sudden undoing of its democratic enemies. But not so in a democracy. When peace—so called—comes, a democracy relaxes, demobilizes, and goes back to normal. Otherwise why *have* peace, even so called? Thus the democracy which makes peace with a Fascist enemy merely lays itself open to the final crushing blow.

The impossibility of such a peace was lucidly stated by Walter Lippmann yesterday. After describing the deadly surprises which a Fascist state forges in secrecy, Mr. Lippmann continued, "No form of security and no kind of guarantee of peace can ever exist between a free nation and a totalitarian state. The impossibility of knowing what is being planned, the possibility of organizing an attack and concealing it until it is launched, the fact that the free state cannot conceal any of its preparations, the fact that it must debate publicly all its policies before they can be adopted—these things preclude any kind of peace between the two kinds of states except a victorious peace or a temporary armistice."

That, I submit to you, is the plain, unvarnished truth. There may have been irreconcilable human conflicts before, but there has never been one so totally irreconcilable as this one. If the totaliarians have the power, there is not the slightest chance for Britain to escape a crushing, final defeat. But suppose that the British, having won the edge, should grant Germany a truce. What would it mean? Would it mean that the dozen nations already conquered by Germany would remain under her heel to help prepare the next blow against Britain? Would it mean that the Nazis would be forced back within their own borders and left in control of seventy million Germans—to plot and plan and arm again with the same furious intensity with which they have driven the Germans for seven years past? Is there any point at which the British can stop, short of the liberation of the people of Europe from the ruthless rule of the warmakers?

Where, too, does our own interest lie? Do we wish the British to give the Germans and the Japanese ten years in which to consolidate their gains? Not even Mr. Ford can wish for British defeat, for that would merely make South America the battleground between us and the three Fascist powers. Nor could the conflict stop there, especially if we fought a losing struggle against very great economic and propaganda odds. Our own citadel in North America would assuredly be assaulted, first by the propaganda armies and the economic shock troops.

Here, too, Mr. Ford's inability to see anything in the present war which distinguishes one side from the other suggests disquieting questions. If triumphant totalitarianism flooded out across the Atlantic—and Pacific—would Mr.

Ford discern any danger to our free institutions? And if a strongly organized and financed Fascist movement arose in this country, would Mr. Ford see in it anything reprehensible? Would he still continue to be neutral, between Fascism and democracy? Would he rally at the eleventh hour to the defense of freedom? Or would he conclude that a dictatorship which would wipe out all labor unions wouldn't be such a bad thing?

In the struggle which already engulfs half of all humanity it is not possible to be neutral. The conflict has gone too far for that. Every man who is still free is in favor of stopping the spread over continent after continent of rule by club and gun and bombing plane, or he is not. There is no middle ground. The professed neutral in a free country is unavoidably on the side of the totalitarians. One is either for the rule of brute force alone, or he is in favor of defending the free, humane institutions which make up civilization itself. There was a time when that fateful dilemma could have been avoided by the administration and wise enforcement of the peace which we won in the last war, but now the conflict between force and law is world wide and it must be fought to a conclusion. The future of every people on the globe—free or slave—is at stake, and the full resources of every people, free or slave, are already engaged in the struggle. When it is over, there is the strongest kind of probability that we shall find almost the whole of the earth ruled by a few brutal despotisms or the great bulk of mankind again free to develop civilized life.

We have already recognized that stupendous fact by the unprecedented preparation for war which we have just begun. But in the meantime the decisive battles of the war are already being fought—in the skies over England and Germany, on the seas around Britain, in the Mediterranean, and in the Far East. In these battles the main decision can be made before spring comes or it may

129

be delayed for years. In either case, as I see it, we should understand clearly that the decisive struggle for the world itself is already well along and that what we do to affect the result may have to be done more quickly than we have thought since we recovered from the shock of the fall of France.

Our scientists have made the earth a unit for the purposes of trade and war. We can never reverse what they have done; but if the present war can be won, we can establish institutions of world government strong enough to control the destructive forces which have been turned loose. It is upon the solution of this problem that all future progress depends.

Our government lent China a hundred million dollars on November 30, the day Lorraine was formally annexed to Germany. President Roosevelt promised Greece all possible aid. On December 10 the United States further decreased the flow of war materials to Japan by requiring export licenses for iron ore, pig iron, ferro alloys, and certain manufactures of iron and steel.

London was blitzed again on December 27. Germany continued to mass troops in Hungary on the border of Jugoslavia. The Italian armies were driven out of Egypt. Anthony Eden became British Foreign Secretary on December 23, and Admiral William D. Leahy, retired, arrived in Vichy, France, as our Ambassador. Hitler declared that "the year 1941 will bring consummation of the greatest victory in our history." In his message to Congress, on January 6, President Roosevelt again stood for the four freedoms and called for all-out aid to all peoples resisting aggression.

THE PRESIDENT'S CALL TO ACTION
January 8, 1941

NEVER IN OUR PREVIOUS HISTORY HAS ANY PRESIDENT DELIV-
ered two messages within ten days which were as important
as those just spoken by President Roosevelt. What do these
messages mean to you and me? Are they based upon facts?
Do they constitute a call to action which we can disregard?

In the first part of his message to Congress the President
reviewed our history to show that our future has never
been threatened as it is today and that we have always
fought to defend our place in the world. "What I seek to
convey," said the President, "is the historic truth that the
United States as a nation has at all times maintained opposition to any attempt to lock us in behind an ancient Chinese wall while the procession of civilization went past.
Today, thinking of our children and their children, we
oppose enforced isolation for ourselves or for any part of
the Americas."

There is the nub of our danger, and in looking it in the
face we should also remember those leaders who are largely
responsible for our present predicament. Twenty-four
years ago we fought a great war to defend our rights upon
the sea, to keep a ruthless militarism from dominating Europe, and to make the world safe for democracy. Then as
soon as the fighting was over a group of men in control of
the United States Senate told us that making and keeping
the world safe for democracy was not our business. All
we had to do was come home, slam the gate behind us, and
"mind our own business." Do business as usual with the
whole world, lend money to all nations to promote our
business—that was the proper policy. But allow no "political" entanglements; assume no responsibility for keeping
the peace of the world. To be sure, the men who induced
us to follow this policy did not intend that twenty years

later a deadly, enforced isolation, backed by the military resources of a billion people, should threaten to close in upon us. They only wanted a voluntary isolation whereby we would live a carefree, irresponsible life of our own, enjoying all the advantages of living in our economically unified world without bearing any of the burdens of keeping it in order.

Today the chickens of world disorder which Senators Lodge, Borah, Knox, Reed of Missouri, Johnson of California, McCormick of Illinois, and others helped to hatch have come home to roost. And, true to form, the heirs of these men are now telling us that there is still nothing to worry about. "In times like these," continued the President, "it is immature—and incidentally untrue—for anybody to brag that an unprepared America, singlehanded, and with one hand tied behind its back, can hold off the whole world." This is a plain reference to the efforts of Colonel Lindbergh, former Governor Philip La Follette, Senator Wheeler, and others to convince us that we are safe now because there are a hundred and thirty millions of us.

Such reasoning overlooks entirely two things: (1) that Germany and Japan are just at the brink of securing control of the labor and resources of half a billion people each; and (2) that nothing counts in the total anarchy we have allowed to develop except armed power. Good intentions alone have no value whatever. Strong manhood is of little use in itself. Unarmed men are as helpless as children, and men that are not thoroughly trained in using mechanized weapons are almost useless. The bravest and most righteous nation is helpless now without tanks and artillery, warships, planes, and bombs—and it does very little good to have these things unless you have more of them than the aggressors have. The fact that there are a hundred and thirty millions of us means very little. Our real hope is that we can get our great potential industrial power organized in time. Everything depends upon that. France didn't do

132

it; England began almost too late; and we are just starting. For seven years, one half of all the labor expended in Germany has gone into arms. Lately the British have arrived at that point, but we are now spending only about thirty minutes of our working day in making arms. At present we are sending the British two hundred million dollars' worth of war materials a month, but the Germans are getting twice that much every month from France and other conquered democracies. Last year we sent two and a half million tons of steel to Britain, but the Germans got the same amount from microscopic little Luxembourg.

Such facts are determining whether we shall live a besieged life on this continent after the world has passed into the control of utterly ruthless men who know how to make their subject peoples produce as many arms as they may need. It is because the furnaces and factories of German Europe are roaring for the conquest of England that the President calls for "a swift and driving increase in our armament production."

I would not have anyone think that I take satisfaction in the waste of the earth's resources in weapons of destruction. But I should take a thousand times less satisfaction in living in a world dominated by brute strength used to enforce intolerance, racial persecution and strangulation, organized looting, and the suppression of every free thought.

That is why I welcome the three-point policy proposed by the President, as follows: (1) an "all-inclusive national defense"; (2) "full support of all these resolute peoples everywhere who are resisting aggression and are thereby keeping it away from our hemisphere"; and (3) rejection of any "peace dictated by aggressors."

The second point gives expression to the principle upon which any tolerable existence on this planet must rest. It is a law which no nation can ignore except at the cost of its own peace and liberty. The submarine and the bombing plane, backed by a constant increase in the effectiveness of all weapons, have put it beyond the power of any set of men anywhere, even in the United States Senate, to live safely without helping to defend their fellows. The impossibility of escaping this law was realized in 1919, and after, by the many millions in many countries who tried to establish international agreements for mutual defense against aggression. But our isolationists, along with those in other lands, would not hear of it. "It might cost us something," they said. "We might have to do some fighting or spend some money. No enforcing of the peace for us." Thus, instead of taking small risks and making small sacrifices, along with scores of other nations, we now find ourselves confronted with unlimited danger and compelled to make enormous efforts. Instead of helping an organized world to stop aggression when it was far off, we must now become the arsenal for every people which is still free, in order to avoid fighting alone. Never did a great nation miss so great an opportunity as we rejected in 1919. Now, instead of spending a few millions through the League of Nations, we must spend tens of billions to defeat aggression which is already swollen to world proportions and which threatens to break through the thin barriers and engulf the continents and seas which surround us.

The President's second point is vital to any decent world, and his third point is no less important. It reads: "Our security will never permit us to acquiesce in a peace dictated by aggressors and sponsored by appeasers." By this time the futility of making treaties with the aggressors should be apparent to everybody. It is not enough to remember that Poland, Norway, Holland, and Belgium all had treaties and promises from Hitler. The basic difficulty is that the Fascist racket is openly committed to the making of treaties only as ruses to advance conquest. No treaty signed by any Fascist regime, whoever the leader, can have the slightest validity, for it can have no other purpose than to gain time for a new aggressive onslaught.

If anyone doubts that this is true, let him compile a list of the peace treaties and promises which Facist Italy and Germany have made and broken. I emphasize the point because I believe that our future safety depends on our understanding that any Fascist machine, once created, becomes a frankenstein of force and terror which can only go on looting and abusing people until it is crushed by superior force. Built upon force and guile, it is incapable of keeping faith. It can never turn back if it would; it cannot behave decently without permitting the return of democracy and free living. That is why any thought of peace with a Fascist regime is an illusion.

It is high time that all of us ceased to flutter about hoping to appease or pacify men who long ago burned all the bridges of peace behind them. We cannot deal with them, and we can defeat them only by setting our faces firmly to defend the essential human freedoms which make life worth while.

Here again the President has given us objectives worthy of the best in our past and the best that is in us. He bids us to work now, with all our might, for a world founded upon four indispensable freedoms: (1) freedom of speech; (2) freedom of worship; (3) freedom from want for the people of every nation through generous economic intercourse; (4) freedom from the fear of menacing armament.

These objectives are clearly beyond our power to obtain by ourselves alone. We must have the help of other free nations to secure them for ourselves. That is why the President calls us to defend with our whole resources the others who are grimly holding the forces of violence in check. Nor does the President dodge the necessity of working with the other free peoples after the forces of rapine and aggression have been defeated. "The world order which we seek," says the President, "is the co-operation of free

135

countries working together in a friendly, civilized society."

There is nothing new about that. It is the lesson which the first World War should have burned deeply into our consciences. Then many of us called it an ideal. Now that we have seen the alternative, we know that "the co-opera-tion of free peoples working together in a friendly, civi-lized society" is an inescapable necessity. The President speaks truly when he says, "To that high concept there can be no end save victory." We do not intend to see our free world destroyed and to live besieged by enormous predatory empires.

THE ALL-AID-TO-BRITAIN BILL
January 15, 1941

THE AMERICAN PEOPLE HAVE REACHED A VERY CRITICAL point in their relation to the swiftly moving world crisis. The presentation to Congress of the lend-lease bill com-pels us to decide whether we are going ahead full steam with the policy of aid to Britain or whether we are going to reverse that policy. What is our state of mind now that the decision must be made?

For many months past every poll taken has shown that more than 90 per cent of us want Hitlerism defeated. Upon that there is virtual unanimity. But the majority which is convinced that our future safety depends on a British vic-tory is somewhat smaller—68 per cent according to the latest Gallup poll. On the crucial question, whether help-ing England is more important than going to war our-selves, the majority is, naturally, smaller still. The poll fin-ished last week gives a nation-wide vote of 60 per cent in favor of backing Britain even if it leads to our participation in the physical fighting.

136

Omitting the small percentage which is wholly pro-Nazi or anti-British, this leaves about 35 per cent of us who have not made a clear decision. The people in that group want Hitler defeated but are not sure that they want to go further in helping to defeat him. It is natural that a large minority of us should continue in this state of mind. It has been abundantly demonstrated in Britain, France, and elsewhere that in a democracy a large percentage of people cannot decide to fight while any hope can be found of avoiding war. That is democracy's chief weakness in opposing the totalitarians, who never have to decide that issue, since they are permanently committed to war and aggression.

Sixty per cent of our people have made up their minds that we cannot permit the British to be defeated. But in the Midwest and Great Plains area the percentage is only 55 per cent; that is, a minority of 45 per cent have not been able to resolve the conflict within them. Why is the minority larger in the Upper Mississippi Valley than anywhere else?

There are, I believe, two leading reasons. First, the people who dwell in this region are far from the sea; they live in a vast interior basin where great land distances unavoidably influence all thinking. In this environment the bombers that are blasting away at our Western civilization are certain to sound farther away than they do in New York or San Francisco, even through the ears of the radio. People in the heart of the continent find it hard to believe that their own security is really involved. They think not only of the oceans but of the two mountain ranges which enclose them, and find it difficult to realize that, if the gangster empires are allowed to sweep the rest of the world, their bombers will have the power to reach Chicago and St. Louis within a comparatively short time.

This natural influence of geography has been strongly reinforced, especially in the Chicago area, by the vigorous isolationist teaching of anti-British newspapers, notably the

Hearst press and the *Chicago Tribune.* As most people well know, this paper has been a constant and powerful influence for many years. On last Sunday, for example, the *Chicago Tribune* printed a front-page editorial entitled "A Bill to Destroy the Republic," in which the pending aid-to-Britain bill was termed one "for an unlimited dictatorship with power over the possessions and lives of the American people, with power to make war and alliances for war. . . . . Mr. Roosevelt's power to do anything he pleased with the person and property of an American citizen to aid any government he pleased, in any conflict he chose to make his own, would be unlimited. . . . . From that cradle the American dictator will arise," continued the *Tribune.* "Mr. Roosevelt decides and his decision is final. He would be above the law."

What is this bill that would destroy the Republic, according to the *Tribune?* The bill authorizes, "notwithstanding the provisions of any other law": (1) the sale, leasing, lending, or "other disposition" of war materials to any country whose defense the President deems vital to our own defense; (2) the outfitting or repair of any defense article, including warships, belonging to a friendly belligerent; (3) the manufacture or release of any defense article to a friendly government; and (4) executive discretion to determine what kind of repayment should be made for materials leased or loaned.

These are drastic powers, and it is fitting that we should scrutinize them carefully. It may be that the bill can and should be amended in some particulars, but it is vital that in debating amendments we should not lose sight of the bill's purpose. What is that purpose? It is to give the President the power to proceed as rapidly as possible with the fullest possible economic aid to the people who are fighting the triple alliance. We have reached the point where, to use a sand-lot expression, "we must put up or shut up." We have already helped the British a great deal. First we put arms in their hands after the Dunkirk disaster; then we bolstered their navy with destroyers—in exchange for immensely valuable naval bases—and we have sold them other war material as such material has happened to be produced. All of these transactions have been on a cash-and-profit basis—a basis which we cannot stand upon much longer, from either the economic or the moral standpoint. The crisis of world war is at hand, most probably within six months, quite possibly within ninety days. What we do must be done quickly and smoothly without a long series of interminable debates in Congress. We can afford one debate of reasonable duration, but we cannot afford one long-drawn-out squabble after another. As the *Cincinnati Enquirer* said last Sunday, "It is not practical to keep this authority in Congress, for it is unthinkable that we should have a public debate on every request the President might make. That would be to inform the German government of every new accretion of strength to its enemy well in advance of the delivery of the goods."

Either this democracy must give its elected chief executive authority to make us the effective arsenal of democracy or we must prepare to live as a lone island in a world of totalitarian violence. The British are doing magnificently. At this moment they are manufacturing three times as many warplanes as we are, in spite of a nightly rain of German bombs. But the industrial machinery of all Europe is being driven night and day to overwhelm Britain. Our aid is required on a great and mobile scale and required at once.

In giving it we should understand perfectly that we are not doing anything altruistic. We are not helping the British. We are defending our own future, and by that I don't mean the remote future. One of the worst results of the isolationist propaganda of the past twenty years has been its constant insinuation that anything we did for the peace of the world was a pure favor to other peoples. "We ourselves are so strong and so safe that we don't need to care about the world's peace," they said.

Now we know that that line of reasoning was false. It was not true in 1920, and it has been less and less true every year since then. It was always true that the largest and wealthiest of the free peoples had the greatest interest in world order. Today we have let things drift to the point where we must defend our world living space and do it at once or it will be gone—for generations, perhaps centuries. So don't let anyone tell you that in lending or giving arms to the British and Chinese we are doing anything magnanimous or bighearted.

We are living in a brutal, rapacious world in which we cannot avoid unpleasant choices. It is natural and unavoidable that the President's opponents on domestic policy should dislike the large increase in power which this bill gives him. Nobody could expect Wendell Willkie, with his strong convictions on home affairs, to relish that prospect. But Mr. Willkie has weighed it against the danger which faces the nation and made his decision that the President must be given the power to act. That is the statesmanlike decision which, as I see it, most people who are troubled in their minds must make.

But, say the objectors, the bill gives the President the power to make war. Is that true? Undoubtedly, replied the *Cincinnati Enquirer*, but "that is not a novelty. Every President possesses abundant power, as Commander-in-Chief of the Army and Navy, to lead the country into war."

It does not follow, however, that the President intends to send another A.E.F. to Europe. On the contrary, it is unquestionably the hope of both the President and the Congress that powerful aid to Britain now will defeat the gangster powers on the other side of the ocean and prevent any large-scale fighting on our part. Here again we are realistically selfish. We want the fighting done now in

Europe, not later in West Africa and the Azores, in South America and North America. With scientific warfare shrinking time and space every year, it would be pitiable shortsightedness for us not to look considerably beyond our noses.

During the coming debate we shall need to be particularly on our guard against appeals to our own personal fears. Senator Wheeler has already appealed to the fears of American mothers by his charges that the President plans "to plow under every fourth American boy" and perhaps to receive payment for the aid sent to Britain in the form of American boys in their caskets. If there are some mothers who can consider nothing beyond the immediate physical safety of their sons, Senator Wheeler's tactics will be completely effective with them. But I am disposed to believe that the large majority of American mothers and fathers, daughters and sons, will recognize that gangsterism is loose in the world on such a scale that the future of everyone's children is threatened, along with Christian civilization, humane living, and free government in every part of the world.

We are long past the time when any man can assure us that no American boy will ever have to fight. The only thing we have left to decide is how best to defend the national heritage which a hitherto free world has enabled us to possess.

On February 8 the lend-lease bill was passed in the House, a month after it was introduced, by a vote of 260 to 165, largely on party lines. Earlier, on January 21, the State Department had lifted the "moral embargo" levied against Russia in December, 1939, during the Russo-Finnish war. This action allowed planes, materials for their manufacture, and patent processes for making aviation gasoline to go to Russia.

In Rumania the Fascist Iron Guard broke loose again, after having murdered sixty-four former officials on November 27, and two thousand people were killed before the government regained control on January 24. Great Britain severed relations with Rumania on February 10. In France, Marshal Pétain met Laval, whom he had dismissed as Vice-Premier on December 3, and reconciliation was reported. Admiral Jean Darlan was, however, appointed Vice-Premier and Foreign Minister on February 9. February 13 Pétain held a three-hour conference with the Spanish dictator, General Franco, who had just established "complete identity of views" with Mussolini during a meeting in Italy.

In the Far East a Japanese-instigated, undeclared war between Thailand and French Indo-China was settled by Japan in favor of Thailand. A pact between Japan and Indo-China gave the Japanese virtual control of the country, which was being turned into a military base, especially in the north, along with Hainan Island. At Singapore several thousand Australian troops debarked and moved up the Malay Peninsula.

SHALL WE HELP DEFEND SINGAPORE?
February 26, 1941

THERE HAS BEEN A SERIES OF ALARMS LATELY IN THE FAR East which have reminded us that Japan may make her final bid for control of East Asia this year. Should she make a thrust for Singapore at a time when our attention is focused on a great German drive on England, what would our reaction be? What could we do in the Far East? What should we do?

The recent appearance of Japanese warships in the Gulf of Siam and the Japanese seizure of the airport at Saigon, the capital of French Indo-China, was plain notice that the Japanese intend to take over all of Indo-China. No one

142

had doubted that they would do that, but their advance to South Indo-China also brought them some seven hundred miles nearer to the great British base at Singapore, which they must reduce if they are to rule the South Seas. For two years Japan has been edging southward, but this latest step brought sharp reactions from the other Pacific powers, all of which realized that Japan could not be allowed to creep nearer to Singapore without resistance. The British publicized the arrival at Singapore of large forces of Australians completely equipped, who at once moved up the Malay Peninsula to block the path of the Japanese. It was announced also that the waters around Singapore have been mined. The Dutch have closed some of the harbors in their great empire in the East Indies near by. The Australian cabinet had an emergency session, and the premier flew to London, making it clear that Australia would fight with all her power to defend Singapore. Australia's power to turn out planes, tanks, and other war equipment as well as the best soldiers in the world is now no mean item in the Far Eastern balance of power.

On our part, Washington again urgently advised all Americans throughout the Far East to return home, and on February 20 the House of Representatives at last voted some five million dollars to improve the harbor and build bombproof shelters at Guam, our island in the Far Pacific, about thirteen hundred miles from Tokyo. While this does not mean the fortification of Guam, the first step in that direction now provided for was rejected by the last two Congresses on the ground that Japan might not like it. Now no one raises that objection, and the suggestion that Guam be made into a great Far Eastern Gibraltar does not raise the opposition it used to stir. Our Pacific fleet at Hawaii is also to receive many new warplanes of the latest type.

These simultaneous activities by the British, Dutch, Australians, and Americans were intended to warn Japan that the period of retreat before her is over. Even the Vichy

143

government stiffened up enough to reject a Japanese attempt to give a large block of Indo-China to Thailand.

The reaction of the Japanese was characteristic. When ten years of constant aggression had finally resulted in strong defensive reactions, the Japanese complained of "encirclement." Why all the excitement, they asked? It was the joint conferences between Secretary Hull and the British and Australian diplomats which touched off the encirclement cry, for heretofore the Japanese had been going on the assumption that we would not fight to defend our interests in the Pacific.

What are our interests in the Pacific area? As I see it, they are: (1) our legal obligation to defend the Philippines until 1946 and our moral obligation not to turn our wards over to the exploitation of Japanese rule immediately after 1946; (2) our right to a legitimate share of friendly trade and commerce with China; (3) free access to the rubber, tin, and quinine of the Dutch Indies, at present the only adequate source of these indispensable commodities in the world; and (4) the right to live and trade with all the peoples on the other side of the Pacific without having to deal with one tremendous Japanese empire exploiting the labor and resources of half a billion non-Japanese to create a vast, truculent naval empire which would be a perpetual danger to us, especially if matched by the the domination of the Atlantic Ocean by a huge Nazi empire.

Do these four interests, taken together, constitute something which we are bound to defend? It seems to me that it would be very difficult for anyone who looks ahead to take the position that we should not resist Japanese pretensions to dominate the whole of East Asia and with it the Pacific Ocean, both north and south. But there are some who say we are not strong enough to oppose the Nazis and the Japanese at the same time. Therefore we must let Japan overrun East Asia, if she can, and deal with her later, after the Nazis are defeated.

There can be no question that Japan's chief role in the triple alliance is to make a lot of noise, with three purposes behind it: (1) to divert our attention from the main battleground in Europe; (2) to divert some military and naval supplies from England; and (3) to frighten us with the idea of war in both oceans at the same time, with the result that we will do nothing effective to block either the Nazi or the Japanese thrusts for world empire. A year ago one would have had to conclude that the bad boys of Europe and Asia stood a good chance of keeping us confused and inactive; but today it is clear to us that the time to save ourselves from permanent imprisonment by Nazi and Japanese naval empires is *now*, while we have powerful friends on both sides of the ocean. The passage of the lend-lease bill will signify our complete understanding of this principle so far as the Atlantic is concerned. We do not intend to see the Nazis dominate the Atlantic, both north and south, if our aid to Britain can prevent it. But are we as clear about the issue in the Pacific?

It seems to me that we should be. Japan is trying to do there exactly what the Nazis are attempting in Europe, and with far less power to back it up. For the past ten years Japan has been using up the accumulated wealth of generations in an attempt to conquer the enormous country of China. Japan's economy is already seriously strained, and yet Free China is stronger today than ever. Japan occupies the best part of China, but she can get little from China to compensate for the great drain of the war she does not know how to win, unless the other Pacific powers will allow her to take over the immense areas of the South Pacific, thus bottling China up and ending her hopes of freedom.

This same Japan is particularly dependent on world trade to keep her war going, and 75 per cent of all her trade is with the United States, Britain, the Dutch Indies, and Australia. Without oil from the United States and the Dutch Indies her war machine must come soon to a complete and disastrous stop. Japan's dependence on us for the other sinews of war—machine tools, iron, and copper—is almost as great. In 1939, 75 per cent of the iron ore imported into Japan came from the Philippines and British Malaya. We are still buying Japanese silk at the rate of a hundred million dollars a year, money which helps powerfully to keep Japan's war machine running. In short, Japan is in the position of being able to conquer China, Indo-China, Singapore, and the Dutch Indies, preliminary to taking over the Philippines and Australia—with the aid of materials and money obtained from the very peoples whom she wishes to despoil.

Many people find it difficult to believe that Japan will do more than take over Indo-China, at least while Britain is unconquered. But Japan's war leaders face the strong probability of seeing all their efforts at world conquest slowly but steadily fail—unless they make one final gamble in the grand manner for Singapore and mastery of all East Asia, for victory that would enable them to avoid retreat to oblivion.

If Japan's warmakers should decide on a final plunge for Singapore, we would be compelled to decide promptly: (1) whether to take the chance that Japan would occupy the whole of the Orient and establish a huge closed empire, from which it would be exceedingly difficult, if not impossible, to eject her; or (2) whether to add our naval power to the already great military, naval, and air power which our friends now have in the Singapore area, with the purpose of keeping control of the Pacific Ocean while we have it.

On March 1 Bulgaria became the seventh nation to join the Axis. German troops occupied strategic places throughout the country, as a note from Russia expressed displeasure with Bulgaria's action.

ARE WE TO BE FATALLY DIVIDED AGAIN?

March 5, 1941

A SITUATION HAS DEVELOPED IN THE UNITED STATES SENATE which must give grave concern to every person who wants Hitlerism defeated and the world, including our own people, freed of the oppressive fear of its brutal conquests.

For two months now the lend-lease bill providing for all-out aid to Britain and other free peoples, has been before the country. It has had five weeks of hearings before the House and Senate foreign-relations committees, a week of debate in the House, and two weeks in the Senate. Formal debate in the Senate appears to have ended, but some twenty-odd amendments still remain to be dealt with, upon any one of which there may be a whole series of long speeches. Meanwhile Hitler has taken over Bulgaria; his troops now press heavily upon the frontier of Greece, one of the nations whom we propose to aid under this bill; and the full weight of his diplomatic offensive, backed by half a million troops, falls upon Yugoslavia and Turkey. What must be the feelings of these desperately beset peoples as they see the American people unable to record a decision to back with their industrial power the nations which will fight for their lives and freedom?

Hitler has won his smashing victories in large part because the democracies which he mows down have talked while he acted. Of course it is impossible for democracies to avoid talk, discussion, debate. We must have debate,

147

and even in times of extreme urgency we should be loathe to restrict debate. But in such times the minority must also be conscious of its responsibility not to block action unduly long. It is important that the opposition have the chance to say every reasonable thing which can be said, but it would be disastrous for them to prolong debate when only stirring passion and division in the nation could result.

Inevitably, Senator Wheeler and his colleagues are tempted to try to repeat the feat of the Senate opposition to the League of Nations in 1919, that is, to reverse the national opinion and to turn a public opinion strongly for the lend-lease bill into one against it. Though the present opposition has steadily denied that it is filibustering, Senator Wheeler declared in the Senate yesterday that requests for a filibuster were justified. "I intend to fight this bill any way I can," he said, and predicted that "there will be such a public uprising as has never been seen here before."

We have clearly before us the strong possibility of a dangerous division of national opinion, one which might be as paralyzing as the long-drawn-out fight on the League of Nations Covenant from 1918 to 1920. It was in the middle of December, 1918, that Theodore Roosevelt, Henry Cabot Lodge, and others agreed to conduct a war of attrition against any League of Nations agreement which President Wilson might bring back from Paris. Before a line of the League Covenant was written, they agreed that they would attack it with reservations and amendments, gradually whittling it away.

At that time the senators knew that public opinion was overwhelmingly in favor of a League of Nations to prevent other world wars from breaking out and spreading around the earth until only the United States could stop them. But bitter, questioning speeches began at once in the Senate and continued at intervals for sixteen months, until the final blow was administered to the League.

On April 29, 1919, two months after the League Covenant had been framed and published, Senator Lodge, the elder, and Senator Borah had a conference in which Lodge said it was "perfectly obvious" that any attempt to defeat the treaty of peace by a straight vote in the Senate would be "hopeless." It would have to be done by amendments and reservations. In his book *The Senate and the League of Nations* Lodge says that most of the nation's clergymen, teachers, editors, and writers "were friendly to the League as it stood and were advocating it." [1] George Harvey, arch foe of President Wilson, has also recorded in his *Henry Clay Frick, the Man* that the nation's business leaders were "literally unanimous in their advocacy of the League." [2] In other words, the whole leadership of the nation, excepting only some politicians, was for the League, as were the newspapers and the people.

But Andrew D. Mellon and Henry Clay Frick, two Pittsburgh multimillionaires with practically unlimited funds, were persuaded to finance a nation-wide fight against the League. Senators Johnson, Borah, and others traveled to the big cities, conducting great mass meetings, just as Senator Wheeler threatened on February 24 to do again if the lend-lease bill passes. At these meetings the League was denounced in the strongest language and the name of President Wilson was hissed and booed just as the names of President Roosevelt and Wendell Willkie were booed and hissed at the mass meeting addressed in New York City on February 20, 1941, by Senators Wheeler and Nye. It is notable, also, that at the same meeting the names of Hitler and Mussolini were mentioned by another speaker without a sign of disapproval from the audience.

In 1919 speeches continued in the Senate and over the country for more than a year—until our people were deeply divided, confused, and embittered; until they were sick of the whole controversy and finally persuaded to wash their

[1] P. 147.
[2] P. 325.

hands of all responsibility for the peace of the world in order to concentrate on "minding their own business," narrowly and selfishly defined.

We all know what the disastrous fruits of that policy have been. We gambled ourselves into the great depression of 1929, which precipitated Hitler's advent to power and the steady downhill rush of our whole civilization from 1929 to the present. Never did a great nation have such an opportunity for constructive leadership as we had in 1919 —an opportunity which was lost in bitter, endless controversy such as in this dangerous time lays democracy wide open to destruction.

There is still time for us to hear protest against the lend-lease bill, but we do not have time to fight out an interminable contest of wills between the leaders of the minority and the majority. The future of every person in the whole world of free nations for many decades to come will be determined by what happens on the battlefields in Europe and Asia during the next six months. We are on the eve of the most savage and ruthless assault upon free peoples which the world has ever seen—not sometime in the future, but now. Upon the outcome will depend whether we are to live a permanently besieged life on this continent, militarized as we have never dreamed of yet, constricted in our economic life, pouring our substance into arms, and submitting to rigid controls in an effort to defend ourselves in a gangster world. Make no mistake about it, either; the dangerous division which is already registered in the Senate would be only the beginning. As determined groups reached for control of our policy, every appeasement-, Fascist-minded element in the land would raise its clamor for power, confident that totalitarianism triumphant in the rest of the world could not be denied here.

Every poll which has been taken has shown a popular majority for the lend-lease bill, but the latest polls do show that the percentage of confused and uncertain people is increasing under the constant assertions in the Senate that the lend-lease bill means dictatorship and war. There is in the Senate a clear majority for the bill, but the bill can be killed by amendments as well as by outright defeat. When the final vote in the Senate is taken, we shall know whether we have the power to block Hitler and his allies now—the only time it can be done—or whether we have compromised with the Senate opposition until we can do nothing decisive. When the bill is voted, also, the gallant peoples who are holding back the dictatorships will know whether we are behind them or whether we shall have to have another long debate in the Senate whenever any important step is to be made.

At this moment democracy is on trial for its very life all over the world—and not least in the United States Senate. In 1919 the Senate talked us out of peace and thereby registered a disaster in our national life which we cannot afford to repeat. Today it is beyond the power of any group of men to keep us out of war by talk. War is loose in the world on a scale, and with weapons, never seen before. Before this year is over, war will sweep up to our own shores on both the Atlantic and Pacific—or it will be met and held at bay on the other side of both oceans. It is too late for talk to save us; only action can do it.

There is every reason to believe, too, that a strong majority of our people are for action and action now. But the mail of senators says the contrary. The desks of senators are covered with the harsh, violent protests of the opposition, while those who favor the bill trust to their senators to know how they feel and to stand firm. Some senators will stand firm, and some will conclude from their mail that compromise or retreat is the better part of valor.

For the past twenty years our destinies have been dominated by the men of uncompromising isolationist convictions. In 1919 it was the Senate irreconcilables, the "bitter-enders," who carried the day, and now their successors are equally adamant. But today there will be no ten-year interval before the results of national paralysis on our part become evident. The earth itself trembles beneath the tread of millions of marching men and under the impact of the bombs of the air navies. This is a crisis year such as the world has not known for centuries. This spring, as never before in our whole national life, "time marches on"!

After three weeks of debate the Senate passed the lend-lease bill on March 8 by a vote of 60 to 31, mainly on party lines. It became law on March 11, 1941.

THE END OF AN ERA
March 12, 1941

THE PASSAGE OF THE LEND-LEASE BILL IN THE SENATE ON Saturday marks the end of the era of isolation for the United States which began in 1919 and the beginning of a period of close co-operation with other nations. We have tried the policy of isolation and found it wanting. Now, as the opposite policy comes into operation, it is fitting that we look backward a moment to see from whence we came and then ahead to see what may lie immediately in front of us.

Much as I dislike the bitter fruits of isolation, it is a fact that many senators and others have always believed during these last twenty-two years that the United States was a world apart, instead of a part of the world, and that we could be a law unto ourselves. There were many isolationists who became such out of hatred for President Wilson and who rationalized arguments to justify their opposition to him—arguments which they later came actually to believe. But there were and are sincere isolationists. It is natural to dislike large and distant responsibilities. All of us have enough cares already. Perhaps all of us would be isolationists if the policy could be made to work.

Why is it that isolation will not work? Why has it so disastrously failed? As I see it, there are at least two reasons, the validity of which each person can judge for himself:

(1) The inventors are destroying time and space at such a terrific rate that we can no longer depend on distance to protect us. In 1919 it was clear to great numbers of us that this was true. Every year makes it less possible to doubt that our physical security is disappearing and that this process will go on in the future beyond the power of any group of men to stop it. Only by combining with other peoples to re-establish order in the world can we regain our security.

(2) Our power is so great that there can be no order in the world unless our strength is exerted on the side of order. When the world's strongest nation, controlling a good third of the earth's resources, is held aloof from the preservation of order, there can be no order. Everything is out of balance. No other power is strong enough to keep the peace—or to organize others for that purpose. The result is anarchy in which every ambitious dictator is free to set the world afire. When we try to resign from the world the result is chaos; and world chaos is a dangerous state of affairs for the richest nation, especially since it sets lawless forces loose to grasp for control of the earth itself.

These are the forces which doomed to failure our attempted retreat into isolation. But, in addition, our sincere isolationists suffered from two other illusions. First, they thought that they could control the future by erecting paper walls and saying what we would not do in the future. If world chaos should result from the policy of isolation, no matter; we would pass a law saying that it is not our concern. If predatory forces should begin to range over the earth, we would—and did—pass a law to forbid our citizens to go abroad. If world war should start to engulf us again, we would enact strong neutrality laws and have nothing to do with the war. All that we needed to do was to will isolation strongly enough and we would be successfully isolated. Undoubtedly for Senator Hiram Johnson the bitterest part of the recent vote in the Senate was the discovery that laws could be thought up to nullify his isolation laws. Johnson got a law to make it impossible for us to lend money to Britain again. But eventually we have discovered that nobody wants to lend money to Britain again—that the only thing that matters is to get arms to the British, pay or no pay. And the law which Senator Johnson thought would do a lot to keep us isolated does nothing at all. We just forget that it was ever passed. It is true that laws passed to hold us inert in a future world crisis can delay our future action somewhat, perhaps dangerously, but they cannot prevent action. Surely we will not again put our faith in resolutions not to do this or that in future world crises—in conditions which nobody can really foresee. We should not need to learn again that paper promises of passivity will be swept away by swiftly moving events.

The second illusion which deceived many of us is akin to the first: it is the belief that nations can close their eyes to right and wrong. No one would suppose that society inside the nation could be held together if we took this attitude—if we all silently witnessed murder, robbery, and every other crime; if we ignored the beating and persecution of helpless men, women, and children. Inside the nation we do not dare, in our own defense, to shut our eyes to crime and take no interest in the enforcement of law. But we have been told these last twenty years that nations were immune to all moral laws. When a helpless small nation was attacked, we were told to look the other way; it was not our business. When conquest and rapine ran riot over half of Asia, we had only to be neutral. When Christian civilization itself was assaulted in the heart of Europe, we had to remember only to be neutral. We must not attempt to identify the aggressor or to take any measures against him. We must be neutral.

It is this policy, insisted upon for two decades, which we have just repudiated in the lend-lease bill, in which we proclaim our determination to help all free nations which resist aggression. That is the only basis upon which civilization can exist on a constantly shrinking globe. The contrary policy was bound to result in the uncontrolled spread of international brigandage until everything was swept away in vast predatory wars of conquest. Wrong does not become right simply because it is perpetrated on a vast scale; it becomes more dangerous than ever. Neutrality between law and order on one side and brutal aggression on the other is as morally wrong as it is perilous. In a world in which civilized nations have the power to enforce even a rough degree of peace and justice, neutrality is immoral and self-destroying to the nation which tries to practice it. By his silence the neutral aids and abets the aggression, helping it to grow constantly more dangerous.

The collapse of the policy of isolation is now so complete that it does not seem likely that we shall try it again. But what about the postwar reaction? Will we forswear the world again? There is one disquieting thing about the Senate vote on the lend-lease bill: the vote was sixty to thirty-one—one less than the two-thirds majority necessary to approve a treaty. If this bill had been a treaty of peace, the isolationists could have defeated it outright or whittled it away by emasculating amendments as they did the League of Nations Covenant. Are we to have, a little later, another determined band of irreconcilables in the Senate, both able and willing to do what the bitter-enders of 1919 accomplished?

As we try to understand the humanness of the isolationist position, we are compelled to remember constantly the enormity of their error. The three great democracies had both the responsibility and the power to put their victory in the last war to constructive purpose. It was their duty to give us a workable world order that would last for generations at least, if not for centuries. Never had a need been so cruelly demonstrated on such a huge scale, and never was failure so great. The responsibility for the failure is divided between the shortsighted men who ruled Britain and France in recent years and the United States Senate, but the first and most fatal offending was ours. It was our isolationist leaders who gave the world its first big push back onto the road to chaos.

Today we are still on that road, but now that the remaining democracies are pooling their power, there is an increasingly good prospect that the gangster regimes will be defeated and a world of free nations restored. This result will not be accomplished unless the President makes the fullest use of his powers under the bill to transfer war equipment now in our possession to the fighting fronts and to speed the manufacture and delivery of new weapons. It will not be enough, either, merely to make the weapons; they will have to be delivered successfully against the most powerful sea warfare which modern Germany has ever organized. It may be that the British can keep their supply lines open; but as the summer season advances, the loss of ships may mount to the point where we shall have to decide to convoy our supplies to the British.

If this step becomes essential in order to avert defeat, will the Senate isolationists again offer all-out resistance? Presumably they will. Tentative plans have been announced for speaking tours to prevent the policy of aid to the democracies from advancing any further than authorized in the lend-lease bill. It is the right of the minority to continue opposition of this kind; doubtless they consider it to be their duty. But in speaking their minds the opposition will need to take into account that we are now non-belligerent participants in a desperate world war which will reach its climax this year. There will hardly be time for two months of debate on every major decision which must be made during this decisive year. The time for action has come, and the major action should not be impeded by too many rear-guard engagements on the home front.

The leaders of the Senate isolationists may well remember that they are the wave of the past—in a far stormier ocean than that from which it emerged in 1919.

As Hitler Attacked Russia

MARCH 30—JULY 2, 1941

On March 19 and 24 the House and Senate appropriated seven billion dollars for lend-lease supplies. On March 25 the government of Yugoslavia signed a treaty making the nation the eighth member of the Axis. Revolt at once flamed throughout the country.

THE YUGOSLAVS RESIST
March 30, 1941

It is quite possible that thursday, march 27, will prove to be the turning point in the war. At any rate it appears to mark one important turning point.

For weeks past, indeed for years, we have witnessed Hitler in his old, familiar role of turning the heat on a small nation. First it was Austria, bulldozed and overrun. Then Spain, Czechoslovakia, and Poland. After that the list lengthened rapidly. In several cases—Denmark, Norway, Holland, and Belgium—the small nations were simply overwhelmed, suddenly in the night, by tremendous military assaults. In the case of Rumania the softening process was long employed. Then the country was partitioned between Hungary and Russia and the embittered, divided remnant occupied by the Nazis in the name of order, as Austria and Czechoslovakia had been. Just lately Bulgaria was co-ordinated, easily and not unwillingly as far as her controlling elements went.

158

By this time Yugoslavia was almost surrounded. Austria, Hungary, Rumania, and Bulgaria all bordered on Yugoslavia. Each time Hitler took over one of these four countries, he advanced the encirclement of the Yugoslavs. At last he had them almost entirely penned in—Italians on the north and on the south in Albania, Germans on their whole eastern flank, and the rock-bound Adriatic coast on the other side. Only a small window opened southward into Greece—the hard-fighting Greece that Hitler was moving to smash for the impertinence of defeating his Italian ally.

Then concentrated Nazi diplomatic pressure upon the isolated Yugoslavs—come into camp or else! Day after day the same relentless heat. Give us passage down your Vardar Valley to Greece and we will give you Salonika after the war! Demobilize your army and give us transit for our war material and we will respect your independence after the war. Otherwise—you know what happened to Poland! Think what the devastation of your country will mean.

There are some who say that the whole series of events in Yugoslavia was cleverly stage-managed by the British to gain time for Yugoslavia to mobilize and for the British to entrench themselves in Greece. That is possible, but I am inclined to think that the Nazi pressure on Prince Paul and the Yugoslav Cabinet is enough to explain their eventual capitulation. Some of them were not strong men; and the pain of decision, with such terrible consequences involved in resistance, was enough to bring them to the point where they could no longer resist—especially since the fears of the Croats in the north weighed upon them. So they went to Vienna with leaden hearts and signed what they thought was a bargain which might keep their country from being either occupied or devastated, but which actually would have been only the first of a series of surrenders on their part.

Meanwhile, the agony of the Yugoslav people was no less acute, but with the difference that the simple, common man, having nothing to lose but his life and home, preferred to risk both rather than surrender his freedom to an inhumanly efficient tyranny. The Army too, soldiers of one of the toughest, most virile people in the world, could not submit to the tyrant in Berlin who has made everything in his conquered realm, including Germany, either *ersatz* or *verboten*.

When the Yugoslav Army struck, at two o'clock Thursday morning, it moved with such speed that within an hour all strategic posts in the city were manned with tanks, machine guns, artillery, and the ministers were rounded up and deposed while the young King took power and installed General Simovitch at the head of a new Cabinet.

At first the few people of Belgrade—and all other cities —who were awake thought that the regime of Prince Paul was acting to hold down the bitter and rebellious people. When the truth was learned everyone rushed into the streets in what the correspondent of the *New York Times* called "the most moving and heartfelt demonstrations of pure joy and thanksgiving" that he had ever seen. The roar of their enthusiasm increased until in one great center of the city ten thousand, then thirty to forty thousand, shouting, singing people shook the surrounding buildings with their cheers.

Everywhere there were flowers for the troops. In Ankara, Turkey, too, the Yugoslav Embassy was showered with flowers and congratulations; and the spot in Marseilles where the young King Peter's father was murdered several years ago was heaped with flowers by the French people, in spite of the efforts of the Vichy police to prevent it. In this total war, flowers are one of the few weapons which the conquered peoples have left. In Lyon, in central France, the Germans have torn down the statue of a woman executed by them during the last war, but they have not been able to prevent the French people from silently depositing flowers on the spot where the statue stood.

In Berlin, where nobody ever lifts a finger, let alone his voice, unless he is commanded, the outburst in Belgrade was thought to be very strange. Solemn words were spoken about the pact which the constitutional government of Yugoslavia had just signed. The press spoke ominously of outrages against Germans in Yugoslavia—just as it did before the Nazis took over Austria and Czechoslovakia. In both of these earlier cases the whole atrocity campaign of the Nazis was manufactured. The poor Austrians and Czechs were only too desperately and pathetically anxious not to give the German juggernaut any excuse to roll over them.

But at long last the Nazi press does not have to create its alleged insults. In Belgrade the German and Italian travel bureaus were smashed. Nazi and Italian flags were torn to shreds and pictures of Hitler and Mussolini trampled in the streets, while German automobiles bearing the swastika were overturned and wrecked. Thousands of husky German "tourists" who had invaded the land lately began to mill about the railroad stations, with fishing rods and hunting rifles still unused, in the greatest haste to return to Germany. Even the German minister who stormed into the Yugoslav Foreign Office left six minutes later.

By all past precedents such defiance of the terrible-tempered head of the new master race will bring the most swift and brutal retribution upon the Yugoslavs, especially since Matsuoka is now in Berlin being shown the invincible might of the Nazis and commanded to go back home and make war upon the British and Americans without further delay. Matsuoka can never have his Greater East Asia, he is being told, until the Anglo-Saxons are disposed of, so he had better return and concentrate on the main business lest he find himself without a friend after the forthcoming German victory.

For the Serbs the outlook is bad enough. They will probably have to see their people slaughtered and their land laid waste because they have dared to reject the slavery of the Nazi "new order." It is a hard decision to choose death to subjection, and it is a terrible commentary on the shortsightedness of those who won the last war that men must still make it.

Yet we do progress. When the Serbian people rose, our government instantly and openly promised them all the aid we can send if they have to fight for their liberty. That is a total revolution in the foreign policy which we clung to until recently—a revolution which I am confident the great majority of Americans are glad has been made. No longer are we compelled to stand by while small nations are brutally destroyed, telling ourselves that we are not our brothers' keeper, that it is "not our business." Of course there is risk and responsibility in standing against what is abominably and powerfully wrong. Of course, too, we are pursuing our true self-interest in helping to resist aggression wherever it occurs on this constantly shrinking globe. We do it primarily because we know now that we shall be the last victim of the law of the jungle if we do not help those who are willing to fight for their freedom. We seek to avoid for ourselves the real and deadly kind of isolation in which Yugoslavia finds herself today. But the wisdom of the new policy does not destroy the fact that it is also right.

On April 3 Count Teleki, Premier of Hungary, committed suicide, apparently to escape the odium of breaking a newly signed treaty of friendship with Yugoslavia. On April 5 Rus-

sia indicated her feelings by signing a five-year treaty of friendship and nonaggression with Yugoslavia. The next day German forces attacked Greece and Yugoslavia, and Hungarian troops joined the invasion on April 11.

Meanwhile, adversity dogged the British in North Africa. Between January 22 and February 6 their forces had swept the Italians back through Tobruk, Derna, and Bengazi. Then Nazi General Rommel was sent to Africa with German troops, and by April 14 Rommel led his Axis armies back across the Egyptian border.

Four days later, on April 18, the Yugoslav army capitulated, its resistance ended except for the very considerable forces which escaped to the mountains. Belgrade had been laid in ruins by air attack, after being declared an open city.

Foreign Minister Matsuoka of Japan arrived in Berlin on March 26, traveled to Rome and from the Axis capitals back to Moscow, from which capital it was announced, on April 13, that Russia and Japan had concluded a five-year neutrality pact.

THE GLOBAL WAR
April 20, 1941

THE RUSSO-JAPANESE NEUTRALITY PACT CONTINUES TO BE the most important of recent diplomatic events. This treaty states that "should one of the contracting parties become the object of hostilities on the part of one or several third powers, the other contracting party will observe neutrality throughout the duration of the conflict."

Two principal interpretations have been put on this pact. By the first, Russia is seen as freeing herself of the Japanese threat in her rear in the event that she has to fight Germany. Like Germany, Soviet Russia has always feared war on two fronts, though lately the Japanese have been so involved in China that the risk of an attack on Russia has been reduced. Still, a great many of Japan's best troops have been maintained on Russia's Siberian borders throughout Japan's war on China; and, with Germany steadily outflanking them in Europe, it would doubtless be a real comfort to the Soviets to have these Japanese armies removed. No Japanese promise of neutrality would have much weight in Moscow; but if Japan could be induced actually to take her troops away, that would be important.

On her side Japan is almost frantically anxious to scoop up the riches of the South Seas while Britain is fighting for her life and the United States is somewhat divided about what it can or should do. But can Japan trust Russia not to move into Manchuria if she moves south? There is where German pressure on Russia comes in. Doubtless Hitler has told Matsuoka that if Russia should attempt to go back on her bargain he will hurl a diplomatic blitz at Stalin's head that would stop him dead. Quite probably Hitler has told Matsuoka that he is going to attack Russia soon anyway and that he needn't worry about Russia's having any time or energy to take over a weakened Manchuria.

The treaty therefore pleases Japan, Russia, and Germany. They all feel that they are more likely to get what they want or, in Russia's case, to be able to keep what they have.

For us the treaty is undoubtedly bad news. If executed in the only way it can be, by a Japanese move to the south, it will undoubtedly confront us with the grave necessity of deciding whether Anglo-American naval power is equal to the job of holding both the Atlantic and the Pacific. It has been my belief that we should do so, if it can be done, by the utmost efforts of which we are capable. Yet it is possible that we may have to revise our position and decide to use our full naval power in defeating the Nazis in the Atlantic, leaving until later the troublesome job of ousting Japan from the great raw-material areas of the South Seas. That is a decision which we ought to make only in the most urgent necessity, but it is vital that the greater enemy be defeated.

The Russo-Japanese treaty also removes any lingering doubts that we may have had that the triple-alliance treaty was aimed at us. There was never any question that it was, but it was apparently intended to put the same kind of squeeze on Russia. Now Russia is apparently excused from the squeeze, and there is nobody left to whom it applies except us. It has just one purpose left, to intimidate us into permitting Britain's defeat. Will it succeed?

That is a question which will be decided in a very few months. One question which has a bearing on the answer has, it seems to me, been settled with finality this week— whether the British Empire deserves to survive or not. Free men have often performed prodigies of valor in the past, but never before have men fought against odds as the British the Anzacs, and probably many Canadians have fought in Greece this week. As compared with what they have endured, the battles of the last war were static maneuvers. Assaulted by overwhelming masses of metal and men on the ground and from the air, they have done all that the best men anywhere could do to keep Hitler's formalized millions from crushing the life out of another brave and gallant people.

The Greeks themselves have proved that there is something immortal in Greece. No small nation has ever acquitted itself better when beset by huge predatory powers. The Greeks have also put all mankind under bonds to see to it that a flame of liberty which burns that valiantly shall not permanently be extinguished.

Along with the Greeks, the men who speak our language and live by our own free institutions—common to all of us since the time of Alfred the Great a thousand years ago —have shown that the tolerant, liberalizing rule of Anglo-Saxon civilization is also tough enough to deserve to live.

That the future of that civilization will hang in the balance through the remainder of this year is plain enough. The Mediterranean is not yet lost, and it is still doubtful that it can be taken; but the heaviest assaults at both ends of the Mediterranean must be expected—along with a relentless attempt to destroy British cities utterly before our aid can turn the scale. Over and over again we shall have to examine our resources to see if additional air power can be dispatched to Britain during the crisis.

Yet it is the sea war which will call for our gravest decisions. The damage to British shipping has already passed the danger point. Ships are being sunk at the rate of five and a half million tons a year, and a million tons are laid up all the time from air damage. The world's tonnage is disappearing at a rate which cannot be allowed to continue if means exist to reduce the damage. Already cargoes are having to wait throughout the New World, and the delays threaten to become longer.

In Washington many ways of easing the shipping crisis are being considered. Some of them may be effective. Whatever is tried, speed is essential. Hitler has sworn to keep our aid to Britain from being effective, and he will pull no punches. If we are to defeat him, enough vessels must be kept afloat to carry the stream of our aid to Britain and to keep our own defense activities moving.

The British Navy is a magnificent fighting machine, fully as efficient as Hitler's land forces—more efficient, because it is composed of free men who can think for themselves when the thinking above them slips. But the British Navy is not large enough to police the Indian Ocean and the Mediterranean and still have enough ships left to convoy thousands of ships across the North Atlantic. If the aid necessary to win the war is delivered successfully in Britain, we shall have to find some effective means of delivery.

☆

On April 27 German troops entered Athens, and by May 1 eighty per cent of British forces in Greece had been evacuated in a lesser Dunkirk. The next day Iraq troops attacked the British, inaugurating an abortive revolt. But on May 5 Emperor Haile Selassie returned to his throne in Addis Ababa, five years after the Italians drove him into exile. On May 6 the Russian dictator Joseph Stalin assumed the office of Premier for the first time.

IS LINDBERGH RIGHT?

May 7, 1941

ONE OF THE FACTS OF THE PRESENT SITUATION IS THAT many people believe what Charles A. Lindbergh tells them. He exerts a strong emotional pull because he tells us the old story which many of us came to believe again after the last war—that the United States is safe and need not bother about the world and its wars. He has all the advantage of voicing an old tradition; and, though the airplane which made him famous has killed that tradition beyond the power of any man to revive it, it is comforting to hear Lindbergh tell us that we are still safe and need have no fears.

In a world in which every value that we attach to life is disappearing beyond our borders with lightning rapidity, Lindbergh and his associates tell us that there is nothing we can do to stop the destruction—that all we need to do is go on living today and let the future take care of itself. He thus justifies the human desire in us to keep ourselves and our loved ones out of danger today, no matter what tomorrow may hold.

To people who want to be told that they have no responsibility in this world crisis, Lindbergh speaks with the voice of authority. There is not the faintest doubt in his tones. He told a large audience in New York on April 23 that "we cannot win this war for England regardless of how much assistance we extend." If we pass over his implication that we are fighting for England, how does Lindbergh know that the Nazis cannot be defeated by the combined industrial power of the British Empire and the United States?

So far as I know, the only answer to this question is that Lindbergh has been to Germany and found out. He left his own country to escape the newspapers. In England he found a haven. The British people shielded him from publicity, but without winning his affection. Soon, as the Nazi menace boiled up, Lindbergh began to go to Germany. We do not yet know all that he learned there; but, so far as I have been able to discover, nothing that he learned in Germany excited his disapproval. I have followed everything that he has said in recent years as closely as I could, and I have yet to see any suggestion of disapproval for any phase of the return to barbarism which Nazi Germany represents. So far as I have been able to learn, he has made no statement which would suggest that the Nazi system of terror, exploitation, and perpetual war is not the wave of the future.

But we do know that Lindbergh returned from Germany and advised the British government not to fight, for they would certainly be defeated. There were rumors that he was giving that advice at the time of Munich. Now we learn that he was doing it sooner. In his St. Louis speech of May 3 he explains how he tried to tell Prime Minister Stanley Baldwin, before Chamberlain's time, how powerful Germany was. The Prime Minister was very courteous, says Lindbergh, "but he changed the subject immediately. Time and again whenever the opportunity arose, I talked with members of the British government about military aviation in Europe. They were always courteous but seldom impressed."

Eventually, in September, 1939, Britain disregarded

Lindbergh's advice altogether by going to war with Hitler; and Lindbergh has not forgiven her. In his speeches he says, again and again, "I opposed this war before it was declared," and he always carefully makes the point that England "declared" the war.

I believe that he makes the suggestion occasionally that Britain might have been better prepared later on, though in one of his speeches he ostentatiously disregarded Britain altogether as a possible center of air power.

I would be the last person to minimize the folly of the Baldwin and Chamberlain governments in permitting Hitler to take Europe by the throat, but I feel sure that history will be slow to condemn Britain for fighting, at last, when he invaded Poland. Not to fight was to permit him to take Europe by default, one weaker country at a time, with few of them being able to fight at all. Lindbergh asked Britain to permit Hitler to overrun Europe rapidly, organize its resources, and then turn upon France and Britain. But the British felt that if they pursued appeasement to the very end, the end would certainly be bitter. If Hitler got Europe without a fight, he would have all his strength and more for them. It is true that from September, 1939, to date the British have not saved a single people which fought with them. But who can be sure that Poland or Greece or any of the others who fought may not have upset Hitler's timetable just enough to win liberty for them all in the end?

Today Lindbergh is giving us exactly the same advice which he gave Britain. We must let Hitler continue his conquests. He says, "I knew in 1939 that England and France were not prepared to wage war successfully, and I know that America is not prepared today to wage successful war in Europe." The day after Lindbergh made this statement Hitler told us that no pool of industrial power was vast enough to halt Germany's march of conquest. Both Hitler and Lindbergh are certain that we can do nothing to prevent the Nazis from taking over Europe and Africa, to say the least.

But on the same day that their dicta were published seventeen Americans who have made a deep study of this war united in a joint statement saying that "factors of fundamental importance still operate in favor of Britain and her allies and there is no warrant for presupposing a German victory." The seventeen who signed the statement included four admirals who have made a life-long study of war. I recently heard one of them, Admiral William V. Pratt, discuss the whole question of what we can do in this war, and I gained a strong respect both for his knowledge and his judgment. He was very keenly aware of the crucial importance of air power in this struggle.

The seventeen experts list seven reasons for believing that Hitler can be defeated. Briefly, they are: (1) Germany is denied the world's resources beyond Europe; (2) the industrial plants of the Germans are open to British bombing; but ours and those of the Dominions are beyond their reach, while British air and sea power stands between; (3) our power is only beginning to be felt, whereas Germany's is already at the peak; (4) unless Germany wins the Battle of the Atlantic this summer, which victory we have the power to prevent, she cannot win; (5) if there is any people in the world which can surpass all others in the science of mechanized warfare, it is the people of the United States; no people is as machine-minded as we are; (6) the moral factors, those imponderables that Bismarck was so aware of, are against Hitler; (7) even if it were true that Britain is destined to lose, it is imperative that any Hitler victory be delayed as long and made as costly as possible.

The logic of this last point seems to me irrefutable, as Nazi control of Europe and Africa means that the richest part of South America is at their mercy. Apparently Lindbergh is willing to believe that if we let the gangsters have the Old World they would be satisfied, but no responsible official of our government can proceed on that strange hypothesis. From the time that Hitler took control of the Saar Valley in 1933 on down to date he has fooled some by announcing that whatever conquest he was making would satisfy him. Today we know that no rich resources that the Nazis or Japanese can take will remain untaken and that the conflict between their organized gangsterism and our free civilization is permanent and irreconcilable.

No man knows just how or when this war can be won. But when did anybody know just how a close struggle lasting years could be terminated? I am free to admit that one of Lindbergh's points disturbs me. He states with total finality that "it is physically impossible to base enough aircraft in the British Isles alone to equal in strength the aircraft that can be based on the continent of Europe." It is possible that that may prove to be true. But it has not been proved true yet, and as I see it, we should not accept that conclusion while the slightest chance of disproving it remains. Certainly we should not accept it on Lindbergh's word alone, especially since Major Alexander de Seversky, a far more competent aviation expert than Lindbergh, has reasoned cogently to the contrary in the current issue of the *American Mercury*.

We have control of the seas, always the decisive factor in all other world wars. We undoubtedly have the capacity to outbuild Germany in the air if we can gain a little time. Why should we give up the struggle when our power is as yet scarcely felt?

That is the question which will soon have to be answered. Lindbergh, Wheeler, Clark, Nye, and others are addressing large crowds in our cities daily, urging them to wire and write their congressmen. The flood of messages thus stirred is phrased, we may be sure, in the strongest language. Meanwhile, the President is waiting to hear from the country, and the popular majority for seeing the thing through which has been registered on every test so far waits for the President to make the next move.

All would agree, I take it, that the moment is one of the greatest danger. It is now or never for democratic civilization. The sea lanes to Britain must be kept open this summer or the world and its oceans will be gangster ruled up to our shores. If by pulling with might and main we can get through until Christmas, there is every prospect that the score of free nations already conquered will live again. If we do not hold the seas this summer, we shall be a lonely and beleaguered people for a long time. Yet today, at the critical moment of the war, we are on dead center, with those who would accept a totalitarian world filling the land with their voices.

Is it true, as the Nazis confidently believe, that the democracies are all doomed because no two of them will ever be able to pull together until it is too late? As we move toward the final answer to this question, I am reminded that when Lindbergh set out to conquer the Atlantic he didn't begin by telling us it couldn't be done. He took his courage in both hands and destroyed the Atlantic barrier which had given us a sense of isolationist security. He marked in the sky the trail to our cities for the heavy bombers of any gangster dictator who might gain control of Europe. Now he should help us to deal with the consequences before they are beyond remedy.

WHAT IS THE ISSUE?
May 14, 1941

FOR THE PAST WEEK DEBATE HAS CONTINUED AS TO THE PART which this nation can and should play in determining the outcome of the world war which is now in progress. Due to the postponement of the President's speech, the opponents of more active measures on our part have had possession of the field this week—notably in the speeches of Charles A. Lindbergh and former President Hoover. I would like to discuss some of the issues raised in these two addresses.

Lindbergh began his Minnesota address by recalling the fight which his father made against our entry into the last war. This is a bond which Lindbergh has in common with the LaFollette brothers, Senator Clark of Missouri, and others. Their fathers opposed the last war unsuccessfully. Today the sons are strongly determined to succeed. Up to the outbreak of this war, they had complete confidence that they *would succeed*. Under the leadership of Senator Nye this group had convinced the country, largely through the medium of the Nye Munitions Committee, that it had made a mistake in going into the last war and should never do such a thing again. For years all polls registered their victory. They rewrote the history of the last great crisis in one of the most successful propaganda campaigns in our history. They made us believe in the thirties that what we had felt and seen and known during the last war was not true at all. But lately, as brutal aggression began to take the citadels of our Western civilization one after another, our people very rapidly reconsidered the comfortable verdict which the Nye group had established. In April, 1937, 64 per cent of our people thought our entry into the last war a mistake; but in April, 1941, only 39 per cent still held that opinion, whereas 43 per cent had concluded it was not a mistake. This swift shift of opinion presages the end of the idea that we didn't know what we were doing in 1917.

But as fast as the legends which isolationism creates are exploded by the impact of tremendous world forces, new ones are created. Thus in his latest speech Lindbergh lays

173

the defeat of his creed and the present plight of the world to our professors and idealists. He says that after the last war "we left the future of the world in the hands of our college presidents and our idealists." From 1917 to this hour, he says, "the idealist has held sway."

These assertions seem to be the greatest perversion of history yet attempted. It is true that during the last war the overwhelming majority of college presidents and teachers looked that vast tragedy in the face and used their full influence to prevent its repetition. So did the great majority of our clergymen, editors, writers, speakers, businessmen, and bankers. Henry Cabot Lodge and George Harvey have recorded in their books that the whole intellectual leadership of this nation was for the League of Nations "as it stood," to use Lodge's words.

Never in all human history had the need for a step in the perfection of human government been so frightfully demonstrated. It was crystal clear then that the earth had become a unit, for the purposes of both trade and war, and that the perfection of the means of destruction would soon make it forever impossible for any great power to remain aloof from any future world war. Were the vast company of our leaders who recognized these facts in 1919 "idealists"? Were they not rather the most sure-sighted and hard-headed realists who have spoken to us since 1914?

But instead of putting our destinies in the hands of these men who knew what lay ahead, what *did* we do? We cracked down on them, turned our backs on the plainest lessons of the war, and went in for "normalcy." It was the Harding gang which ruled us, not Lindbergh's so-called idealists. We turned our back on the League of Nations, refused many times to enter the World Court, and devoted ourselves to the business of getting rich by any means until we developed a gambling mania which finally exploded in 1929, wrecking the financial and economic system of every nation on the globe, turning the Japanese loose in

Manchuria, and bringing Hitler to power. When he took control of Germany in January, 1933, the present catastrophe was assured.

Today, when we grapple with the titanic forces which blind isolationism turned loose, is a poor time for the younger prophets of isolationism to shift the blame for the postwar policy which their elders imposed upon us.

The situation we face now is that a tidal wave of lawlessness is on the point of bursting all bounds and rolling up to our shores, east, west, and south. In his Sunday address Mr. Hoover said that we are united only in our willingness to defend the Western Hemisphere.

But what *is* the Western Hemisphere? It is time for us to recognize that there is no such thing. Under the conditions of modern warfare the Western Hemisphere does not exist. South America is not on our side of the ocean; it is *between* Europe and North America, and the bulk of it is much closer to Europe than to us, not to speak of a Europe-dominated Africa. The idea that South America is a part of our land mass is a similar illusion. South America is *overseas* to us, just as truly as Europe is, and its ties of language, blood, and laws, ties of religion, customs, and culture are with Europe, not with us. The bulk of its trade, also, is with Europe—and must be.

This is why our responsible leaders are convinced that the Western Hemisphere, as we call it, can be defended only by defeating the Nazis in Europe, by keeping out of their hands Dakar and West Africa and the chains of islands from Africa to Portugal, and by holding the British Isles themselves.

The urgent question which we must decide soon is *how* to hold this first and best line of our own defense. In Mr. Hoover's view the best way is to continue to "give" England the tools of war, but without helping to *deliver* the tools.

And where does that lead? The columnists Alsop and

Kintner have endeavored to tell us in a few sentences. They predict: "If we hold our hands, Britain's merchant fleet will be a third smaller by the end of this year. Within sixty days vital war materials produced by us for Britain will pile up at our docks for lack of ships. And next year, when our output will be sufficient to alter the balance of the war, we shall find ourselves with a vast striking power in our hands, yet with no way to send it against the enemy."

It is my own belief that this prediction will come tragically true unless we use our navy to decrease the destruction of ships and to see the goods over. The British have just admitted that they lost nearly half a million tons of ships during April. They have lost one and a half million tons since January 1. If we are hardheaded, we will expect their losses to increase through the long summer months ahead. If we remain quiet, we gamble that the world's tonnage will not be reduced this year to the point which will mean certain loss of the war.

The question we have to decide now is not whether we shall send a huge army to Europe, but whether we shall use our ships to see that supplies get to Britain. Both Lindbergh and Hoover assume that the Nazi strangle hold on Europe cannot be broken without the landing of huge American armies in Europe. Mr. Hoover demonstrates the impossibility of this by saying that we would have to build forty million tons of ships to land the necessary five million men in Europe.

That would be a large undertaking. But sea power is still in our hands and we have a better than even chance to take control of the air next year—*if* we sharply decrease soon the deadly drain on the world's shipping. We have no reason to believe that the German people will take battering from the air as the British have.

The whole logic of Mr. Hoover's address points toward the submission of Britain to Hitler. Lindbergh continues to demand a negotiated peace. These words sound attractive.

A negotiated peace would relieve us for the moment of taking a decisive stand in this conflict, but it would mean the end of Britain. There is only one conceivable reason that would lead the Nazis to sign a negotiated peace: that they feared defeat and wanted more time—time to build an ocean-going navy larger than Britain's, time to organize Europe and Africa, time to build an unbeatable air force. Every Englishman knows that if he quits fighting now he could not begin again.

If we should be confused about everything else, let us be clear on the point that there can be no compromise between democracy and totalitarianism, between freedom and slavery. They will not mix. It is either one or the other. Lindbergh now says, very belatedly, "I never wanted Germany to win this war," but he still advocates the policy which means total and complete German triumph. When this war is over, world air power and world sea power will rest either in the hands of a German Europe or in the hands of the free peoples, including us.

If the Nazis win, the world will be governed by them. If they lose, we must see to it that we belong to a powerful organization of free nations—not a weak league of nations such as the isolationists of 1920 inveighed against, but a federation so strong that the peace will be permanently kept. If we miss this chance, we are never likely to have another. And if we *get* the chance, we must make sure that the second generation of irreconcilable isolationists does not take it from us. The policy which was plainly wrong in 1920 cannot be other than irretrievably disastrous if it is tried again, for the improvement of the engines of destruction never ceases.

UNLIMITED EMERGENCY
May 28, 1941

IN COMMON WITH MOST OF YOU I HAVE EXAMINED THE President's speech of last night to see what he means for us to do. The time for words is almost past. Words can still help to assist action, but our action or inaction will determine soon the nature of the world we are to live in. What does the President propose to do?

First, he rejects the idea of a victor's peace for Hitler to be forced by us upon the British. Every line of this part of the speech is the obvious truth. He forecasts exactly the fine promises that Hitler would make to us and how many of our people would snap up those promises in the hope of the profitable trade which the Nazis would pledge.

It seems fairly clear that the Nazis would like to arrange a truce now, one which would give them Europe and Africa and leave Britain ostensibly in control of her empire. They dread the full weight of our power against them. But the President sees clearly that such a truce would be merely to give the Nazis time to build a naval and air force intended to master the oceans. Meantime, as he says, "they would fasten an economic strangle hold upon our several American nations. . . . . They plan to treat the American nations as they are now treating the Balkan nations." No one, as I see it, can doubt the truth of that parallel. It would be economic domination by barter methods first and then military conquest if necessary.

And for us? Here again, there can be no reasonable doubt. In the President's words, "wages and hours would be fixed by Hitler." Our farm surpluses would be permanently unsalable except on Nazi terms; and no tariff wall could save us, for there would be a much greater Nazi-Japanese wall to keep us in. Said the President, "The whole fabric of working life as we know it—business, manufacturing, mining, agriculture—all would be mangled and crippled under such a system. Yet to maintain even that crippled independence would require permanent conscription of our manpower; it would curtail funds" for every constructive purpose. "Instead we would be permanently pouring our resources into armaments and, year in and year out, standing day-and-night watch against the destruction of our cities."

This is what is directly ahead of us if the Nazis win. But if the worst does happen, no citizen in our great interior can say that he was not accurately and solemnly warned.

No one can ever say, either, that the method of attack upon us—through South America to the citadel of our power here—was not pointed out. The most conspicuous strain in the President's address is his insistence that the Atlantic outposts of our defense, especially the Azores and the Cape Verde Islands, shall not fall into Nazi hands. He was not quite so positive about Dakar but nearly so. These are places that we will fight for. The Nazis are plainly warned away.

The President reiterates his pledge not to fight unless we are attacked—a pledge he never should have made—but he will not wait until our greatest line of defense is gone before making up his mind that we are attacked. It is suicide, he tells us, to wait in one's own front yard to see the whites of the eyes of enemies advancing in tanks and airplanes. And it is equally dangerous, he tells us, for people in our Midwest not to see that the safety of their homes is bound up with the safety of homes in Brazil. "We are placing our armed forces in strategic positions," says our President, "and we will decide for ourselves when, and where, our interests are attacked or threatened."

On the Battle of the Atlantic he is equally positive. "The delivery of needed supplies to Britain is imperative; it must be done; it will be done." There is no room for evasion or procrastination here; the stuff will be delivered. The blunt truth, he assures us, is that the Nazis are sinking more than twice as many ships as Britain and America can build. These losses must be cut down, he says. Obviously they must or we shall find ourselves unable to deliver the goods a year or two from now when they come off our assembly lines in great quantities.

About these all-important assembly lines the President minces no words. Disputes between labor and labor, by which he means jurisdictional strikes, must stop; and all other labor-capital disputes must be settled without stoppage of work. Warning labor that it will lose everything it has gained if this war is not won, he says with emphasis that "this government is determined to use all of its power . . . . to prevent interference with production." Every laboring man and every labor leader will do well to heed that warning, for with the life of this nation in danger as it has never been, the President will have overpowering public support in any action he may take to keep the wheels of industry turning. No administration has ever done as much for labor as this one, and it is now time that labor should demonstrate both its gratitude and its patriotism. Labor is entitled to good wages, even liberal wages, but the pyramiding of wages cannot go on or it will bring inflation that will eat up labor's gain and defeat the winning of the war.

It is time also for some straight thinking by the group of our citizens that is obstructing the national policy. That policy was fixed clearly and unequivocally in the lend-lease bill, which by heavy majorities in Congress and in the country put our power squarely behind those nations which are fighting aggression. This is a clear, intelligent policy—the only one which offers us a chance of saving our free American way of life. But a determined minority of objectors, in the Senate and out, refused to accept the policy. They took to the stump as if nothing had been decided and have been giving the impression that this is a divided and confused nation—too divided to act. They would paralyze the nation into inactivity.

Without mentioning it by name, the President grants the sincerity and patriotism of the America First Committee, but he calls attention to the sinister support it is receiving from "the Bundists and Fascists and Communists and every group devoted to bigotry and racial and religious intolerance."

It is no accident that these open enemies of democracy who throng many of the meetings of the America First Committee echo "the words that have been poured out from the Axis bureaus of propaganda."

For some weeks the minority which is attempting to block our action in this supreme crisis has been calling itself the majority and demanding that we attain national unity by agreeing with it.

That would indeed be self-strangulation for our democracy. The President has issued a clear call for national unity on the basis of the policy adopted by our whole government of seeing to it that the remaining free peoples are not destroyed. "Your government," says the President. "has the right to expect of all citizens that they take loyal part in the common work of our common defense—take loyal part from this moment forward."

That is an admonition which has not come any too soon. It puts every objector to the policy of seeing this conflict through under the heavy obligation to examine his attitude afresh to see if it squares with the rules under which democracy must operate if it is to live.

The President has issued a clear call. He says: "We will not accept a Hitler-dominated world." That is the issue, and every man must be on one side of it or the other. There is no longer any middle ground. If one is not against a Hitler-dominated world, he is for it. To take no position is to decide for a Nazi world. Inaction is action in Hitler's behalf. Opposition to opposition to Hitler is action for his cause.

That is not a pleasant conclusion for anyone to be compelled to make, but there is no time to lose in making it. The British people must have powerful help from us before this summer is gone. They are living under a burden of world-wide strain that we cannot safely allow to continue. We have told them often that we would give them the tools of war, but they are being defeated on one battlefield after another for lack of the tools. Now it is up to us to deliver them and to furnish whatever additional support is necessary if we wish to have fighting friends left when this year is ended.

If I read the President's speech rightly, he is telling us that the time for talking about what we are going to do has been used up. The emergency we are in is unlimited, and we must act accordingly.

On June 5 Hitler gave an interview to our former Ambassador to Poland, John Cudahy, who had gone to Berchtesgaden to ask Hitler if he intended to invade us. Hitler laughed at the idea and explained that enough ships did not exist for such an undertaking. On June 14 the President ordered frozen all assets in the United States belonging to Germany, Italy, and the Axis-occupied countries. On June 16 all German consulates and travel and propaganda agencies were ordered closed. On June 21 a similar order banned Italian agencies.

WHERE ARE WE HEADED?
June 18, 1941

I WOULD LIKE TO SAY IN BEGINNING THAT I AM TRANSCRIBING this talk electrically a little in advance in order to attend a conference on war problems and Canadian-American relations at Queen's University in Canada.

Tonight I would like to attempt a survey of the whole world scene to see if we can see where events are heading. I begin with Russia because of the general feeling that something important is brewing there. In spite of many denials from both sides it is apparent that for more than a month Germany has been increasing pressure on Russia. German troops have been piling up on the whole Russian frontier, including Rumania and Finland. Late dispatches from Sweden tell of fleets of twenty-five transports going from Germany to Finland on successive days.

What then does Hitler want of Stalin? The ultimate answer is, of course, the domination of the whole of Russia or of such part as would not be given to Japan. But immediately Hitler needs three things from Russia: (1) the wheat of the Ukraine; (2) the oil of the Caucasus; and (3) passage around Turkey to Iraq and Egypt. If Hitler is demanding anything of Stalin, we may be sure that these three are included in his demands. Let us consider them.

The Ukraine is the greatest black-dirt plain on the Eurasian continent. If great amounts of wheat are needed, here is the place to get them—and great amounts of wheat *are* needed in the Europe which Hitler has bombed and ravaged from end to end. Hitler urgently needs wheat to feed his huge armies and the dozen nations they hold down, but he also needs wheat for another purpose—to enable him to wage a long war with Britain and the United States. Now that our resources are fully pledged to defeat him, there is only one place in the world that Hitler can get

183

anything like comparable resources with which to balance ours. That place is southern Russia. There is to be found not only the wheat but the greatest oil deposit in Eurasia. If Hitler could finally take the oil fields of both Iraq and Persia, he would not be much better off because of transportation difficulties. Even if the British were driven entirely from the Mediterranean, there would still be a very long and devious haul. Besides, the quantity of oil in these fields is not huge, and Hitler needs oil in great quantities to keep his vast war machines running and to fill the motor requirements of all Europe. The oil he needs lies at the eastern end of the Black Sea in Russia, from where it could be transported by both sea and land out of range of British bombers.

Hence it becomes a question of how much wheat and oil Stalin will agree to deliver to Hitler peaceably. The amounts must be very large to satisfy Hitler. But Soviet agriculture and life generally have been motorized. Russia needs nearly all of her own oil, especially for her own huge war machine. There are also a hundred and eighty million Russians, and bread is none too plentiful among them. Indeed, there have been a couple of big famines in Russia during the last fifteen years, and there could be again. So what is Stalin to do?

One report has it that spring wheat planting in the Ukraine is short by fifty million acres. Is this due to a desire to reduce Hitler's temptation to take the Ukraine? Or is it due to the disorganization in Russia caused by big mobilizations? In either case, the prospect of a grain shortage in the Ukraine means to Hitler that he must send his efficiency boys into the Ukraine to see that production does not lag again. And is not a heavy infiltration of German experts into the Russian oil fields required? But if these armies of Nazi "experts" once get control of his breadbasket and powerhouse, will Stalin be able to get them out again? Will Hitler be satisfied, either, with any arrangement that requires him to pay for the wheat and oil? And if his troops are permitted to go through that part of Russia to Iraq, will they not remain?

These are the questions that Stalin has to decide, probably soon. Most reports credit him with such fear of Hitler's war machine that surrender is to be expected. It has always seemed to me, however, that he can hardly yield his great treasures to Hitler without a fight.

But whether he fights or not, there has been issued this week from the Brookings Institution in Washington a report which brings the problem home to us. That highly reputable research organization says that even if Russia were included in Hitler's empire it would still have to get vast quantities of raw materials and foodstuffs from the rest of the world. Otherwise, the diet of his empire would be monotonous and very seriously deficient in fats.

Virtually nothing would remain of Europe's great textile industries. Machines and machine tools would deteriorate. There would be little or no asbestos for automobile brake linings or mica for spark plugs. The European empire that Hitler is grasping for would still have to import immense supplies of essential goods.

Here, of course, is where South America would at once come in should Hitler conquer Russia and Britain. In South America lies all the food and fats that he needs and many of the rarer materials. Would the master of Eurasia and Asia refrain from taking these things? Why should he when looting on a colossal scale had succeeded everywhere else? That he would have the power to take what he wanted below the bulge of Brazil hardly needs elaboration, for if he can sink the American ship *Robin Moor* in the narrow waters between Africa and Brazil as things stand now, what could he do if in secure possession of Dakar and the shoulder of Africa? But an equally grave question remains: would the proved master of the world need to take over his Latin American victims by force of

185

arms? Would not his enormous buying power and his terrific propaganda pressure be sufficient? Is there a country in South America that would refuse his economic domination when to do so would mean that its wheat and meat, cotton and coffee could not be sold at all?

This is the real meaning behind Hitler's published statement that two worlds are in conflict and that one of them must break asunder. This is also the basic reason why we must exert our full power to defeat that world which intends to live by looting and plunder. We must not forget either that Japan is an integral part of that world. Beginning in 1931 she set the pace of aggression and conquest and she is still at it to the full extent of her power. I do not doubt that many of the businessmen of Japan would like to take Japan out of the hunting pack temporarily at least, but it is always to be remembered that it is the Army and Navy which rule Japan and that, whenever they desire, these armed services simply run amuck wherever they like. I see no reason to doubt that Japan will stick to the plunderbund until the end. If the gangster powers win, the mastery of all East Asia will be hers; if they do not win, Japan is due to be driven back to her islands to stay a very long time as a third-rate power.

But what of Nazi Germany? As I see it, the greatest marauding expedition in all history cannot succeed unless we fail to use our power. Britain's war production is still rising. Ours is just beginning. Germany must have a hundred and fifty thousand tons of rubber a year and can hardly produce synthetically more than a third of that amount. As time goes on, German Europe—even including Russia—will grow shorter and shorter of copper, tin, nickel, chrome, cotton, and wool, to mention only some things. These key commodities, together with unlimited quantities of foodstuffs, lie in the oceanic world, which is controlled by the American and British navies. It is our side which possesses the sinews of victory, and, if we have the resolution to use and defend our control of the seas, the strength of the aggressor combine is due to decrease steadily until the outraged peoples of some fifty nations have a chance to take control of the world again.

That time may not come for several years, but it is not too soon for us to begin to think about "what then?" A recent Gallup poll shows that sentiment is rising very rapidly in favor of a new and stronger League of Nations. A dispatch from Washington declares also that our government fully intends that such an organization to police the peace shall be created. Surely by the time this thing is over there will be few who will deny the overwhelming necessity of a federation of free nations to defend the common peace. It is unthinkable that we should be betrayed a second time from going through with that job.

It is essential, too, that we should begin to think about the kind of world we mean to organize. It must, for example, enable the great energies of the German people to have scope in constructive channels. There must, of course, be drastic control of the weapons of destruction, but we shall not be able to make a new world order endure unless we provide really free access to all the world's resources for all the world's peoples. We shall not get peace unless we ourselves are ready to give up some of the narrow economic nationalism which is partly responsible for the present wars. Hitler's method of gaining economic self-sufficiency by conquering the world cannot be permitted to succeed. But afterwards we must provide a better way for the nations to live without economic war.

The sinking of the Robin Moor, *about which the President sent a special message to Congress on June 20, seemed to bring*

us to the point of shooting war; but two days later an epochal event occurred which greatly eased the concern of Americans about the future. On June 22 German armies invaded Russia on a two-thousand-mile front.

THE WAR VIEWED FROM THE MIDWEST
June 25, 1941

FOR SEVERAL DAYS I HAVE BEEN READING THE NEWS OF THE world crisis from the Middle West while traveling through that region. What I have to say tonight was sent to you by electrical transcription from Detroit on June 20.

The atmosphere in this region is, of course, somewhat different from that in the South and other parts of the country. There is not quite the same agreement here as in other sections that the triple alliance must be defeated and control of the seas kept in our hands. The oceans are far away from the Midwest and do not seem so vital to the national health. Yet the national viewpoint prevails here as elsewhere. The number of people who are willing to let the predatory powers take over the world may be a little larger, but the majority of Midwestern people want the threat of Fascist strangulation removed from our future and realize that that threat cannot be canceled without very powerful efforts on our part.

The impression that the Midwest is different from the rest of the country on international issues is kept alive, and to some extent kept a reality, by the *Chicago Tribune*, as I well know from a number of years' residence in Illinois. Foreseeing that the result of this second world upheaval in twenty-five years is likely to be a world federation to prevent the recurrence of such catastrophes, both the *Tribune* and the *Chicago Herald-American* are carrying on a crusade against Clarence Streit's plan for "Union Now." Both represent Streit's plan for a federation of the democracies as British propaganda, and the *Tribune* features it as "a subversive plot to change our form of government." No newspaper in the world did more to defeat the League of Nations twenty years ago and to invite the return of the present world anarchy; and though world anarchy still more dangerous to us has returned, the *Tribune's* position is just the same. Nothing that has happened has changed its attitude in the slightest. Just as Woodrow Wilson was fought for trying to organize the nations against future world wars, so now President Roosevelt is portrayed in front-page cartoons as planning to make himself the first president of "Anglamerica."

Editorially the *Tribune* terms the idea of outbombing the Nazis fantastic and seeks to show that this is not a very serious war for Britain or she wouldn't be trying to maintain export trade—one of the chief sinews of war. The President's recent moves to curb Axis activity in this country are also represented as steps toward war which the President is wantonly taking. Says the *Tribune*: "It is no secret that Mr. Roosevelt wants a war and that he seeks to provoke one."

Naturally the *Tribune* features the charges of Senator Nye to the same effect, to which charges the *Chicago Daily News* replies that Nye "misses no opportunity to make out the best possible case for Hitler," and notes that, though Nye has retracted his statement that it was probably the British who sank the *Robin Moor*, he has not retracted his assertion that it was probably the British who bombed Dublin.

In Detroit the owner of the *Free Press* has changed its isolationist policy to conform to the national determination that Hitlerism must be opposed.

The ousting of the German consuls from this country, with care that they do not ooze out in the direction of

Latin America, is a step which few of us will oppose. In charging the Germans with subversive activity, the *St. Louis Globe Democrat* notes that the German consulate in St. Louis had twice as many staff members after the war started, though commerce with Germany had practically disappeared. That these swollen staffs were doing their best to develop a fifth column here is no news to anyone. This effort will of course go on, financed liberally, but it will now have to go underground. The additional executive order this week designed to keep all new Axis agents from entering the United States will not keep our Nazi organizations and their allies from getting direction from Berlin, but at least we are closing the open avenues of infection. Only the German embassy in Washington, with its large staff, remains—and in this connection it is well to remember that it was the military and naval attachés of the German embassy, Captains von Boy-Ed and von Papen, who directed the sabotage of our industries during the last war.

It took the Germans several days to arrange some specific charges against our people in closing American consulates in Europe. During this interval the Nazi press raised a loud wail about the "illegality" of our actions in expelling their agents and freezing Axis assets. The cry of illegality from the Nazis is indeed amusing after they have destroyed the very idea of law as a means of regulating civilized international relations.

Similar reflections inevitably occur to one in connection with the Turkish-German pact signed on June 18. In this treaty the Nazis promise to do nothing directly or indirectly against Turkey for ten years. But far from being reassured the Turks will know that they are in a more dangerous position than ever. When Hitler guarantees to act in a civilized manner toward a small nation, it is from that moment doomed, if he has the power to strangle it. His first treaty was one with Poland, to whom he made the same promise—for ten years. The roaring Nazi war against Poland was suddenly called off—only to be turned loose again long before the ten years was up. The German-Polish treaty of nonaggression and friendship merely served to lull the Poles until Hitler was ready to ravage and destroy their country as no land has been devastated yet. Now for two years the Nazis have been making every effort to exterminate the Polish people by every means short of continued mass slaughter.

It is ominously reported that the German-Turkish treaty of friendship calls for the cessation of unfriendly comments in press and radio. This, too, will seem to the Turks like the handwriting on the wall, for the Nazis made the same agreement with the Poles—until they were ready to destroy Poland. Perhaps by hushing their people into silence the Turks may put off their own evil day a little. Even so, there is a warning here for us, for if Hitler masters the bulk of the world, he will most certainly demand that our press and radio stop saying anything critical about him. Nothing infuriates him so much as the criticism of his crimes by people who are still free.

The chief service of the mild Turkish-German pact to Hitler is that it may weaken a little the resistance of Stalin to his demands. The majority of the commentators still believe that Stalin will fold up and give Hitler the grain and oil he must have if he is to have a fair chance of winning a long war. Yet I am still unable to see how Russia can give up her food and oil to the Nazis when she has none too much for herself. If the Nazis must have these things, so must Russia. Walter Duranty vouches, too, for the fact of a remarkable industrial upswing in Russia somewhat comparable to our own defense effort.

It is difficult to foresee, either, what Stalin could gain, beyond saving his own skin, by turning Russia over to Nazi control. But the advantages to Hitler from a giant blitz against Russia would be very great. Presumably he could get a military grip on the coveted grain and oil, which would be better than any arrangement with the Soviets. But beyond that, the political advantages of a war against the Reds could decide the whole world struggle in his favor. The British Tories swallowed his anti-Red crusade for years, and if he really went through with it many of them would want to stop the Anglo-German war and help him. When Russia attacked Finland a year ago last winter, the French Conservatives forgot all about the Franco-German war they were supposed to be fighting and did their best to turn the war into an anti-Red crusade.

It is to be remembered that in this country, too, a powerful segment of our people felt the same way. Their indignation against the Reds was so great that they forgot what Hitler was doing. Should he now attack Russia, a large and influential element in our people would be likely to lose sight of the menace of Hitlerism in the hope of getting rid of the Red specter, for that specter haunts the sleep of many wealthy Americans as nothing else does. A Hitler war against Russia would therefore offer a good chance of delaying our decisive participation in the war by causing turmoil and division of opinion among us.

To ward off a Hitler victory by this route it seems to me that we should try to keep one thing clearly in mind: that it is the Nazis who for the past eight years have been trying to conquer the world by every known means—not the Reds. I do not discount in the slightest the effort of Moscow to use the Communist parties of all the nations of the world to her own interest, but it is a matter of record that fear of a two-front war has been the dominating feeling in Moscow for the whole of the Hitler period. I make that statement in full confidence that the history of the last ten years will substantiate it. I do not say that the Soviets would not have recovered the former Russian territories, from Finland to Bessarabia, for other reasons, but I think it is clear that they took back that great strip of territory in all haste to begin fortifying it against Hitler. It may be that Russia will become sometime a raging, tearing conqueror, but that role is now plainly filled by Hitler and his Nazis. That is the central fact which must be kept in mind at all cost. It is a Hitler world we have to fear now, not a Communist one.

But the clearest impression that I have from a week's reading and listening in the Midwest is that Hitler is not going to win this war. A German seizure of Russia may prolong the struggle for years, but I believe that Hitler and his chiefs know that they have lost the war. They have won stupendous military victories and can still do that—bigger ones than ever—but, lacking control of the seas, they cannot organize Europe and feed and operate it. They know now also that we are not going to surrender control of the seas to them and that we have the power to keep it.

In the meantime, the gathering might of American industry is rapidly demonstrating that we are still the greatest industrial power—and the most machine-minded people—on earth. When Hitler sought to take control of the world by machines, he started something that we shall finish—if we can keep Britain fighting strongly until winter comes—for we have the power not only to keep control of the seas but to take control of the air, a combination which means the disintegration of the Hitler empire.

Finland had ordered full mobilization on June 20, two days before the German attack on Russia, and on June 26 she joined in the war against Russia. Vichy France broke off relations with the Soviets on June 30. But Prime Minister Churchill at once welcomed the Russians as allies, and on June 24 President Roosevelt pledged them all possible aid.

193

HITLER'S WAR ON RUSSIA
July 2, 1941

THE GERMAN ATTACK ON RUSSIA IS UNQUESTIONABLY THE most important event of the war since Hitler failed to win control of the air over Britain last September—and it brings before us equally grave decisions. There are a great many people who fear and hate Russian Communism more than they do Nazism—because of its repression of capitalism or because of its war on religion. I have not been surprised to find here in Toronto, Canada—from which city I am sending this talk by electrical transcription—that some people were gravely disturbed to hear Prime Minister Churchill declare that whoever fought Nazi Germany is Britain's friend and whoever aids her is Britain's enemy. Finding themselves suddenly on the same side as the Reds was a considerable shock to conservative Canadians.

Yet in my judgment Churchill has never made a more statesmanlike decision than in announcing his unequivocal determination not to be deceived by Hitler's master stroke. There never was a time when we needed more to keep our eyes on the main issue, which is, "Shall Nazi Germany rule the world itself, for all practical purposes?"

For the moment, the pressure on Britain and the Western World is relieved. It is just possible, too, that Russia will use up so much of Hitler's strength that he cannot return for a knockout blow against Britain. But the Nazis are wholly confident of the opposite result. They expect to get from Russia the sinews of war for a successful conquest of the West—and by the West they mean far more than Britain. They mean Africa and the bulk of South America. I am convinced that it is a fact that the Nazis cannot find, either in Russia or Africa, enough resources to make their so-called "new order" stick; but if they can secure a firm grip on both Russia and Africa, they will be in an im-

194

mensely better position to reduce Britain and to seize, by one pressure or another, the abundant resources of South America. We would, therefore, be woefully blind if we regarded the Russian campaign as anything more than a preparation for the final struggle.

Fortunately, it does not appear likely that Hitler will be able to deceive many people with his effort to represent this campaign as a holy crusade against the Bolsheviki. Before he had overrun all of Western Europe, the most civilized and Christian part of Europe, he was quite willing to put aside his anti-Red crusade and to split the loot with Stalin. It is too late now for Hitler to represent this greatest of his aggressions as anything better than that. He wants the wheat and oil and manganese of southern Russia and means to take them. There is nothing about this onslaught that makes it any more moral than the rape of Austria and Czechoslovakia or the seizure of a dozen other countries since 1937.

We cannot afford to be deceived, either, by his talk of restoring independence to Latvia, Estonia, and Lithuania and of returning Bessarabia to Rumania and the Karelian Isthmus to Finland. What has just happened ought to make it possible for us to view the recent and future fate of these lands in a different perspective. In doing so, the first thing to note is that these territories were all Russian before the last war and that during the last twenty years Russia never asserted any desire or intention to recover any of them except Bessarabia, and for several years before 1938 the claim to Bessarabia was put completely into the background while Russia attempted to co-operate with the Western powers against the growing Nazi threat. It was not until Russia had been expelled from the councils of Europe at Munich that the question of the Baltic states came up. Then when Britain and France went to Moscow for an alliance, the Russians asked: "What about these small Baltic states, all too weak to defend themselves, all largely controlled by Germans, and all ready to be taken over by Nazi infiltration exactly as Austria and Czechoslovakia and Spain have been?" Russia maintained that she must make certain about these entry points into her territory, but the Allies would not agree to Russian control. Nor would the Poles agree to admit Russian armies to Poland in their own defense against Germany. Russia accordingly made a truce with Germany which gave her these lands and the half of Poland which was Russian and Ukrainian and which never should have been included in the new Poland.

The evidence all indicated at that time that Russia was seizing these countries in order to use them as shock absorbers against German attack. The Russians knew well enough that it was Russian resources that the Nazis were after. They had never made any secret about that. So the Reds hastily reoccupied the strip of land from the Baltic to the Black seas and feverishly fortified it against the attack which has just come. This additional belt of territory may not save Russia from conquest; but when the final history of this war is written, it may be recorded that it was this wide belt of new defenses which kept Hitler from delivering a knockout blow. In any event, when aggression was loose in Europe on a scale never before prepared, it would have been strange if Russia had not sought to fortify herself against it as strongly as possible. And the fate of these same lands under Nazi domination would be something like a living death—as the fate of Poland has amply demonstrated.

Nazi propaganda has achieved many astounding triumphs, but in a world which has been plunged back to the jungle by cold-blooded aggression it can hardly persuade us that the aggressor himself is the leader of a Christian crusade.

As the *Toronto Weekly Saturday Night* suggests this week, the government of Russia is certainly not Christian;

but the government of Italy has not pursued a notoriously Christian policy of recent years, from its killing of Ethiopians with poison gas to this moment. The Nazis make no secret that they are completely un-Christian, in both dogma and morality. The government of Japan is also non-Christian, but it is not the profession which counts; it is the conduct which a nation exhibits to other nations. It is not the internal ideology of a nation which determines the attitudes of other nations toward it; it is its external conduct.

From this standpoint the record is too clear to be misread. Soviet Russia might some day become a world conqueror. If that happened, then everybody else would be compelled to go against her. But as matters stand, the only aggression—if we can call it that—which stands against her is the recovery of a belt of former territory, upon which she is now fighting for her very existence; whereas Germany and Italy and Japan have for years attacked almost every neighbor which was weaker than themselves.

It is these three powers also that are bound together in an alliance which is directed against the United States. It would be a serious threat to Alaska if Russian Siberia, just across the Bering Strait, should fall into the hands of Japan. It is in the Pacific, too, that we have some power to aid Russia if she is attacked there.

Meanwhile, the Battle of the Atlantic goes on in full intensity. The British Admiralty has announced the sinking of a million and a half tons of ships by the Nazis in the past three months. That is a rate of sinking which spells victory for Germany in the place where victory must be finally won. It means that when our lend-lease materials come off the assembly lines in really great quantities, a few months hence, there will be dangerously fewer and fewer ships to carry them. Until the sinkings are drastically reduced in the only way they can be reduced, by naval and air action, we cannot look forward with any confidence to the final defeat of Hitlerism.

Perhaps the greatest danger in the German attack on Russia is the danger that we might slacken our efforts. But as I see it, the contrary result should follow. Hitler is attacking Russia because he knows that he can't win unless he can conquer resources somewhat comparable to ours. We are still in a race against time, but on a bigger scale. If we give the Nazis time to take the resources of southern Russia and to develop their use, then we must look forward to years of war. On the other hand, the attack on Russia has opened up the first real hope of defeating the aggressors fairly soon. Now is the time for the democracies to move as never before.

The Debate Continues

During the month of July the German armies rolled over the vast plains of Russia with apparently irresistible force. As great Russian defense lines were broken and cities fell almost daily, Japan added several hundred miles to her progress toward Singapore by taking over South Indo-China.

SHOULD WE APPEASE JAPAN FURTHER?
July 30, 1941

FOR EXACTLY TEN YEARS NEXT SEPTEMBER 21, JAPAN HAS been openly marching toward the mastery of the whole of East Asia, from the Arctic Ocean to New Zealand. When she took Indo-China this week our government and the governments of Great Britain, the Netherlands, Canada, and Australia, decided that the time had come to stop Japan's march toward the South. The five governments therefore froze all Japanese assets, canceled all remaining trade treaties with Japan, and prepared for a final showdown.

Our government, along with several others, has decided that Japan cannot be permitted to master the Orient. Is this decision right? Is it one that we must take? Or should we block Japanese expansion to the South but permit her to take the vast Siberian region from Russia?

199

A tolerant course toward Japan's conquests has been suggested in two recent radio broadcasts to a national audience by Mr. Upton Close. On July 20 he fixed upon Russia as Japan's true quarry. There was no question, he said, that Siberia was Japan's real aim. That was settled. She must drive Russia back two thousand miles, behind Lake Baikal, in order to be safe. The only question was what we were going to do about it. The Japanese had concluded that we would probably fight for the Dutch Indies, but not for Siberia. Would we?

Mr. Close indicated clearly that we should not. He spoke of our action in restraining Japan from taking Siberia during the last war as the action of one Woodrow Wilson, who was the ally of Lloyd George, who was the ally of Kerensky of Russia. Close approved of England's failure to take action against Japan when she took Manchuria in 1931 and began the series of predatory wars which are today reaching a climax. In 1931, said Close, England "looked at things rationally." But we Americans apparently cannot look at things rationally. We did not get excited, he said, about Japan's invasion of China or about the *Panay* affair. But now, he added, "when there is the least good to be done we become the most excited." Were we now going to smash Japan for taking Siberia and drive her into Communism? Close had just been talking to the Japanese minister to London and echoed his sad comment: "Too bad."

On July 27, after Japan's seizure of Indo-China, Close deplored the stoppage of commerce in the Pacific by what he called "this sudden economic offensive of ours"—action which, he said, "puts Japan on a very thin line." He thought Japan had been tempted into Indo-China by Hitler, reminded us that nobody in Japan wanted war with the United States, suggested that Japan had enough American oil stored up to take over Siberia if she can avoid war with us, and stressed—three times—that Japan's first job is to take Siberia.

200

We thus have the alternative presented to us of being understanding with Japan while she takes Siberia. Is that a policy which we should pursue? Let us examine it from the viewpoints (1) of the South Pacific, (2) of China, and (3) of our own interest in Siberia. There seems to be widespread agreement that Japan's steady aggression southward must be stopped. Otherwise she can take over the Philippines at some convenient time when it would be most awkward for us. But more important still, Japan will take the Dutch Indies with the world's main supplies of rubber, tin, quinine, and other key products unless she is stopped now; and Australia would also be at the mercy of Japan. Moreover, if Japan is allowed to move on into Thailand, she will be in position to attack Burma, close the Burma Road, and finally strangle China.

These consequences would make Japan the absolute master of East Asia, except in Siberia, and they would of course put her in position to bite off Siberia at some favorable time. The Japanese policy of grabbing territory and then sitting back for another propitious chance is too well known to need elaboration. Do we want Japan to establish a master-slave relationship over some half a billion people in China and the South Pacific?

It is difficult to think of any reason for accepting that result. Before Japan began the present world war in 1931, she had proved herself a bad colonial ruler in Korea and Formosa. But it is in China that Japan has fully revealed herself in a way which the American people have watched with deep indignation and, I venture to say, lasting memory. It was at Shanghai in 1932 and again in 1937 that a modern city was first made a shambles. Then all the great cities of China suffered the same fate of burning and looting, killing and raping. The Japanese proved to everybody that they could not be trusted either with firearms or with power over other people. The effort to debauch the Chinese people with opium, and otherwise, still continues.

The kind of China that the Japanese want is a vast mass of poor peasants and cheap factory workers, all working for Japan permanently. But that is not the kind of China we want. We need a strong, free China, developing her own resources and trading with all of East Asia and with the rest of the world on a basis of equality.

From the second standpoint, that of China, our interest clearly lies in stopping Japan now before it is too late. But shouldn't we let the Japanese have Siberia, at least? It is true that Vladivostock, seven hundred miles away from Japan, is a potential aerial menace to Japan, just as every point in the coast line of Europe is to the British, but only, in either case, if there is a predatory power on the continent which is bent on destroying the island empire. For the past twenty years there has been no such power opposite Japan. Soviet Russia has whipped Japan in Manchurian border battles whenever the Japanese attacked, but Russia has sold her railroad in Manchuria to Japan and pursued no policy of aggrandizement in East Asia.

That Japan might use Siberia if she had it may be true, although the Japanese have shown no aptitude or ability to live in cold countries; but that is true of almost any neighbor's lands. Most people could use their neighbor's property if they had it. It is perfectly true that Japan has a population problem, one that the Japanese will have to do something about sometime. They cannot always produce people for conquest purposes. But the real solution of Japan's economic troubles is peaceful trade with all her neighbors. Toward such a Japan we would be under tremendous obligation to lower our tariffs and be a good neighbor in every respect, but toward a Japan which is trying to turn the clock back by creating a vast aggressive empire on our borders we can have only one attitude. We do not want to squander our resources forever in building navies and armies to check a triumphant Japan, a Japan in control of the labor and resources of half a billion people.

Japan's aggressive ambitions, too, are all of one piece. As everybody knows, she is out to take anything in any direction. If she got Siberia, she would then be in a strong position to complete the strangulation of China from the north and south. Then it would be only a question of time until she would turn south again and clean up the South Pacific. The Japanese military have staked everything that Japan has on conquering East Asia. They have gone much too far to turn back. They dare not bring their discontented armies back home from China to a Japan impoverished by four years of futile war. It is often said that Japan is a poor nation, but like Germany she has had wealth enough to terrorize and ravage a continent—wealth which if devoted to constructive purposes in Japan would have given the Japanese a far better standard of living than they had in 1931 or in 1937. Think what could have been done in Japan with the money and materials and manpower which have been wasted in war by Japan. But Japan cannot revert to peaceful building now. It is now world conquest or downfall. The Japanese expansionists cry out that they are encircled—by our navy, by our Aleutian Islands, by everybody. And indeed they are completely encircled by opponents which their aggression has created, encircled without a friend in the world that can aid them—unless Germany can smash Russia so completely that the Russian armies in Siberia lose all will to resist Japan.

Should that happen, Japan may get Siberia, but then we would have exchanged a neighbor across the Bering Strait from Alaska whom we have had no cause to fear for one which has already complained, unofficially but vocally, that our naval base in Hawaii is a threat to Japan. We can hardly desire a close neighbor of that kind, one able as the master of East Asia to build a really immense navy and air force.

☆

All petroleum products, except certain furnace oils in pre-war quantities, were embargoed to Japan on August 1. An Economic Defense Board headed by Vice President Wallace was created, partly to oppose the Axis in Latin America, where Nazi plots boiled up in six different countries during the week. The Fascist government of Spain sent propaganda notes to all Latin American governments preaching Hitler's holy war against Russia in defense of "Occidental Christian civilization." Isolationist Senator Clark of Idaho said that we should take control of this whole hemisphere, including Canada, and set up puppet governments which would put our interests first.

WHO ARE THE WARMONGERS?
August 6, 1941

FOR MANY MONTHS SOME OF OUR PEOPLE HAVE BEEN BUSILY engaged in calling others, especially our national leaders, "warmongers." This practice has gone so far that it seems to me time to identify the warmongers. Who are they? What are they doing? Why?

Like all epithets, the term "warmonger" needs defining. Let me attempt a common-sense definition. A warmonger is a person who wants war, either for war's sake or because he thinks war will do him some good, and who works actively to bring about war. How many people are there who fit this plain, unvarnished definition of warmonger. Very few, I believe. In some countries which have been poisoned by years of Fascist education you could find many people, especially deluded young ones, who believe in war for war's sake, who accept it as the chief purpose of life; but who can name any influential American who believes such things? In countries with huge peacetime armies it is possible that some of the less thoughtful army officers might desire war for the sake of action and promotion, but I have heard no such charges about any American officers—and I doubt if the officers of any army on earth will hereafter be able to regard war with anything better than reluctant resignation. The scope of the carnage has become too unmanageable.

But may there not be Americans who think they could make more money if only the United States were engaged in a shooting war? There may have been a time when businessmen thought they could make money out of bloodletting, but not lately. It is notorious that the business and banking interests of Great Britain backed the Chamberlain policy of appeasement until that policy failed pitiably, because they feared the effects of war on their fortunes. Our big business interests also feared this war and they had to have the payment for their new plants assured by the government, in the main, before they would undertake large defense orders. Businessmen all over the world know now that while war may bring profits it will also bring enormous taxes, vast destruction of property, and great danger of drastic social changes. Few businessmen have anything to gain from a shooting war.

Who then are the warmongers? The President and members of his Cabinet are continually called this name. There is a constant campaign of assertion and innuendo directed at Secretaries Knox and Stimson. Are these three men plotting war? For what purpose? To get people killed, bankrupt the country, and be hated forever? Surely no one would be so stupid. The truth is that the President and his Cabinet believe that the whole future of this nation is directly at stake in this war and that we have got to see to it that brutal aggression on a world scale is defeated. That is why they take, and must take, the risk of being burned up later by the hatred of people who don't like war and its sacrifices, as Woodrow Wilson was consumed in 1919 and 1920. Whenever we hear the charge of "warmonger" leveled at the President and his aides, we should reflect that they are responsible for the life of this nation and that they dare not gamble on its destruction. They cannot take the chance that the colossal aggressions now raging on both sides of us might not destroy or cripple our future permanently. If they err at all, it must be on the side of putting an end to the bedlam of slaughter and looting which now rages over the earth. The men who are engaged in a deliberate campaign to break down the confidence of the country in the characters and abilities of Secretaries Knox and Stimson are not doing their country any service. They are endangering it in a time of peril. The vast majority of our national leaders could be mistaken about the dangers which face us, but they can have nothing to gain from driving or leading the country into bloodletting. It is perfectly true that a large majority of our leaders in all walks of life believe that it is better to fight, with guns as well as all the other weapons we are now fighting with, if that is necessary to defeat the predatory powers. But that is a vastly different thing from fomenting war. I know of no one who wants us to take a shooting part in this war because of any satisfaction or profits that would give him.

Why then do we hear these perpetual charges of war-mongering? The real reason is that the men who make these charges daily are the proponents of a bankrupt policy, the failure of which has left them high and dry. The war-mongering charges are their defense for the failure of their policy. If we would find the men who have "mongered" this war, we must go back a little. This war did not originate in 1939 or in 1937. Our real warmongers are the men whose policies resulted in the present state of world war and international anarchy. This is a definition of war-mongering which some will resent, but keep it in mind and test it by both the past and the future: A warmonger is a leader whose acts and policies lead to a state of world anarchy and war.

There is no use in blaming the men who have to put out

the fire after it is already a raging conflagration. If we are sensible people, we will inquire who planted the tinder. And if we do that, we in this country inevitably come upon that band of senators and their helpers who tried to isolate the United States again after the last war. It was just as clear then as now that the ever-more-rapid improvement of war machines would destroy the physical security of every country on the globe. It was abundantly proved in 1919 that only the power of the United States could stop world wars, and anybody who thought knew that the world's greatest trading and manufacturing nation would have to help stop any world wars which did get started. But a dozen determined men in the United States Senate gambled with the future of their country and forbade it to have any part in organizing peace and order in the world. Bent mainly on political gain and political revenge, these men took their chances on "mongering" the next war and on incurring a responsibility for that war which would rest on them so heavily that it could never be removed.

Then a group of younger leaders joined the older men, and they all exhorted us continually to "mind our own business." Shortsighted, self-destroying selfishness was exalted into a smug virtue. Year after year we minded our own business while the postwar peace machinery languished and then was slowly broken to bits. While a world war was brewing that would cost us fifty billion—maybe a hundred billion—dollars, these leaders told us that it might cost us something to help keep the peace. Simultaneously, they created a false legend that we had been jockeyed into the last war by the international bankers. Today they know *that* one is exploded and they are now shouting that the movie industry is getting us into war. "Getting us into war" has become their new shibboleth—that and "keeping us out of war." They intone those words as if any five words repeated often enough would save a nation—or the reputations of completely discredited leaders.

But this strategy will not work. The people who have to pay the fifty billions of new war debt can't be told again that all we have to do is selfishly to mind our own business. They will know that world government is the most important business we can possibly have—business that can't be neglected without incalculable loss and strain and danger. Nor will the millions of young Americans who have to do military duty be fooled again. They will know that plundering wars of aggression, raging over the earth, mean uniforms, drill, and army life for them. They will suspect everyone who tells them to mind their business until war grips every continent and who then try to save themselves by shouting "keep us out of war"—long after there is any salvation in wishful cries.

It is natural that men whose policies have resulted in world tragedy of immeasurable proportions should conduct the best rear-guard defense that they can. It is natural even that they should become fanatical peacemongers, long after peace has ceased to exist. But we cannot afford to be deceived by words. Peace cannot be defended or established by the continually chanted desire to keep out of war. Something far more substantial is required. Indeed, the professional peacemonger who would "keep us out of war" by will power alone, instead of by solid labor for world peace, may become far more dangerous than any warmonger that might be found in our midst.

It would add to our national strength and unity a great deal if the credentials of every person who cries "warmonger" or "keep us out of war" were examined to see what he has done to establish and defend *world* peace—the only kind of peace that can ever have any value to us.

IS THE MOTION-PICTURE INDUSTRY
A WARMONGER?
October 1, 1941 [1]

FOR A MONTH NOW THERE HAS BEEN PROCEEDING AT INTER-vals in Washington an investigation which should have the close attention of every alert American citizen. I refer to the activities of a subcommittee of the Senate Interstate Commerce Committee against the movie industry. This group of four isolationists and one administration supporter is attempting to indict the movie industry for "warmon-gering" and to deter the movies from making further anti-Nazi pictures or others which might rouse the spirit of the American people. This inquiry, so called, is one of the most dangerous undertakings launched in Washington in years, for two reasons: it attempts to impose a censorship upon freedom of expression, and it takes a Fascist line.

The current attempt to intimidate the movies grows out of the suspicions of the isolationist senators that the Jew-ish executives of some movie concerns have given us anti-Nazi pictures because of what the Nazis have done to the Jews in Europe. It happens that some of our Jewish citi-zens are powerful in Hollywood; hence the isolationist in-quisitors are drawn to attack the movies as improperly try-ing to get us into war for European reasons.

The present crusade was inaugurated by Senator Nye in a speech at St. Louis on August 1, in which he charged that "at least twenty pictures have been produced in the last year—all designed to drug the reason of the American people, to rouse them to war hysteria. . . . . The movies," continued Nye, "have become the most gigantic engines of propaganda in existence to rouse the war fever in America

---

[1] This talk is advanced out of chronological order because of its re-lation to the preceding one.

and plunge this nation to her destruction." Nye named eight pictures as being of this dangerous and subversive character from his point of view: "Convoy," "Escape," "Flight Command," "That Hamilton Woman," "Man Hunt," "I Married a Nazi," "The Great Dictator," and "Sergeant York."

These pictures are not all alike. Some of them portray heroic events of British or American history. The majority of them are definitely anti-Nazi, and they do powerfully portray the iniquities and dangers of the Nazi regime. Is this treason?

Let us consider the charge. For eight years past the most monstrous tyranny ever invented in human history has been rapidly extending its sway over the world. First it undermined and took over nations without a shot, deceiving some of the governments of the big democracies themselves, deceiving powerful people in every country. Then the Nazis proceeded to that open career of conquest and looting which has crushed nations literally by the dozen and which can only end in world dominion by the Nazis or in their destruction. If they win, there cannot be the slightest doubt that the whole world is in for the most frightful experience it has ever undergone. The daily news of the mass killing of innocent people called "hostages" in all parts of Europe is advance notice and evidence of the way in which the Nazis would exterminate whole peoples in order to seize their lands and property. It is plain notice of the way in which they would kill off the leaders of the conquered peoples and reduce the remainder to helpless slavery to the German "master race." If the Nazis win, too, we shall not only be besieged in North America but we shall have to fight Nazism from within the country every day of our lives.

With the situation rapidly developing before our eyes, what would Senator Nye have the movies do? Should they stand dumbly by and continue to entertain us with fairy tales having no relation to the deadly danger so rapidly spreading over the earth? Should our American motion-picture industry quail in terror until some Fascist dictator takes it over and makes it an engine of total repression, as in Germany? Must the movies remain inert until the Nazis have conquered the earth and until some American Goebbels decides what lies shall be portrayed in every picture?

When catastrophe is sweeping over the earth, literally on the wings of the wind, it is the duty of every medium of expression that we have to warn the people of what is afoot. It is impossible to imagine that in this period no moving pictures should tell us how Western civilization itself is being undermined and destroyed. No senator has alleged that the many pictures in question are not true to life—the objection is that they have told us the grim truth and given us glimpses of nobler episodes in our history than those of the isolationist 1920's.

The Clark subcommittee alleges, of course, that it is merely trying to see if a few movie magnates have not conspired to get us into war. The animus of the Clark group, of course, is isolationist. They hope to repeat the feat of the Nye Munitions Investigation Committee of 1926, which temporarily convinced the American people that they had been hoodwinked and bamboozled into the last war by British propagandists and by the munitions makers. These were false conclusions. We went into the last war because the acts of the Germans and Austrians convinced us that they could not be allowed to win. The Austrian ultimatum to Serbia that was plainly intended to be rejected, Austria's swift declaration of war against Serbia, Germany's quick onslaught on France and Russia, her cynical violation of Belgium, the sinking of the "Lusitania," and the whole course of the submarine war—these were the deeds which spoke louder than any words of propaganda possibly could; these were the deeds culminating in the final German decision to break all promises to us and engage in unrestricted submarine warfare. We fought in 1917 because public opinion demanded that Germany's high-handed drive for world domination, especially of the seas, should be defeated. I say that as one who lived through those days intensely as a student of history and who has since read a shelf of books about our entry into the last war.

Today the situation is fundamentally the same. We have fully made up our minds that Nazi Germany must be defeated because we know that, far more than in 1917 even, German control of the world would be a mortal danger to our free way of life. It is the crimes of the Nazis, culminating in their conquest of France and Western Europe, which has determined our attitude toward this war beyond the power of anybody's propaganda or antipropaganda to prevent.

It is perfectly true that Senator Nye succeeded for a time in selling us a revised version of why we entered the last war. As a people we had a bad conscience because we had pulled out of the peacemaking and had done our best to kill the League of Nations. Never in modern history had a great nation ever made so grave a blunder. We knew that in our hearts and so we were open to any reinterpretation of history that gave us some justification. The story that we had no business in the last war at all gave us the "out" we sought, and Nye also supplied the scapegoat—the wicked munitions makers.

A small group of our congressmen never forgave us for entering the war. Then their sons in Congress, actual or intellectual, took up the fight to keep us out of future wars; and they are still determined to do it, regardless of consequences to our national future. Plainly, Senator Nye is trying to repeat his former success—a success which has now evaporated under the impact of world events. Instead of the munitions makers as the devil to be hated, Nye now points his finger at the movie magnates, Jewish at that. They are the new devil that all true Americans should crack down upon, instead of the Nazis, who are at the point of enslaving half the human race. There is no one whom Hitler hates with such venom as the writers, speakers, and artists who have told the world his misdeeds—not a fraction of them really, but enough to encompass his eventual defeat.

Will the new Nye crusade succeed in deterring us from defeating Hitler? Will it intimidate and silence the movies? If it does, the same clique of isolationist censors in the Senate Interstate Commerce Committee will unquestionably move on the radio commentators until they have silenced every voice that speaks out for a policy of resisting Fascist aggression while there is time. If the movies and the radio can be controlled by isolationist intimidation or pressure, then newspapers and public speakers will be in line for control. Certainly the publishers of the anti-Nazi novels dramatized by the movies would be strictly disciplined, and the authors of anti-Nazi plays would have to be penalized—all of which points clearly to Fascism itself, as does the anti-Semitism which is in the movie witch-hunt.

One remaining question, I am sure, will puzzle many. How is it that the isolationists on Senator Wheeler's Interstate Commerce Committee have been able to stage this prosecution of the movies when the Senate is as anti-Nazi as the American people are? The answer is that the whole inquiry is going on under a subterfuge. Not only is the subcommittee packed by Senator Wheeler with isolationist irreconcilables; it has never been authorized by the Senate to investigate the movies or anything else. It is proceeding under the guise of attempting to determine whether an investigation is necessary. Yet everyone knows that the members of this "kangaroo court" do not want an impartial inquiry, and there is no reason to believe that more than twenty senators would vote for any inquiry at all. Hence the ruse to evade a vote of the Senate and put pressure on the movies under the pretext of investigating the need of an investigation.

Surely this attempt by senatorial cliques to begin the censorship of what we shall see and say should be brought into the open and either made legal by vote of the Senate or ended at once.

As weeks of furious fighting in Russia passed, it became clear that the Germans had an immensely powerful enemy, one able to engage them fully with many thousands of tanks, guns, and planes. The Russians yielded ground, but their armies were not destroyed. After the armies retreated, the Germans discovered that incessant guerrilla warfare against them continued. It was evident that the Russian people were a unit in their resistance. These developments surprised the Germans and the Western powers as well. We had been taught for many years that the Soviet state was a failure. It was inefficient and weak. Hitler's armies would cut through it like a knife through butter, said our military men. When it became apparent that our information about Russia had been bad, we were puzzled. Some were disappointed; but, in any event, the tough resistance took the pressure off Britain and enabled us to postpone our own military participation in the war indefinitely. We relaxed and awaited events.

IS THE DANGER PAST?
August 13, 1941

ON TUESDAY THE HOUSE OF REPRESENTATIVES EXTENDED FOR eighteen months the service of the selectees, National Guardsmen, and reserve officers by a vote of 203 to 202. The poll could not have been closer.

214

How is it possible that on a question of the greatest importance there could be so close a division of opinion? Party politics undoubtedly had a good deal to do with it. Only twenty-one Republicans, nearly all from the East, voted for the extended draft, although one of their number, Representative James W. Wadsworth of New York, made the most powerful speech for the extension. Said Wadsworth: "If this bill is not passed and these men are discharged, you will wreck unit after unit in our Army—just when the Army is beginning to get good." Wadsworth received a standing ovation from the House for his speech, but his fellow Republicans went right ahead and voted against the bill, 133 of them, and 65 Democrats joined them in expressing the opinion that it didn't make any difference if, in this time of spreading war, the Army were wrecked and scattered to the four winds.

Most of the 65 Democrats and the 133 Republicans who voted "No" live in the great continental interior, where the feeling of safety in a ravaged world is greatest. Chicago is the center of powerful isolationist and anti-British newspapers and propaganda organizations. That had not a little to do with the vote, but there was more to it. The people of the Chicago area feel that no great harm would come if the Army were disbanded. They do not believe that the country is actually in danger. No invading armies have appeared. Not a single hostile bomber has darkened any Midwestern sky. We are at war, by any fair definition, but it is a bloodless war. Hitler has moved east, not west, and is well occupied with the Russians. Therefore we shall be able to ride out this world war without doing any shooting ourselves. Our industrial might will win it, but the boys in the Army won't have to do any fighting—so they might as well come home.

That so many people believe this to be true is, of course, an immense encouragement to Berlin and Tokyo—and to Rome and Madrid. The even split in the American House of Representatives has been received in the Fascist capitals with tremendous satisfaction. It proves the Nazi thesis that no democracy can pull together until it is too late. The Nazis believe that to be profoundly true. They are certain that democracy is just that way. Permit everybody to have his opinion; and the result is certain to be argument, confusion, and fatal division, while the monolithic Fascist state marches on, picking off the foolish democracies one at a time. This is a basic article of Fascist faith, and we need not be in the slightest doubt that there is joy in Berlin over the vote just taken in Washington. It takes no clairvoyant powers to hear Goebbels saying: "Here are the Americans running true to form. We have destroyed nearly two dozen free nations, one or two at a time. We are in fair way to conquer Russia and, with the Japanese, master ninetenths of the people in the world—and the Americans actually split fifty-fifty on a motion to disband their army and send it home!"

Every man of the Axis propaganda armies in Latin America—German, Italian, Spanish, Vichy French, and Japanese—will soon be suggesting to the Latin Americans, subtly and openly: "You see how the wind is blowing. In the face of our iron resolution and steady marching ahead, the Americans decide by one vote in 405 not to send their army home. You should be able to judge for yourselves how this thing is going to turn out." And many canny Latin Americans will govern themselves accordingly.

On the final showdown the Axis propagandists will be mistaken, for this nation is committed to their defeat and will do whatever is essential to that end—not because we want to but because the Germans and Japanese will give us no choice. They have staked everything that they have on world mastery. Each of them has so abused and embittered half a billion people that they must go on. Both the Germans and Japanese are now obliged to master half the world or destroy themselves in the process. The two master peoples have burned all their bridges and must now dominate or suffer the consequences of disrupting the life of every people on the globe.

What then are the present probabilities that the aggressors will finally win through? Undoubtedly, the lessened sense of danger which was registered in the House of Representatives is due to the magnificent fight which the Russians are putting up. Maybe they will wear the Nazis out and save us from bearing the brunt of the final struggle. Maybe so, but the Germans may seize the wheat and manganese and oil regions which they need and hold on a year until they can get production of those things. They are already talking of an advance upon India.

In Western Europe the German grasp is still expanding. Fascist France has this week announced its determination to crush the democratic elements in France and collaborate with Germany fully. Fascist Spain is ready to join the war at any time and semi-Fascist Portugal can be taken by telephone from Berlin. If, therefore, it suits Berlin's purposes to take over North Africa and West Africa, it can be done at any time.

Will Germany do it? There is one compelling reason to drive her. She is not doing so well lately in the Battle of the Atlantic because of our aid; but with West Africa in her hands she could take a new and perhaps fatal toll of the shipping still afloat. It is still possible that if we send powerful aid to the Free French forces they might take Dakar before the Germans get there, but the time for such an effort is rapidly slipping. Dakar is the perfect jumping-off-place for Nazi pressure upon South America—pressure of all kinds—air, naval, military, economic, and propaganda. If the Germans get and hold Dakar, our control of the South Atlantic will be gone. But will they give us notice of any sudden move? May not the whole job be done so gradually and quietly, through Spain, France, and Portugal, that fifty million people in the Upper Mississippi Valley will never know that it is being done?

In the Pacific, too, Japan is edging toward the control of the South Pacific—just a step at a time, not enough to touch off a big war. And, here again, if a hostile power gets the whole of the other side, any two-ocean navy that we may have will be tied to our own coasts by lack of friends and bases in a friendless world, for if Germany and Japan win, their economic power alone will be irresistible in most of South America—not to speak of the air and naval power that the Axis powers would soon command.

Surely, then, it is too soon for us to settle back and leave it all to the Russians. Two of the boldest, most resourceful, and most desperate military powers in all modern history are out to seize control of the whole of the Old World and of both the oceans which surround us, and they may yet succeed unless we are completely alert and united enough to act when action will save our world position.

That is what is primarily at stake, but there is more than that at issue. Total war is still being waged against all free institutions, and if the total war wins in the Old World we shall fight defensively against a hostile world and internally among ourselves for a long time to come. Half of our people already rebel at thirty months' military duty; but if the war is lost we shall be in for conscription permanently, along with all the pains and frustrations that go with living in a closed, military economy in a world permanently at war.

In such a situation what is the part of wisdom? Shall we begin cracking down on the whole defense program with the idea that if it gets too big there might be danger of Americans' being sent to fight overseas? Shall we be very cagey and determined not to be too well prepared? Shall we help those who are shedding their blood in rivers—or bearing up in blasted cities—just enough to keep them alive?

Shall we resolutely refuse to believe in danger until it is visible in the sky overhead?

Or shall we remain determined that the world of the future is going to be a free one and that decent trade and free dealings between all peoples is going to be the rule again? Though the events of the week have given ground for considerable uneasiness, I am confident that in the end we shall be substantially united, from Mexico to Canada, on the real issue of a free world versus a predatory, totalitarian one.

President Roosevelt and Prime Minister Churchill met at sea off the Canadian-American coast and drafted the Atlantic Charter. Senator Gerald P. Nye, speaking at an America First rally in Chicago on August 13 declared that "whatever these leaders may wish America to do, she will not permit her sons in this foreign war." As Hitler's armies plunged deeper into Russia, Congress restored, on August 15, about half of a $1,-347,000,000 cut in appropriations for tank and plane production. The next day the New York state convention of the American Legion voted against sending any aid to the Soviets, citing the anti-Communist charges of the Dies Committee; but on August 19 Supreme Court Justice Frank Murphy, a Catholic, urged aid to Russia because Nazism had proved itself the world's "overshadowing menace."

In Russia the city of Smolensk fell and the Ukraine was deeply invaded.

HOW DANGEROUS IS IT TO HELP SOVIET RUSSIA?

August 20, 1941

THIS IS A SUBJECT WHICH I APPROACH WITH A GOOD DEAL OF reluctance. Many Americans fear Communism more than anything else in the world, and some of them will be unable to believe that any circumstances could justify aid to Communist Russia. The amount of antipathy in this country toward Red Russia is enormous, both on social-economic and on religious grounds. These antipathies have been strengthened during the past two years by the belief that Stalin was acting as an ally and accomplice of Hitler.

It is, therefore, a deep shock to countless Americans to find themselves, not only on the same side as the Reds, but actively aiding them. There are strong chances of a new and dangerous cleavage in an already divided nation. That makes this subject a dangerous one to discuss, but it also makes it imperative for us to face it. So I make my contribution in the knowledge that what I say will have to stand up both under present scrutiny and in the future.

To begin with, all but a microscopic fraction of us agree that we want neither Fascism nor Communism for ourselves. What we want is a continuance of our own system of free enterprise and political democracy. We want a state strong enough to protect our essential liberties, both within and from without, but we emphatically do *not* want our liberties to be devoured by the state—Fascist or Communist. We want to keep and perfect that which we have.

With this basic understanding, we have two questions to consider: (1) Is it to our advantage to aid Russia *as a nation* in her present war with Germany? (2) If Russia wins, will Communism devour us? The two questions are related, but I think it is essential to try to weigh them

220

separately. It has been my strong belief, stated many times publicly, that Russia, considered as a nation, has *not* been an international menace and is not likely to be. I believe that the record of the past twenty-five years shows that Soviet Russia has been consistently concerned with military defense, not offense.

✗Fear of outside aggression has been a fixed obsession with the Reds—literally a mania at times. This fear began when the Bolsheviki had to fight a series of wars from 1918 to 1922 against Czarist armies, financed and supplied by Great Britain and France. Three or four different times large armies of several hundred thousand Russian Whites, with strong Allied backing, almost defeated the Reds. The Russo-Polish War of that period also struck deep into Russia before the Poles were defeated. At that time, too, Japan was occupying Siberia and was finally forced out only with great difficulty.

These heavy struggles convinced the Red leaders that the capitalist world would never permit a Communist Russia to survive. It became a fixed article of faith with them that the capitalist world would attack again, from both sides, at the first opportunity. Hence everything else in Russia—even the Communist experiment—was subordinated to building up the Army and to constructing defense industries to back it. That singleness of purpose explains a great deal about Russia that has seemed strange to us. It also explains, at least in part, the Russian control of Communist parties all over the world—to spread the world revolution, yes, but first and foremost to use as allies in Red Russia's coming struggle for existence. Lenin always maintained that Communism had to take the offensive and conquer the world or eventually it would be stamped out in Russia.

Stalin broke with this doctrine in the late twenties and there was a brief period when Soviet Russia felt strong enough to be relatively secure. Then the Japanese broke loose in Manchuria and Hitler in Germany, renewing all

221

Russian fears of a war on two fronts. Indeed, there could be no reasonable doubt that this was precisely what was ahead of Russia.

The Soviets, therefore, turned to the West. They joined the League of Nations and made every effort to make the League work as it was intended to work—not, of course, because they loved the League, but because they hoped it would help them to survive. During a period of four or five years, Russia was the best great-power member which the League had. I have many times heard Litvinoff speak in English at Geneva the words which the British and French leaders should have said.

But the hatred and suspicion of Red Russia was so great in the Chamberlain-Daladier regimes in Britain and France that they preferred to coddle Mussolini and Hitler and egg them on toward a great Fascist-Communist war in which the democracies would be bystanders. This policy came completely into the open at Munich and led directly to the Hitler-Stalin deal which permitted Stalin to recover a wide belt of buffer territory, from Finland down to Bessarabia, while Hitler was busy in the West. Some of these seizures, especially the one from Finland, seemed brutal enough to us; but the territory seized gave the Russians their present chance to wear down the Germans without themselves being destroyed.

Today, it is only because of the might of Russian resistance that we can look forward to peace at all. Otherwise, the full brunt of defeating Hitlerism would rest upon us— as it *will* rest on us again if Russian resistance should collapse. If the Russians are defeated, we can look forward to nothing but years and years of war; and no one of us can say that the sending of American armies overseas would not then be essential to prevent a smashing world victory for the Germans and Japanese—a victory that would enable the Fascist powers to encircle North Ameri-

222

ca and subject it to both external and internal peril indefinitely.

That is why it seems to me clear that we must take the chance of helping Red Russia to the full extent of our ability. If the Fascist powers are defeated, a Communist menace may arise; but we can meet that when the time comes—and we shall have the British Empire, and many, many other peoples left to help us. That is a far different prospect from being left alone in a predatory Fascist world.

But there is no certainty that a world Communist menace will develop. If Soviet Russia emerges from the war freed of the fixed fear of being crushed between a Japanese-dominated East Asia and a German Europe, she may settle down within her own vast borders to live in peace, to nurse her wounds, and to develop her own system. There is also another possibility which it seems to me no open-minded American ought to overlook—the possibility that Communist Russia, living alone in a democratic world, might evolve toward democracy herself instead of trying to convert the world. And if our democratic institutions are sound and progressive, no Communist propaganda can ever convert us.

The contrary development—that Soviet Russia might become an aggressive, invading, conquering power—must also be considered; but if the democracies really help Russia to pull through a desperate struggle for existence, they will have claims upon the good will of both the Red leaders and the Russian people that could not be lightly disregarded.

In any event, Russia is a land power, and there is no present evidence that she would or could aspire to take control of the seas and thus dominate the world as the Japanese-German combination fully intends to do and still has at least an even chance of doing.

In a speech to the Knights of Columbus at Atlantic City yesterday, Justice Frank Murphy of the United States

Supreme Court put the relative danger to us of Communism and Nazism into a pungent paragraph. Said Murphy: "We know that Nazism, with its superior competence and perverted intelligence, its extraordinary energy and missionary zeal, its profound belief in racial superiority and destiny, its fanatical intolerance and, above all, its tremendous military power and skill, is by far the greater menace to free nations and free institutions."

Surely that is the present situation, and it is one about which we cannot afford to be easygoing or indifferent. We have no reason to believe that the Russians can win the war for us without prompt and powerful aid from the outside. How can we expect them to carry the whole brunt if they could? It may be necessary to open up a strong fighting front in Western Europe if the Soviets are to be kept in the war. But at the very least it is imperative that arms and supplies be rushed to them as promptly as possible. We and the Russians are dealing with the most dangerous military machine ever constructed on this planet. The situation is critical and it will become worse if Japan strikes Russia in the back as she may do at any moment.

The Russians blew up their great Dnieper River dam to prevent its use by the Germans, who soon crossed the river. Russia and Britain jointly occupied Iran.

To propitiate the anticonscription feeling, the Army announced on August 30, that it would release two hundred thousand men by December 10. Appropriations for defense passed fifty billions.

From Tokyo came a new Ambassador, Admiral Nomura, bearing a note from Premier Konoye. The tariff on Japanese crab meat was raised 50 per cent, and the too-numerous Japa-

nese shops in the Panama Canal Zone were closed. Chungking was bombed for the 142nd time.

On September 5 the destroyer Greer *was attacked by a submarine near Iceland.*

WHAT FOLLOWS THE GERMAN ATTACK ON THE *GREER?*

September 10, 1941

WHAT SHOULD BE THE REPLY OF THE UNITED STATES TO THE attack of a German submarine on the American destroyer *Greer* on September 4? What will be the consequences of this incident?

The answer to these questions has been affected strongly by the discovery yesterday that an American-owned ship, the *Sessa,* was sunk without warning off Iceland on August 17 and by the news on Tuesday that the American merchantman *Steel Seafarer* had been sunk by air bombs near Suez.

My first reaction to the attack on the *Greer* was that it was a mistake by the German submarine commander. There is every reason to believe that Hitler does not want a full-fledged shooting war with the United States. From the very beginning the chief problem of the Nazis has been to achieve world mastery without provoking the United States to all-out war. They had almost every reason to expect, too, that they would succeed. From 1933 on, American public opinion was clearly hostile to the Nazis and their deeds, but our determination to keep out of any more European wars was so strong that with each advance of the Nazis we passed a law designed to enforce peace upon ourselves when the final storm broke. These neutrality laws convinced the Nazis that they could conquer Europe, at least, before we could possibly reverse our isolationist policy and arm ourselves enough to stop them.

What the Nazis did not count upon was the adoption by our government of a one-step-at-a-time policy. The Nazis thought they had that patented. For five long years, from 1933 to 1938, they waged undeclared war, furiously and determinedly, by taking one step, declaring themselves satisfied, then seizing something else and issuing another reassuring statement. By this method they marched from victory to victory——through secret, then open, rearmament; through the fortifying of the Rhineland; the recovery of the Saar Basin; the conquest of Spain; the seizure of Austria; the crucifixion of the Czechs; and so on, down to the war on Poland, which touched off the world conflagration.

This was a game which appeared for years to be unbeatable—until we began to play it, too, by aiding the enemies of the Nazis, one step at a time, just enough to block German victory. By this process we have advanced to participation in the war by every means except shooting. Everyone knows that we have left neutrality behind us long ago and that we are a belligerent with everything except the shooting of guns. We are turning our whole national economy over to the making of guns, with the purpose declared by the Congress in the lend-lease act and often reiterated by the President that these guns shall defeat the Nazi thrust for world power.

Yet the Nazis still have the most powerful reasons for seeking to keep us from going all out for war. By turning against Russia they have greatly promoted division among us and lulled us into a sense of security. We are quarreling more and producing less—which is the best the Nazis can possibly hope for. Should we now resort to total war, there would be a vast spurt of national energy which would make Nazi defeat certain. Not only that; the whole world would know that the Nazis were doomed. The Russians, the Japanese, every conquered people, every neutral people, and especially the German people, would know that the game was up.

That the Nazis do not want that is indicated by their claim that the destroyer *Greer* attacked their submarine first. For hours on end their official press and radio called the President a forger and the American Navy a liar. These sustained tirades had two objects: first, to escape responsibility before the German people for the starting of shooting with the United States; and second, to rouse the American isolationists to block retaliatory action against the Nazis by the President. Adopting the very language of our isolationists, the official German news agency said on September 6: "Roosevelt thereby is endeavoring with all the means at his disposal to provoke incidents for the purpose of baiting the American people into the war."

The Nazis, like our antiwar groups, are trying to "keep us out of war." Why then did they attack the *Greer*, for only a handful of Americans will believe the professional liars of Berlin over the word of their own Navy. Some have suspected that the attack was intended to rouse the Japanese, who are in the process of deciding whether to shoot the whole works in the Pacific now. That may have been a contributing motive, but it seems a bit farfetched. At the same time, the theory that the attack was an accident is cast into question by the subsequent sinking of the *Steel Seafarer* in the Red Sea. That was hardly an accident. The ship was well illuminated, and it was sunk from a height of only 150 feet on a moonlight night. Our ships have been going to Suez for months and one of them could have been sunk long before this had the Nazis desired it. Have they decided, then, that our aid to Britain is being delivered too effectively and that they must do something to check its flow? The three attacks coming close together would seem to indicate that.

In any event, the attack on the *Greer* has advanced our participation in the Battle of the Atlantic. Things cannot be the same again. The President is Commander-in-Chief of the Navy, and no one will expect him to jeopardize the lives of our navy men by ordering them to hold their fire hereafter when any German craft is near, whether it be submarine, surface vessel, or aircraft. The stage of shooting war is definitely here, and by the act of Germany. That is apparently what makes the Nazis so enraged. They had hoped when the shooting did start to pin it on us.

Now that the shooting has begun, what is to follow? There is no evidence that we shall at once go on to total war because two torpedoes were shot at the *Greer*. There will be no explosion of American anger. We shall not fight, with guns as well as all other means, because of any incident. Nor should we. But we shall do whatever fighting is necessary to win the Battle of the Atlantic. We have committed ourselves, by every known means, to holding control of the Atlantic. We know that our whole future depends on that. We cannot accept the changing of our whole way of life by permitting the Atlantic to become a German lake. We now have, from Newfoundland to South America, in Greenland, in Iceland, and, above all, in the British Isles, a great circle of bases which ensure our future control of the Atlantic. Every one of these bases keeps Hitlerism, or any other predatory European regime, far from our shores. We shall not give up these bases to Hitler or any other conqueror.

But there remain the details of defending them, and this defense now clearly calls for the repeal of the remnant of the neutrality law of 1937, which forbids our ships to go to England. That law was, from the isolationist viewpoint, a logical attempt to keep us out of this war by preventing attacks on our ships such as gradually forced us into the last war. An isolationist Congress was determined that we would not go to war again because of any incidents involving our ships in the war zones. We would simply stay out of war by keeping our ships and citizens out of fighting waters.

This was a very popular decision, but it was always a wrong one. By passing that law we gave Hitler the green light to plunge ahead until he involved the whole world in war. We said to him, "Go ahead! Do your worst! Burn the world down if you wish; it shall be none of our business. Whatever you do, we won't interfere. We are through with European wars, once and forever!" It is no wonder that the Nazis are now considerably peeved that we have recanted from that craven position and thrown our whole weight against them.

But in encouraging the Germans to believe that this time they could murder as many nations as they liked with impunity we did an even worse thing. By abandoning our right to use the seas in the waters around the British Isles, we abandoned our right to free seas everywhere, for the Nazis have extended their operations until they cover the oceans themselves; and but for Russia's splendid resistance, Japan would now be joining them in sinking our ships in every one of the seven seas without exception. When you once begin to yield ground to gangster elements, individual or national, there is no stopping place.

That is now perfectly clear. Either we defend the freedom of the seas everywhere or we shall lose it everywhere, except perhaps in the waters immediately surrounding our coasts.

But there are more immediately urgent reasons for repealing the remains of the neutrality law. Even if the Nazis do not step up the sea war, the strain on the world's shipping is going to be beyond calculation next spring when our war materials really pour forth in great quantities. How to get them to Britain and to the Near East, both for British and Russian use, will be a problem almost beyond solution unless we use every means at our disposal. The hauls to the Near East are very, very long—even if Japan does not erupt. In this situation the winning of the war may depend on our taking over the Atlantic patrol from

Iceland on to Britain and using our own merchant ships all the way to Britain to supply that indispensable bastion of our defenses and to free British shipping for the vital supply lines to the Mediterranean, Near East, and Far East.

This, of course, means naval shooting on a considerable scale, but it does not mean going to war because some of our ships are sunk. It will be the reverse of that. We are already in the war and will accept the loss of some of our ships by German action in order to win the war.

That remaining part of the neutrality law which forbids our ships to go to England has served the only purpose it could serve. It is now as obsolete as the arms-embargo and cash-and-carry ideas which went with it and which we abandoned long ago. Its repeal is now essential to winning the Battle of the Atlantic—especially since it contains a provision forbidding the arming of any American merchant ship. That means that every American cargo vessel going to Iceland or to the Near East must go completely at the mercy of German submarines and planes. Not a gun can be mounted. When a Nazi submarine appears, that is the end of the American ship, as in the case of the *Robin Moor* last May. When a German plane appears overhead, it can bomb the helpless American ship under it at will. The American can carry no antiaircraft gun with which to make the German stay high and give the ship a chance of escape.

This is a state of affairs that can hardly continue much longer. Wars are not won that way. The three recent attacks on our ships do not automatically mean total war, with that huge expeditionary force to France which is our principal fear, but they do call for strong countermeasures on our part in the naval war, which is our chief concern.

☆

On September 12 the President ordered the Navy to shoot on sight any Axis warships found in the waters necessary for American defense. "No matter what it costs," he had said in a radio address the night before, "we will keep these defense areas open." Willkie applauded the President's stand. Nye and Lindbergh denounced it. The latter saw a plot for war by British-Jewish-Roosevelt groups and declared on September 11 that England could not win. Senator McCarran asserted the President's action was "nothing short of an unauthorized declaration of war."

On September 16 Herbert Hoover made a major radio address from Chicago disapproving of the "edging of our warships into danger zones." We should save our strength until "Hitler collapses of his own overreaching." The "fratricidal war between Hitler and Stalin" was daily weakening both. Hitler's kingdom could not "live even though he has no military defeat on the continent." While awaiting his collapse we should stop calling names and taking provocative steps. There should be a minimum of interference with economic freedom by preparedness policies and aid only to the democracies.

SHOULD WAR BE DECLARED?
September 17, 1941

THERE ARE A GREAT MANY AMERICANS WHO ARE IRRECONcilably opposed to the foreign policy which our government is pursuing because they simply do not believe that the Nazis could ever do any real damage to their homes and interests in the deep interior of the country. There are some whose dislike of President Roosevelt is so deep that no foreign policy which he espouses can win their approval, though this group is balanced by a great number who oppose his domestic policies but heartily back his foreign policy. In addition to the President's bitter opponents, there are many who are deeply troubled by the creeping nature of our participation in the war. We are a strongly legalistic people. We have hitherto had no difficulty in knowing when we were at war, when at peace. There was always a declaration of war which marked the transition. Now we are a long way into the present war, yet there has been no declaration. Everyone knows that the Constitution says the Congress shall declare war, yet the Congress has not been asked to do so. Maybe it won't be—at least until it is too late for it to do anything else. There are daily charges that the President is deliberately dragging us into war, step by step. Are these charges true? And would a declaration of war clear the air and substantially unify us?

To begin with, it might as well be recognized that in a time of world turmoil any strong American president has the power to involve us in war. His powers to conduct our foreign relations and to command the armed forces are so great that he could deliberately create a state of war if he wished. That is one of the central facts of our Constitution, and it can only be changed by making the president a figurehead and placing all power in a sovereign parliament—the kind of parliament which prepared France for her downfall.

We do not want to take that course, nor are we likely to amend the Constitution to give the people themselves the right to block war or initiate it by a national referendum. Such a procedure would be both dangerous and unworkable at a time when others are waging gradual, permanent, and finally total warfare. In such a time no democracy can hope to survive without strong leadership. We would certainly be lost, as France was lost, without it.

This is the key to our dilemma. Our real grievance is not against Washington but against Berlin, Rome, and Tokyo. It is the total dictatorships in these capitals, unrestrained by any powerful congresses, which have destroyed the distinction between war and peace—deliberately and entirely. They have outlawed peace altogether. Over and over again they have declared peace to be a vicious, ridiculous thing, and they have made every act of life an act of war. To be sure they masked the war for years under appeals to self-determination, under a crusade against Bolshevism, and by various other camouflages; but for ten years war has been loose in the world on both sides of us, waged by every means—by industrial production, by every act of trade, by every device of deceit and propaganda of which the mind could conceive. We do not know when this total war will end, but we know the precise date when it began. It began exactly ten years ago tomorrow, the day on which the Japanese began the conquest of Manchuria.

Our government, under President Hoover and Secretary Stimson, knew then that the world was breaking up; and they fought the breakup by every diplomatic means in their power. Diplomacy was not enough: President Roosevelt finally came reluctantly to that conclusion in October, 1937. Since that date he has been doing his best to arouse his people to defend themselves against ever-spreading world anarchy, and, aided by the recurrent impact of world aggression, he has led us step by step to the point of naval warfare against the predatory powers. There was no other way by which he could lead us and by which he could checkmate the aggressors. It had to be step by step.

We all know what the principal steps have been. The first big one was the repeal of the arms embargo, whereby we had actually legislated that the British and French could not buy a dollar's worth of arms here for their defense against ruthless regimes that had been piling up arms for years. Is there anyone now who regrets that repeal? Would anyone say that it would have been either right or wise to keep that law on the statute books? Who would say, either, that the fifty old destroyers we traded for a chain of new defensive outposts in the Atlantic was a bad thing or that we are less safe than we would have been if Britain had not been kept fighting?

There can be no question that we realized, after the conquest of Western Europe by Hitler that the British Isles and the British Navy are the most powerful Atlantic outpost we shall ever have. That realization was registered overwhelmingly in the lend-lease act. That was our real acceptance of war against spreading world despotism. It is now said by very prominent Americans that it is all right to give the British the arms but that we must not deliver the goods. Yet surely no one really supposed that we would make billions' worth of arms to be sunk by the Nazis to the bottom of the ocean.

Such a policy would not only be foolish; it would defeat our real object, which is the destruction of Hitlerism. If anyone is in doubt that that is our object, it is not because the President has failed to proclaim it many times. Some of us deny that Nazism can be defeated, but no one knows how to make peace with it. As I see it, nothing is more evident than that the Hitler empire cannot make peace. It must go on and on until it masters the bulk of the world or is destroyed. It does not know how to make peace, is not prepared for it, does not believe in it. The Nazis are condemned forever either to seize more available loot or to strike down some living challenge to their tyranny which still stands a little farther away. If Russia is mastered, then Africa will be next in line, followed by South America.

I am never more troubled than when people ask us just to be a good, quiet example to the wicked world. There is no more dangerous role that we could attempt. Any free nation which sets an example of quiet, good living is a flaming challenge to the gangster regimes—a challenge to conquer the impudent people who assume to be free, a challenge to loot a people who are so naive. Far from being a defense, a policy of being the world's good example is positively dangerous in the world we live in.

The day when we could be a passive beacon light to a wicked world is gone forever and it will never return.

But we are not yet totally at war. Very many people feel that we should be, that the war cannot be won without total effort on our part; but there is no evidence that the President is so convinced. He is fully determined that Nazism shall be beaten, but he does not yet know what it will take to beat it. For months it was clear that he hoped to win the war without fighting. What greater achievement could he possibly aim at? Then all factions would be mostly satisfied.

Lately Hitler's sea challenges have compelled the President to accept some fighting, but how much? Perhaps the effective delivery of vast supplies to both Britain and Russia—Russia now being in greatest need—will be sufficient. Doubtless it will be essential soon to repeal the remnant of the neutrality law which forbids our merchant ships to be armed or to go to Britain, our chief fighting outpost. It may be essential to occupy the Azores or Dakar eventually. It is possible that we may need to occupy Eire in force, in agreement with the Irish, as with the Icelanders. It is possible that we may have to send a strong army to Norway or to Spain. It is conceivable that another tremendous A.E.F. may be in the end the only way to terminate the war.

But these things are still in the future. In his address last night Herbert Hoover deprecated at least twelve times the sending of our boys to fight overseas, meaning in Europe. But no one really wants to do that. The President and all his advisers have every incentive to win the war without the belligerent use of troops if they can, and with just as little use of troops as possible if they must be used.

Should we have a declaration of war by Congress? At what point would it be plainly imperative? At what point would it unify us to see the thing through? At what point would it be no longer avoidable? Doubtless there is such

235

a point, but are we certain that it is here now or when it will arrive? Our sense of timing may be good, but is it better than the President's? All factions among us should be able to agree that so far he has dealt with the world crisis adroitly and—so far—successfully. If anything is certain, too, it is that in this desperate emergency we must have strong, able, and patient leadership. Can those of us who reject the President's leadership be certain that we are right in doing so?

Total War Comes to Us

SEPTEMBER 24—DECEMBER 10, 1941

The national convention of the American Legion voted to repeal the law forbidding the use of the Army outside the Western Hemisphere and rejected a motion opposing aid to Russia by a vote of 874 to 604. United States-British missions went to Moscow to investigate Russia's need as Kiev fell and the Crimean peninsula was cut off. A new six-billion-dollar lend-lease bill was introduced on September 19.

September 22 the American-owned steamer Pink Star, *Panama-registered, was sunk off Iceland. The flag did not matter, said the President. It was our declared policy to aid those who opposed the forces trying to dominate the world.*

THIS ENCIRCLEMENT GAME
September 24, 1941

FOR MORE THAN TEN YEARS THERE HAS BEEN PLAYED ON both sides of us the most momentous game ever played in human history. The prize of this encirclement game is nothing less than control of the world itself.

The encirclement game is a deadly one for player and victim alike. It is like the dope habit: once you begin, you cannot quit. You must go on to get more morphine regardless of the cost or results. But where the drug habit victimizes its thousands, the encirclement game destroys or maims its tens of millions. It is a game of which no person

237

who hopes to live a decent, secure life can afford to be ignorant.

Its operation, too, is simple. Let us see how it works. From 1930 on, the German Nazis developed an encirclement complex. Germany, they said, was encircled by nations which disliked and distrusted her. Therefore she must smash the disarmament clauses of the last peace treaty and build up a vast army, air force, and navy.

Of course this argument was a ruse. No single one of Germany's neighbors dreamed of attacking her. She was perfectly safe, even though disarmed; but the encirclement cry greatly helped the Nazis to power and popularized their terrific rearmament drive from 1933 to 1937. In every week of this period it was perfectly evident that their object was conquest unlimited; but they deceived the controlling classes in France and Britain, causing them to believe otherwise until Germany was ready in March, 1937. Then the Nazis suddenly pounced upon Austria in the name of self-determination. Who, asked Chamberlain Englishmen, could object to that? But the seizure of Austria encircled Czechoslovakia with German territory on three sides. It is too far away really to concern us, said Chamberlain; and Czechoslovakia was sacrificed in 1938. But then this conquest and the simultaneous Nazi domination of Hungary encircled Poland, and Poland was massacred in 1939.

In the Balkans, Bulgaria was readily taken over by nonwarlike pressure, and Rumania was then encircled. Already conquered from within by the Nazi Iron Guard mobsters and by hordes of Nazi agents and "businessmen" —hard, cold, and ruthlessly efficient—Rumania was first divided and then occupied. A wealthy, easygoing land was stripped clean by the Nazis as by an all-devouring cloud of locusts—as Austria and Czechoslovakia had been, and as all Western Europe was soon to be.

In the west, Norway was taken first—by ruse and

treachery in dead of night. Then Holland and Belgium were overrun—and France. Spain had already been conquered. The Spanish Republic had been deliberately strangled to death, actually with the aid of the British and French governments and a special arms embargo law hastily rushed through the United States Congress to make it certain that Spain should have no arms with which to defend herself. No one of the three great democracies was Spain's keeper.

But the death of Spain plainly meant the doom of France; and when France fell, Britain found herself encircled with a great half-moon of German air and submarine bases all the way from Norway to Spain—all of which might have been prevented by firm action in defense of Manchuria in 1931, Ethiopia in 1935, or Spain after 1936.

The successful encirclement of Britain roused the American people from their delusions of isolation. Suddenly it became apparent that the United States was about to be dangerously encircled.

Consider also what had been happening on the other side of us. In 1931 Japan had suddenly seized North China, then Central China, then South China, then North Indo-China, then South Indo-China—until all that was left of Free China was encircled by hordes of looting, raping Japanese troops.

This, however, was scarcely half the story, for the recent seizure of Indo-China encircled Thailand, and the fall of Thailand would enable Japan to complete the encirclement of China and also of Singapore and the Dutch Indies, from whence come some of our most indispensable supplies. So the isolationist Americans united with the British, Dutch, Australians, and Filipinos to draw a cordon around Japanese aggression in the South—a cordon sealed by that stoppage of trade with Japan which should have taken place in 1931, in 1937, and in every intervening year.

Now Japan, the great Eastern encircler, is herself completely encircled. With Russia an ally of Britain, Japan is entirely ringed about with powers which are wholly fed up with her aggressions and which are incapable of putting the slightest confidence in anything that she says. The coalition that Japan has welded around herself is, moreover, powerful enough to see to it that Japan's predatory encirclements are ended for generations to come, and—unless the coalition is incredibly shortsighted—it *will* see to it that Japan threatens nobody's peace for at least a hundred years. Japan's only hope now lies in German victory in Europe.

In Europe, alas, the game is far from played out. Some of the later details of it are almost too sickening to recount. There was Yugoslavia, weakened by economic conquest, propaganda penetration, and treason, entirely surrounded by the Axis—by Italy, Germany, Hungary, Nazi-ruled Rumania and Bulgaria. Only to the south did the Yugoslavs have a narrow window connecting them with the free air of Greece. But there was something contagious about the air breathed by the immortal Greeks, who had whipped Fascist Italy soundly for months in the cruelest, coldest mountain fighting in any age. Without any hope of success the Yugoslavs defied the Nazi boa constrictor and fought—fought in vain except that they disrupted the Nazi timetable for a month and saved their own souls. After that Greece was hopelessly encircled and her mighty warriors crushed, but at the price of two precious months nicked from Hitler's timetable.

Once the big nations thought that they could let the little ones be killed and remain safe themselves, but by this time they knew better. As soon as Greece was finished, giant Russia found herself encircled from Finland to Greece; and there began that titanic struggle upon the outcome of which hangs the fate of all human civilization.

For the moment the treacherous assault of Germany on Russia has had the effect of encircling the Nazis themselves—as completely as the Japanese are encircled. Germany is today blockaded in the Atlantic; held out of the Mediterranean; shut out of the Near East by Allied control of Iran, Iraq, Syria, and Turkey; walled in by Russia on the east; and besieged by Arctic waters on the north. At last the great European encirclers have succeeded in encircling themselves with a ring of foes, behind whom is the gathering power of the United States. Today the Nazis are threatened with the exact retribution which they so richly deserve—to be encircled and strangled as they have strangled other nations by the dozen. If the anti-Nazi coalition has the power, it should see to it that German aggression does not again terrorize the entire human race on every continent for a very, very long time.

But does the anti-Nazi coalition have the power to defeat the mightiest aggression which has ever disrupted the lives of a billion and a half people? Today there is no prospect that the Russians and British can keep the ring drawn around the Nazis without tremendous supplies of war material from us—supplies delivered quickly to Suez and the Persian Gulf. Plans will not suffice; promises will not save the day; good intentions will not produce results. Nothing but really powerful aid, delivered at once where it is most needed, will keep the Nazi encirclers encircled.

Today the world has both of the encirclers beaten at their own game—but time is at present running against us. If Russia can be knocked out in the next six months, that will make an enormous difference. Even before that we may see a successful German effort to overrun North Africa. Libya is already in German hands; Fascist Spain is ready for the pay-off, ready to grab a chunk of North Africa for itself. Vichy France is holding all of North Africa and West Africa for German occupation. A railroad is being rushed to completion across the Sahara Desert; a new port is being hurriedly built to supplement Dakar.

If the Germans win in Russia, they have every reason to believe that West Africa will be theirs and with it the domination of the narrow waters between Africa and Brazil. To reap their final reward, the Nazis must defeat Britain too—as from West Africa they would have a greatly increased chance of doing by sinking her ships from Iceland to South Africa.

Should Germany defeat Britain, there is no man alive who can tell how the Nazis could be prevented from dominating the twenty republics of Latin America by the overwhelming massed buying power of half a billion Europeans, by propaganda backed by the prestige of world mastery, by military force if necessary. But few believe that Nazi troops would be necessary.

Thus everything hangs in the balance. If the Russian and British lines which dam in the Nazi flood can be made to hold, all will be well. But if not, within ten years the aggressors will win control of the world itself, saving only North America, which would be encircled for whatever fate of slow strangulation—by economic pressure, by the pressure of militarization, and by triumphant propaganda—the conquerors might arrange.

There is no stopping place in the game of encirclement. Once it is begun, the player must go on to world conquest or downfall, and which it will be now depends on the power and speed with which we Americans can throw our weight into the scales.

That would seem to be self-evident, but something else stands out from this ten-year story of tragic encirclement warfare. As I see it, it is this: no nation, however big and theoretically isolated, can be safe unless the smallest of the nations is safe. On a planet which perpetually shrinks for purposes of war, not even the richest and most comfort-loving nation can be safe unless everybody else is safe. In other words, no nation, not even the biggest, can live in peace and security hereafter unless there is enough world government really to prevent world wars from starting. That is a law the operation of which no nation can escape.

"Unless man adapted himself to changing conditions he might become extinct. There is no question of remaining as he is," warned H. G. Wells on September 29.

The next day Chairman Connally made a radio appeal for repeal of the neutrality law and return to freedom of the seas. Willkie urged his party to take the lead in repeal on October 7. Three days later the President asked only for authority to arm our merchant ships, which was granted by the House on October 18, 259 to 138, as the destroyer Kearny was hit by a torpedo off Iceland. A Gallup poll showed 62 per cent in favor of the shoot-on-sight policy and 28 per cent opposed. On October 21 three Republican senators proposed the outright repeal of the neutrality act of 1929. Three American-owned freighters were sunk in the Atlantic.

The American-British missions to Moscow on October 2 promised to supply all Russia's requests. On October 4 Hitler boasted the conquest of Russian areas twice the size of Germany. Transport was the only remaining problem. Russia *"is already broken and will never rise again."* Bryansk and Vyazma fell on October 13. Two days later the Germans were sixty miles from Moscow. On October 20 they took Taganrog, and Stalin ordered Moscow defended to the last man.

The House passed the second lend-lease bill on October 11, defeating 162 to 21 a move to bar help to Russia. On October 20 the Dies Committee sent the Attorney General a list of 1,124 federal officials whom it charged with *"aiding Communists"* and *"undermining the American system of government."*

On October 16 a spokesman for the Japanese Navy declared that Japanese-American relations were *"now approaching the final parting of the ways"* and the Japanese fleet was *"itching for action." On October 19 General Tojo headed a new "crisis" Cabinet in Japan.*

WHAT IS OUR NEXT DECISION?
October 22, 1941

IT IS ALMOST CERTAIN THAT WE SHALL HAVE TO MAKE decisions of the greatest importance soon. The time when we can debate the war as an urgent but somewhat academic proposition is nearly over, for critical developments are in the offing on both sides of us. Tonight I want to try to examine the situation as it seems to be shaping up, both east and west.

The Germans have not yet put Russia out of the war; and they are not likely to do so for a long time, if ever. But it is increasingly probable that they can soon disengage a big army from Russia to use in the Near East or to invade Africa in force through Italy or Spain. Churchill warned us weeks ago that the Germans had enough strength to attempt all three of these operations at once, and subsequent events have borne him out. The coming German attempt to break out into the oceans will put the issue squarely up to Britain and the United States. Are we going to surrender control of the oceans or not? That is what it always boils down to, and unfortunately we cannot keep control of the seas if the triple-alliance powers conquer too much land. They already hold Europe and half of East Asia. If they can add the Near East and Africa to their holdings, they will be in a far better position to wear down the sea powers and eventually defeat them, because if they get a firm grip on all the land they are now reaching for, they will have resources so decidedly superior to ours that they can take their time about outbuilding us on the sea. For many years we have wanted isolation; but if the fast-

244

maturing plans of the Axis powers succeed, we shall have forced upon us an isolation more deadly than any that our isolationist mentors ever imagined.

Unless all signs fail, Japan is about to take the final plunge in her long career of aggression. Only the Siberian winter, already beginning, could now deter her from an attack on Russia, and its severity seems likely to be outweighed by the need of striking while oil stocks are high and while German power is still expanding. The real masters of Japan, the militarists, have come out into the open in the new Japanese Cabinet. The so-called moderates have been pushed into the background as they always have been and always will be when the army is ready for another aggression. Now Japan is confronting us with a choice of turning over the whole of East Asia to her or of doing something to prevent her taking it.

What is our decision to be? The *New York Times* reported that news of the appointment of a military cabinet in Japan led State Department officials "to say that the conversations between the United States and Japan would be continued in the effort to find a basis for negotiations. The aim of the negotiations would be to work out an adjustment of the basic differences between the two governments."

I must confess that I found this dispatch distinctly disquieting, unless the officials quoted meant merely to stress our pacific desires or to gain time. For what are the basic differences between the United States and Japan? They are at least four: (1) Japan wants to take over the vast Chinese population and enslave them permanently, drawing off their wealth to the coffers of Japanese militarists and industrialists and pouring Chinese minerals and labor into the building of a huge Japanese navy to dominate the Pacific. (2) Japan wants to take over Malay and the Dutch Indies, together with a plentiful supply of oil and our supplies of rubber, tin, quinine, tungsten, and several other key products for ordinary living and for national defense. (3) Japan wants to conquer Siberia, seize its great resources to complete an empire of truly enormous power, and become our near neighbor across from Alaska. (4) Japan wants to tear up every treaty ever signed with us and reduce life in the Pacific area to the jungle principle that he who is strong enough is entitled to take what he can.

This is what the Japanese have let the whole world know that they must have. Now what can we offer them? We can offer to use our whole influence to see that Japan has full and fair economic opportunities in China, in the Indies, in the United States, and in the rest of the world—after Japan has withdrawn her armies from China and given up her ambitions to conquer the whole of East Asia. This offer could mean a great deal to Japan provided that our people have learned that every high tariff law is a declaration of war and will be so regarded by other countries, but is there one chance in a thousand that the Japanese Army would consider it?

There can be but one answer to that. Japan's army leaders put aside all idea of living by peaceful commerce in 1931 and have never thought of doing so since. But, some may say, we could offer them something more. What could it be? Can we betray the great Chinese people, whom we have been supporting ever more firmly? Can we permit the Japanese to take over and monopolize the strategic wealth of the Indies? Can we let them move to Alaska—another storehouse of great wealth?

If the answer to these questions is negative, are we ready to use our naval power and air power to block further Japanese aggressions? These are the next questions if we wish to keep Japan in the iron ring she has so successfully forged around herself. We now have powerful friends—Russia, Britain, the Dutch Indies, Australia, New Zealand, and the Philippines—to help us settle the Japanese question. These present allies are all armed and ready to see the

thing through. Could we ever hope to get a similar combination together again?

In the Atlantic, too, our hour is striking. There a still
more dangerous aggressor is confined within an iron
ring which he has forged for himself. There the British
Empire, Russia, and the conquered peoples are still keeping
the Nazis from breaking out and flooding over the Atlantic
world. But the power of the conquered peoples to help
us will be gone—make no mistake about that—if Britain
and Russia fall; and Russia is being pushed back so far that
her striking power will be gravely curtailed, to say the
least.

More and more the issue is up to us. Are we going to
permit the Nazis to take over the Atlantic and with it the
bulk of South America? Our answer will be given in
Congress soon. The immediate question before the Congress is that of arming our merchant ships—already a truly
academic question. The real issue is the lifting of the ban
on sending our merchant ships to England or wherever they
are needed.

Fearing the effect of another close vote in the House,
the President has not asked for this step now; but three
Republican senators, backed by Wendell Willkie and 124
prominent Republicans, have joined in proposing it, and
a majority of the Senate may well decide that we cannot
strike the shackles of the neutrality act from our arms
too soon.

There is a serious danger, too, that Congress may have
to vote on a declaration of war before the current debate
in the Senate is over. Senator Wheeler has threatened to
offer a rider calling for a declaration of war to the proposal to repeal the ban on ship movements. Wheeler thinks,
of course, that the Administration does not want a declaration of war now and that it would be rejected. Then, he
reasons, the isolationists could take hold of our policy of
defeating the aggressors and reverse it.

But consider what catastrophe such a maneuver could cause. We might all understand here that the rejection of a declaration of war, here and now, did not change our fundamental determination to defeat the aggressors and to prevent them from finally encircling us after all possible allies had been conquered. But would the British people understand that? Could it ever be explained to the Russian people? Could they ever understand that the rejection of a declaration of war did not mean that we had abandoned the fight against the conquerors? What, too, would the effect be on the conquered peoples? Would not despair run through Europe like an earthquake? And what of the Latin Americans? Would they understand the subtleties of our internal politics, or would they make terms with the Nazis? What, finally, of the Japanese army leaders? Would they not conclude that the Americans were "washed up"—too divided to be longer considered? Could there be a better invitation to them to "shoot the whole works"?

As I see it, any thoughtful consideration of these questions leads to the conclusion that if Senator Wheeler persists in his threat to offer a declaration of war, we must face the issue squarely and see to it that the declaration is passed by strong majorities in both houses of Congress. By failing to accept his challenge we would invite the whole world crisis to turn decisively against us—and all the world's peoples to turn away from us.

United States aid to Russia was rerouted from the Pacific to the Atlantic. On October 25 Secretary Knox warned that war with Japan was almost sure if she persisted in her policies. The Army tank program was doubled. Kharkov fell, and Mussolini warned that he would crush us. He promised to shatter

SHOULD THE NEUTRALITY LAW BE REPEALED?

October 29, 1941

THE CONGRESS OF THE UNITED STATES IS ABOUT TO VOTE ON the repeal of the last of the series of laws designed to keep us out of this war. Soon, in all probability, nothing of the so-called neutrality laws will remain except a remnant which compels our private arms manufacturers to obtain licenses from the State Department for the export of arms. That is a provision about which there is little controversy.

How does it happen that all the other neutrality-law provisions have failed to isolate us from this war? Is it because the President has skillfully maneuvered these laws into nullity? Or is it because their purpose was unattainable?

I know that it is not possible for many people to attempt to answer these questions on a basis of reason. Strong emotions will not permit. But it seems to me to be vital for most of us to try to profit by the experience which these laws represent.

Let us recall first what we tried to do and why. We found the last war to be an unpleasant business. By "we" I mean especially the soldiers who took part in it. It was not the thrilling adventure which many had expected. There was too much "K.P." in it and too much picking up of cigarette butts half around the globe. The ocean journey to the battlefields in Europe was long and suffocating, and the French people turned out to be different from us. Many of them actually did not have bathtubs. Al-

249

ways, too, there were unpleasant things to be done. I recall out of my own very average experience having to help dig graves through solid rock on the heights of Brest on a cold, rainy day under the harsh supervision of a very low and vulgar corporal.

So we came home resolved not to go abroad to fight any more, and we thoroughly convinced the younger boys as they came along that that was not the thing to do. After we had failed to enter the League of Nations and to help make the peace and defend it, we had to explain that to ourselves and to the younger people; and to justify ourselves we accepted the thesis of Senator Nye and others that our whole part in the last war had been a mistake and that we should make up our minds to stay out of the next one. Resentment over the stoppage of payments on the war debts—a question most of us never understood—helped greatly to fan this determination. We would simply not have anything to do with the next war.

But having decided to stay out, we had to take some precautions. How did we happen to get into that last war anyway? Senator Nye and other isolationists were at our elbows with the answers. We got in, they told us, because (1) the British cleverly propagandized us; (2) the munitions makers and international bankers wanted us to fight for their loans and profits; and (3) we foolishly insisted on protecting our ships and citizens in the war zones. This version of why we fought in the last war—all of it less than half true—fitted our mood and was accepted.

Then when the Italian invasion of Ethiopia plainly signaled the breakup of world order again, we hastily passed all the laws which might have kept us out of the last war—a law to forbid our citizens to lend money to belligerents; a law to forbid our citizens to travel on belligerent ships, that is, on British ships; a law to forbid our own ships and sailors to go into the war zones; and, most drastic of all, a law to prevent our citizens from selling arms, even for cash, to any belligerent. No friendly people who might be attacked could send their own ships to our harbors and get arms.

Then the Japanese and German aggressions reached the stage of world war in September, 1939, and we saw quickly that it wouldn't do to deny the tardy and negligent democracies the long-established right to buy arms for their defense. That meant the hasty repeal of our arms embargo law. But that was too little to halt the aggressors: they conquered Western Europe. We saw that control of the seas on both sides of us would fall into predatory hands if Britain also fell. The British, too, were about to run out of cash to pay for the arms which they carried from this country in their own ships. The lend-lease bill was the answer to that. It gave United States government credit to the British and to all others who would fight the aggressors, and it avoided the creation of new war debts in dollars that could never be repaid.

The lend-lease policy of course meant ultimate delivery of the goods. We were not so foolish as to manufacture vast quantities of arms for the defense of the democratic world and then permit Hitler to sink them to the bottom of the ocean and win his war for world supremacy. There was time before our arsenal of democracy really got to working for the President to gather in a long string of new defense bases and outposts all the way from South America to Iceland, and to strengthen our navy in the Atlantic until it was ready to proceed from patrol duty to combat service in delivering the goods.

Now the tools of war are beginning to roll from our assembly lines in really great quantities, and we can no longer refrain from sending our own ships and sailors to England, to Russia, and wherever else arms and supplies are required for the defeat of the aggressors. The whole outcome of the war depends on the most effective use of all-too-limited supplies of shipping. The Germans have sunk almost eight million tons of ships, and these sinkings never cease. We are building twelve million tons, but with all we can do there will not be a ship to spare. Our ships must go direct to England and everywhere else under the heaviest convoy we can provide. That is military necessity; but it is also moral necessity, for we cannot win a world war under the rule that the life of no single American citizen shall be risked.

The neutrality laws then have failed to keep us out of this war. But they have achieved their purpose in one respect: they have made it certain that we are not going into this war because of feeling aroused by any incidents on the sea involving our ships and citizens. That was not why we went into the last war. The reasons were broader and deeper—as they are today. But every person of isolationist persuasion should feel better to know that we are in the war for compelling reasons—not because of any series of incidents which could have been avoided.

There has been again a series of incidents involving the sinking of our ships by German submarines, but nobody is steamed up emotionally by these sinkings. When the gangster powers have sunk three thousand ships, when they have killed tens of millions of people, when they have looted and stolen at least fifty billion dollars' worth of property to which they had no shadow of right, when they have terrorized, starved, and abused people by the hundred million—probably four hundred million people to date—we cannot regard the maltreatment of a few of our people on the sea as remarkable.

It is the overwhelming evidence, piled up higher each week, that German and Japanese barbarism is crushing the life out of civilization itself that moves us into action. It is the knowledge that these conquest machines can never make peace, never stop their looting while a free people remains to be looted, that moves us to repeal the last of the neutrality laws. It is the realization that control of the

252

seas means security for us and that loss of control would mean dangerous imprisonment in our North American island which impels us to decide to defend ourselves again on the other side of the oceans—not on this side after it is too late. It is our deepening understanding that Fascism is total and permanent war against every Christian, humane way of life which obliges us to fight it until it is destroyed. It is the inescapable evidence that the constant perfection of the machines of war means the merciless destruction of the great cities of every continent which compels us to decide that the gangster regimes must be brought under control before it is too late.

These are the forces that are now sweeping away the remnants of the laws we passed to keep us out of war. They are forces too vast for anyone to ignore and too devastatingly dangerous to be resisted by any means except the full united power of the world's greatest nation. It is inconceivable that the law which forbids the arming of our ships and their use wherever needed will not be repealed, but the majorities by which it is repealed will make a great difference. If there is a big minority vote in either house of Congress, the enemies of democracy and liberty will take heart in every gangster capital. This is a result which every citizen should take into account in counseling with his representatives in Congress. There is no longer any question that we are going to oppose the gangster powers until they are destroyed; but if a large number of Americans drag their heels, they can prolong the process perhaps indefinitely, and they can make it much more costly and dangerous. Surely that would not profit any of us.

Large America First meetings denounced neutrality repeal as a war measure. La Follette saw all democracy endangered. Lindbergh pictured trickery. Wheeler charged secret pledges. Cudahy called for a peace conference. But the Senate voted repeal, 50 to 37, on November 8. The destroyer Reuben James was torpedoed and sunk off Iceland on November 1 with a large loss of life.

In Russia the fifth German drive on Moscow was hammered to a standstill. Since the Germans wanted a war of extermination, said Stalin, they would get it. Litvinoff became Ambassador to the United States, and a billion-dollar lend-lease credit was extended to Russia on November 7.

On Armistice Day, Undersecretary of State Welles observed at Wilson's tomb that "rarely in human history has the vision of a statesman been so tragically and so swiftly vindicated." President Roosevelt warned that we faced world war again. Knox warned Japan that we would not budge, as Saburo Kurusu, a special Japanese envoy, arrived by clipper.

SHOWDOWN IN THE FAR EAST
November 12, 1941

THERE IS EVERY INDICATION THAT AN END OF MANEUVERING is imminent between Japan and the coalition composed of the United States, Britain, Australia, New Zealand, the Dutch Indies, China, Russia, and the Philippines. Since we are the strongest power in the alliance opposed to further Japanese aggression, the showdown is primarily between the United States and Japan.

This is indicated by the spectacular flight of a special Japanese envoy, Mr. Saburo Kurusu, across the Pacific Ocean. He is to be joined in Washington by the Japanese minister to Canada. These two will work with Ambassador Nomura in telling the United States what she must do to avoid war in the Pacific. For some time there have been hints in our press that three distinguished Japanese ought to sit down with American leaders in Washington to compose the differences between Japan and the United States.

What the Japanese army expects the United States to agree to was plainly stated on November 4 by the *Japan Times Advertiser*, the newspaper which acts as a mouthpiece for the Japanese Foreign Office. According to this authoritative organ, the United States must agree to seven things: (1) All military and economic aid to Chungking must cease. (2) China must be left "free to deal with Japan," and Chungking must be advised to make peace with Japan. (3) Military and economic "encirclement" of Japan must end. (4) Japan's Co-prosperity Sphere must be acknowledged; and Manchukuo, China, Indo-China, Thailand, The Netherlands Indies, and other states and protectorates must be allowed to establish their own political and economic relations with Japan without interference of any kind. (5) Manchukuo must be recognized; "Nobody will undo what has been done there." (6) The freezing of Japanese and Chinese assets must be ended unconditionally. (7) Trade treaties must be restored and all restrictions on shipping and commerce ended.

When added up, these seven demands constitute one more reiteration of Japan's intention to conquer the whole of East Asia and to set its six hundred million people to labor for her imperial glory. It is probable, too, that many Japanese militarists, who in the main don't know much about the world, still expect us to consent to Japan's mastery of East Asia.

That we will not do so is, I take it, as settled as anything can be in these changing times. We do not intend to permit Japan to create a colossal military and naval empire in the Far East which would close the great storehouses of that region to us on any except monopolistic terms dictated by Japan. Since that cannot be unknown to the Japanese Foreign Office, it is to be assumed that Mr. Kurusu is bringing with him some concessions from the full program put out through the *Japan Times Advertiser*. Mr. Kurusu is not flying to appease us in the sense that Mr. Chamberlain flew to Munich to appease Hitler. Japan is in a tight box, but she still expects to get her domination of East Asia. She is, however, willing to concede us some cover for retreat if we will withdraw.

The question before us, then, is which one of the seven demands, if any, should we yield ground upon? Let us consider them in four groups. First, "all military and economic aid to Chungking must cease" and China must be advised to make peace and left "free to deal with Japan." That is, we must abandon China and let Japan have her way there. But this is the one thing we cannot do. We have always been friends with the Chinese. We have always had a valued and important trade with China, especially in key raw materials such as tungsten and tung oil. China is the real pivot in the Far East, not Japan. Japan is trying to throttle the stirring Chinese giant before it can modernize itself and become the really great power of the Orient— one with which we could confidently expect a vast and growing commerce of trade between equals. After having stood for the open door in China for a century, we would be foolish indeed to abandon it just as China is ready to enter into a tremendous modern development—especially since Japan seeks to turn all Chinese labor and raw materials into the service of her war machine.

But, suppose that Japan seeks to keep just a part of China—all of the great cities on China's rivers and coasts, let us say. That, of course, would mean the domination of China. Many Japanese would, I suspect, be glad to get out of the China morass if only they could retain Manchuria and the five provinces of North China. Such a deal would no doubt find some favor in this country, but no Chinese could be expected to agree to it. He could see no reason why his country should be mutilated and divided. There is small reason to believe that the Chinese people will rest content until all of Japan's armies are driven from the continent. The Chinese might agree to extend the war another fifty years, if necessary to free their land, but is that a solution which would be good for anyone? In China, Japan is waging a total war, and there is not much reason to believe that she can avoid a total decision.

What then of Japan's demand number four: that Japan's Co-prosperity Sphere must be acknowledged and Man-chukuo, China, Indo-China, Thailand, the Netherlands Indies, and other states and protectorates must be allowed to establish their own political and economic relations with Japan without interference of any kind?

The meaning here is plain enough. Not only must Indo-China be left in Japan's hands, but we must exit from the Philippines and turn the whole of the Far East, including Australia and the Dutch Indies, over to Japanese domina-tion. Aside from a strong feeling of kinship and admiration for the Australians, we have no intention of seeing the great sources of tin, rubber, quinine, and other key prod-ucts in the Dutch Indies fall under Japanese monopoly, to become aces in her system of closed economy.

We have not the slightest reason to believe, either, that the Japanese could be trusted to rule the twelve million Filipinos whom we have trained for nationhood or the hundred million Malayans in the Singapore area. In China, Japan has demonstrated for centuries to come her complete unfitness to rule any people as subjects. One would have to go back at least to the Middle Ages to find a counter-part of the barbaric cruelty which the Japanese have in-flicted on the Chinese people—men, children, and especially the women. Far from having a God-given right to rule the six hundred million people of East Asia, the Japanese war machine has destroyed its right to rule anyone—even the Japanese people themselves.

The remaining Japanese demands deal with what she calls the military and economic encirclement of Japan.

Japan today is a nation besieged. She is surrounded by an iron ring of eight armed nations—a ring which her own incessant aggression has created. Her trade with all these same neighbors is also cut off. For years we all fed the Japanese war machine with the iron, oil, money, and everything else it needed for the conquest of China and East Asia. But the eight allies have finally stopped financing and supplying Japan's war against all of us, and we are not going to begin again until we know that Japan's power for mischief is ended.

What then does that leave that can be offered to a chastened Japan which has given up conquest as a way of living? To such a Japan we would be under the heaviest compulsion to see that Japanese trade has equal and easy access to the markets and raw materials of the entire Far East and of the world. We do have a heavy degree of guilt resting upon ourselves for the high tariff laws which helped to convince Japan that it would be better to try to conquer markets by force of arms. That effort was always a mistake. Japan has wasted the accumulated wealth of generations without getting anything to show for it. But after Japan's attempt at world conquest has broken down, we shall have only a temporary and fitful peace unless we recognize that every high tariff law passed by us is a declaration of war and that it will be so accepted and acted upon by other nations. Japan cannot hope to raise her standard of living if there are trade barriers all over the world. She must have markets everywhere, just as we must, just as the Germans must, and the British. The whole idea of a "living space" walled off for the exclusive use of the Americans—or the Germans—is a delusion. We ourselves require access to the markets and raw materials of the wide earth itself. Nothing less can satisfy us or the Germans, or the Japanese. The world is an economic unit, and we need not expect to have peace unless it is governed as an economic unit.

Neither the Japanese nor the Germans have been justified in trying to conquer all the raw materials that they could possibly need, but they must be assured freer access to raw materials in all parts of the world on terms of equality with everybody else.

This freer access to the markets and raw materials of a governed world is, as I see it, the biggest thing we can offer Japan—and the only thing we can offer her—but there is small prospect that it will lead her now to give up her effort to take everything in sight. Only defeat in war will end Japan's determination to rule the Orient.

The Armistice Day speeches of Roosevelt, Knox, and Welles jarred Tokyo. They were carefully edited and featured with speeches by Wheeler and Senator Clark of Missouri. On November 17 Premier Tojo demanded that we end the economic curbs on Japan and keep hands off China. On November 26 Washington dispatches stated that the Kurusu parleys revealed no basis for negotiation, and the United States consulate in Tokyo again warned all Americans to leave Japan promptly.

On November 20 Hoover contended that the German-British war was a stalemate. Both the United States and England were safer than a year ago. Sending our armies abroad would be "a futile waste of American life." This "attempt at artificial conditioning of the American mind for war should stop."

On November 27 our terms were given to the Japanese, and two days later Japan was warned that we would not tolerate any new attacks in the Orient. On November 30 General Tojo declared that American and British exploitation of Asiatic peoples and "British-American Communism" must be "purged with vengeance." The President hurried grimly back to Washington from Georgia on December 1. Tokyo dispatches rejected our principles as fantastic. The President an-

*nounced, on December 3, that he had formally asked Japan
why so many forces were being sent to Indo-China.*

IS IT WAR WITH JAPAN?
December 3, 1941

THE FINAL SHOWDOWN IN THE FAR EAST APPEARS TO BE AT
hand. For ten years Japan has been engaged in a campaign
to conquer the whole of East Asia. This has created around
her a ring of armed and resolute opponents who are determined to oppose any further Japanese aggression. On
her part, Japan is ready to begin a new campaign against
the Burma Road, possibly from Indo-China into South
China, more probably through Thailand.

Some writers say that if we now go to war with Japan
the American people will not understand why. Why, they
ask, should Americans fight Japan over the Burma Road?
It does not seem to me that any of us can be unaware of the
fundamental issue between Japan and the United States,
but it may not be amiss to scan the past ten years quickly
for the answer. In September, 1931, Japan started out to
take by force what she wanted. She seized Manchuria.
There was instant alarm in this country and all over the
world because Japan was openly breaking the three most
important treaties upon which the world's peace rested:
the Nine-Power Treaty, the League of Nations Covenant,
and the Briand-Kellogg Pact. If these treaties were destroyed, the world would be back on a jungle basis again.
Our government, through Hoover and Stimson, protested
strongly and refused to recognize Japan's title to Manchuria.

Then Japan edged into North China and began in 1937
a war for the conquest of all China—a war she has never
been able to finish because the Chinese opened up a road

through the back country over the mountains to Burma and the sea. Seldom in human history has such a prodigious job been done mainly by hand labor.

When Japan attacked China in 1937, we protested again, through Secretary Hull, and reaffirmed again the elementary principles of conduct between civilized nations which Japan was violating. But for two years more we continued to sell to Japan the iron and trucks, machinery and oil which she required for the conquest of China. It was not until July, 1939, that we denounced our treaty of commerce with her, and it was another six months before we began by very slow degrees to stop the flow of war supplies to Japan. Not until Japan moved into South Indo-China last June did we make the embargo complete—along with Britain, the Dutch Indies, and Australia.

In the meantime Japan had been proclaiming literally thousands of times her immutable intention to conquer the whole of East Asia—a "Co-prosperity Sphere" she calls it, but no single one of the peoples who would be enslaved by Japan is deceived by the word "co-prosperity." In the meantime, also, the armed strength of the powers Japan proposes to dispossess in the Far East has become greater than Japan's strength, especially in the air.

Japan has, therefore, been staging a diplomatic blitzkrieg to divide her opponents and destroy them singly. This campaign has centered in Washington because the United States is the strongest of the Pacific powers which Japan must overcome. Mr. Kurusu was sent by air in spectacular fashion to arrange our Munich for us. The Japanese know that we do not want to fight them, that we fear Hitlerism more. Why, then, wouldn't a drive to separate the United States from China succeed? It appears to be true, too, that it almost did succeed. Kurusu proposed a temporary arrangement, about two weeks ago, under which Japan would not attack any new country for three months, in return for which we would partially relax our embargo and sell Japan enough iron and oil for her "normal" needs.

On the face of it, this little deal would not hurt anyone much; and if it postponed a war, why not? The reluctance of all Japan's opponents to accept war in the Far East is so great that they all wavered. Britain, the Dutch, Russia, and the United States were all tempted to buy a little more time for the war against Hitler, especially since the Lybian campaign was being held up and Vichy France was visibly preparing to turn North Africa over to Hitler. But actually the acceptance of Japan's bait would have constituted our Munich—the beginning of retreat which could not stop until the last desperate ditch had been reached. In the first place, how much oil would we sell to Japan for her "normal" needs, when Japan has herself proclaimed that she has no normal needs, when she has been busy for years organizing her whole economy for total war. To begin feeding the Japanese war machines again would be to start sliding down a slippery road, yielding a little more all along until the highly effective economic curb on Japan would be whittled away.

Morally that would be a catastrophe for us—and actually as well—for China was so outraged at the idea that she threatened to make a deal with Japan herself. That was precisely what Japan expected. It would have meant the "Vichyizing" of the great people who have frustrated Japan up to this moment, with little but their own bodies to oppose her—the Chinese.

Fortunately we have decided not to sell out China—a decision I am confident we shall never regret. That means that we must help China defend the Burma Road with supplies and planes and pilots, with our navy and air force operating against Japan if necessary.

But we shall be defending far more than the Burma Road. That is only the final trench at which Japan must be stopped. The real issue is whether we shall allow Japan to master the six hundred million people of East Asia and to organize them into a giant military engine against us. That is the issue, and the moment has arrived when we can no longer avoid it. This is a decisive moment such as comes only once in centuries. Today we are the leader of a coalition of powers which surrounds Japanese aggression completely and which is strong enough to end it once and for all. To put an end entirely to Japan's career of incessant aggression will take effort on our part; but we now have seven other powers to help us, including the Filipinos, who will soon be encircled by Japan if we weaken now. We cannot expect the present tight and resolute iron ring around Japan to last indefinitely. Nor is it right that Japan should immobilize indefinitely great forces of troops, tanks, planes, and ships which are needed in the West to defeat Germany.

These are the reasons why we should not be deceived by any short-sighted talk about pulling British chestnuts out of the fire in the Far East. The British and Dutch have the most money invested there, but we have the biggest stake in the future of the Pacific. We have to live in it permanently, and we simply cannot afford to see Japan turn the bulk of the human race against us. Long after Britain and Holland had been driven from the Orient, we would have to stay and fight alone. Our Pacific Ocean frontier is a guarantee of that.

Japanese aggression then must be stopped where it is. That may seem like fighting for China, but it will be far more than that; it will mean fighting for the right to have the Chinese and all the other people of the Orient as free and friendly neighbors with whom we can trade in peace— and without fear of an overriding military power monopolizing the resources of that vast area against us.

In standing firm now we shall be merely exercising the kind of foresight which is necessary to the survival of any great people in a blitzkrieg world. We shall also be helping to settle the present World War as effectively as if we sent two million men to France. It is vital to remember always that this is one war, not two. Japan is formally allied to Germany and Italy, but it is the reality which counts. All three of them are engaged in a total war of looting and conquest, one openly designed to end in their control of the earth. In this endeavor Japan was first in the field, and in an important sense she is the leader of the marauders, though not the strongest of them.

We would have only half a peace if Hitlerism were defeated in Europe but not in Asia. What the whole world requires is that the gangster powers shall all be disposed of and a new beginning made on the basis of law and order—a real new order that will be not only set up but defended by all the free nations, beginning with ourselves. If we should set out to make peace for less than a century this time, we would deserve the destruction that would be in store for us. We have reached the point in human history where civilized nations cannot continue to exist without strong, effective world government. The one certain way to end Western civilization is to invite the continuance of world wars of conquest every twenty-five years.

On December 4 the Japanese news agency Domei declared it utterly impossible to accept the American note. On the same day the Chicago Tribune *and other McCormick-Patterson papers published in full the secret master war plans of our armed forces. On Saturday, December 6, President Roosevelt sent a personal appeal to Emperor Hirohito, after a new Japanese threat to Indo-China.*

THE WAR COMES TO US
December 10, 1941

EARLY ON LAST SUNDAY MORNING THE WAR CAME TO US. It came suddenly, treacherously, without any fair warning, though after preparations so plain that all could see the steady approach of the conflict. On this peaceful Sunday morning high explosives suddenly shattered the bodies of our men and women, as they had the bodies of countless Chinese and Poles, Greeks and Serbs, Britons and Russians over the past ten years. Death was not any worse for our people than it was for the millions who had already been killed and maimed by the Axis powers, but Sunday's action did bring home to the last single American the existence of gangster powers which aspire to dominate the earth.

Nobody doubts now the fact of war with Japan; but the war has been going on every single day of the past ten years, from that day in September, 1931, when Japan defied the League of Nations and began the conquest of Manchuria. From that day to this moment the world has been at war. It is a matter of proved record that Mussolini decided to run amuck just as soon as Japan had defied the world successfully in Manchuria; and it was plain on the day that Hitler came to power, in January, 1933, that we were in for unlimited war again.

The alliance between these three predatory regimes to terrorize and subdue other nations by the score was not signed and published for some time, but its existence was plain enough. For the past ten years Japan, Italy and Germany have been waging an open war for unlimited plunder and loot against the rest of humanity—waging it unitedly and according to carefully concerted plans. They have disagreed as to the details of conquest at times, but never on standing together to wage common war on all others.

Now that Japan has struck, it is of first importance that our people in every state and section should understand that it is one war and that Japan's war on us is only a detail of it. That does not mean that Japan shall escape punishment. On the contrary, the war against her must be fought relentlessly until Japanese military and naval power is completely smashed—smashed so thoroughly that there will be no question of its revival for generations to come. In saying that, I am not speaking in anger against what the Japanese have done to us, but expressing a long-held judgment. There is not in Japan any power with which peace could be made, and there never will be until the military and naval crowds and the ruling clans generally are destroyed by defeat so terrible that their forty-year policy of permanent aggression can never seem attractive to the Japanese again. That means for Japan not merely the loss of a war but a revolution of her people so genuine as to give her an entirely different form of government. The Japanese have proved by their conduct in China during these ten years that they are not a civilized people and that they cannot be trusted with either power over people or high explosives.

We are now united on that, but recognition that the same thing is true of the Germans is absolutely vital. It will avail us little to eliminate the number two gangster regime if we leave Europe and Africa in control of gangster number one. We shall never see a day of peace until they are all accounted for. That is a conclusion which a big minority of our people has so far refused to accept, but its acceptance can no longer be delayed. We would be foolish indeed to allow Japan to divert us from the main job. There must be no hue and cry that our aid to Britain and Russia be lessened while we hurl everything at Japan. That would be exactly what the Axis alliance wants. On the contrary, we ought to declare war on Germany and Italy at once, make a binding no-separate-peace alliance with Britain, Russia, and everybody else who will stand with us, and redouble our efforts to defeat the European aggressors. We need Russia's help in reducing Japan, but we cannot fairly reproach her for avoiding war with Japan if we refuse to go all out against Russia's greater enemy.

What the Axis alliance wants above all things is that their opponents should fight a lot of separate, un-co-ordinated wars against them. But the victory of democracy requires a world campaign directed from one center, as the other side is directed from Berlin. To pursue any other policy is to run grave risk of defeat on all fronts for lack of central direction, or at best of a long-drawn-out, wasteful struggle lasting for many years.

Fortunately we have in Washington a leader who is capable of managing the grand strategy of winning a true world war—a war in which we have the biggest stake of any law-abiding people on the face of the globe. It seems to me, too, that it is time that President Roosevelt should begin to have the gratitude of his countrymen for his leadership in this supreme crisis. But for him, we would not have been even half ready to play our part in it. In October, 1937, when it was perfectly clear that the greed of the three aggressor regimes was boundless, Mr. Roosevelt made his famous "quarantine speech" in Chicago, the place which most needed to hear it. Then a terrific uproar broke loose at the very idea of quarantining the aggressors. There was a roar of commands to the President to stop rocking the boat and mind his own business. The Congress had already done its best to tie the President hand and foot with neutrality laws which turned all the seas and continents beyond our shores over to the aggressors and gave them the green light to conquer the world itself.

As the aggressors plunged ahead from the murder of one nation to another, the President raised his voice and used to the full all his moral influence to prevent each crime. Naturally he did not succeed. But after Hitler had

267

forced all Europe into war, in September, 1939, he was able to secure the repeal of the most iniquitous of the neutrality laws—that which forbade us to sell a dollar's worth of arms at any price to the victims of aggression.

He was already building the two-ocean navy which his critics said would never be needed. The same people laughed when he called for fifty thousand planes after Dunkirk. By using constitutional powers which the isolationists could not take away from him, the President kept Britain in the war, secured the selective service law fourteen months ago, and made us into the arsenal for all democracy through the lend-lease law in March of this year. All along he was gathering in a great string of new American bases from Iceland to South America and simultaneously fortifying all our possessions in the Pacific except the important island of Guam, which Congress repeatedly refused to fortify for fear of offending Japan.

While we were preparing, we did little except protest against Japan's predatory activities; but as our own strength and that of our allies in the Pacific grew, the President began gradually to cut off our economic aid to Japan's aggression, ending it completely last June. Now that the worst has come, we have powerful allies on the other side of both oceans; we have a big army partly trained; an enormous naval building program is well along; our industrial facilities are already half mobilized for war; and we are rid of the last of the miscalled neutrality laws, which fought on the side of the aggressors. Undoubtedly we ought to be very much further along in our preparations, but this much has been accomplished over the opposition of a huge isolationist minority—misled by blind leaders and newspaper publishers—and for this much accomplished, Franklin D. Roosevelt will receive a place in the history of his country second to none.

There will, I know, be some who will continue to say that if we had just kept mum and avoided offending the aggressors, we would have avoided this war. So we would have. We would have avoided it until the arrogant Japanese conquerors of all East Asia had time to prepare truly gigantic naval and air forces to launch against Hawaii and our Pacific coasts. By cravenly keeping quiet while Germany conquered Europe and Africa, we could also have kept at peace in the Atlantic—until South America was at Germany's mercy and also every great city in the United States from Boston to Chicago. So while we are uniting to see the war through, let us be grateful to Franklin D. Roosevelt for leading us unflinchingly against our will to the place where we have an excellent chance to end this bedlam of brigandage and destruction on the other side of the oceans and on our terms. Mr. President, we salute you as the great leader of democracy, as a man great enough to lead us through the greatest peril in our history to victory over the most dangerous dictatorships which human history has thus far seen.

A generation ago we produced in Woodrow Wilson the first world statesman. Then we destroyed him, and we are suffering terribly for that colossal mistake. Today in this greater crisis we have another leader who has a grasp of world strategy sufficient to lead the forces of world democracy to victory again. Let us make certain that this time we defend whatever temple of peace he is able to erect.

171 -1